WHY NATIONS FAIL TO FEED THE POOR

'...Islam precisely analyses how patronage politics affects food security and convincingly identifies the political make-up as the cornerstone of state capacity.'

ARILD ENGELSEN RUUD
Professor of South Asia Studies, University of Oslo

This book examines the political and economic dimensions of food security in Bangladesh and assesses the role of the state in meeting the challenges of food security. The key concern, which is at the heart of this study, is to explore how Bangladesh responds, when its people go hungry. There are no detailed empirical studies that examine the Bangladesh's role by providing an historical cum political analysis; however conventional approaches are primarily concerned with a partial diagnosis of the economic or nutritional problems of food security.

This work provides a detailed picture of the missing dimensions of *stateness* that include the strength of institutions, the scope of state functions, and other important attributes. In doing so, it uses the concept of neo-patrimonialism to explore the political system of Bangladesh. This book explicates the various impediments to food security, ranging from the process of policy formulation to their implementation mechanisms. It unpacks the structural weaknesses of the Bangladeshi state's institutional capacity in promoting food security, and, in the process, argues that the root cause of food insecurity is deeply embedded in the nature of the government itself, and the political institutions that link the state and society.

Mohammad Mozahidul Islam is Professor and Chairperson, Department of History, Jahangirnagar University, Dhaka.

WHY NATIONS FAIL TO FEED THE POOR

The Politics of Food Security in Bangladesh

MOHAMMAD MOZAHIDUL ISLAM

Routledge
Taylor & Francis Group
LONDON AND NEW YORK

MANOHAR

First published 2023
by Routledge
4 Park Square, Milton Park, Abingdon, Oxon OX14 4RN

and by Routledge
605 Third Avenue, New York, NY 10158

Routledge is an imprint of the Taylor & Francis Group, an informa business

British Library Cataloguing-in-Publication Data
A catalogue record for this book is available from the British Library

Library of Congress Cataloging-in-Publication Data
A catalog record for this book has been requested

ISBN: 978-1-032-37694-3 (hbk)
ISBN: 978-1-032-37697-4 (pbk)
ISBN: 978-1-003-34145-1 (ebk)

DOI: 10.4324/9781003341451

Typeset in Adobe Garamond 11/13
by Kohli Print, Delhi 110051

MANOHAR

Contents

List of Tables and Figures

TABLES

FIGURES

Preface

This book attempts to illustrate the political and economic dimensions of food security in Bangladesh and assesses the role of the state in meeting the challenges of food security issues using a political economy approach. The key question which is at the heart of this project is to explore how the Bangladesh state responds when its people go hungry. Upon considering the fact that Bangladesh is a food insecure, under-resourced, and poorly governed country, the study critically examines the causes of food insecurity in general and the state failure and/or inability to promote food security in particular. I argue that food security in Bangladesh has a multidimensional aspect which involves national and international politics. While the role of inter-governmental and non-governmental agencies are important factors, the project particularly focusses on the state capacity of Bangladesh. The thesis explores the neopatrimonial politics of Bangladesh and its impact on state capacity and governance. In other words, in order to examine the 'scope of state functions' in relation to food security, this study is designed to investigate the institutional effectiveness (state capacity and/or governance) to promote food security. In this regard, my main concern is to investigate the different kinds of impediments to food security in Bangladesh, from the policy formulation process to policy execution mechanisms. This study focusses on the state's responses and activities and the ways in which it interacts with the food and agriculture market, agricultural development strategies and activities, farming and non-farming subsidies and the public food distribution system of Bangladesh. It is imperative to note that this thesis seeks to examine the politics of food and hunger in the context of the 'right to food' and a 'social-welfare sense' of economic analysis.

In order to examine the politics of food security in Bangladesh, my research attempts to contribute several important issues at the forefront of the Bangladesh's food security analysis. These are the concepts of neopatrimonialism, linkages between food security and state capacity, institutional effectiveness, 'interest politics' and patronage politics in the making of and implementing of food policies. All of these issues are to some extent linked to the notion of good governance. To this end, regarding governance as an important factor in providing food security of nations, initially my study was aimed at investigating the governance-food security nexus in Bangladesh. My understanding was straightforward and naive: I saw poor governance as the underlying factor behind the poor policy-making process thereby weakening policy implementation mechanisms and resulting in the state failure in promoting food security to hungry citizens. The fact is that in the early stages of my research, I did not grasp the underlying 'politics of the good governance' in relation to the politics of food security.

However, in the course of my fieldwork examining the politics of food security in Bangladesh, I gained new insights into the notion of 'good governance', which is sometimes merely a 'project' allocated to some political actors, and does not always capture the inherent causes of food insecurity in its entirety. More eloquently expressed, as Norris (2011, 2012) argues, good governance is an abstract and vague term which is open to alternative interpretations. During my fieldwork, I realized that the policy failure in promoting food security is not merely the consequence of poor governance, as is commonly thought, but is the inevitable outcome of patronage politics, which in turn is essential for the regime's survival. This dynamic offers benefits/patronage for the ruling elite, and consequently, the failure of appropriate policy formulation for corresponding target groups is inevitable. Therefore, drawing from first hand experiences and practical insights from field research, I began to think about the factors that impede good governance in implementing state functions such as food, health, education and the like. In doing so, my research drew from, and built upon, recent literature on neopatrimonialism, state building and state capacity, state-society relations, state power and the political economy of food security. I attempt to explore the process of making and unmaking of a weak state that has failed to penetrate society, remains unable to carry out basic state functions (food, health, education and so on) and fails to implement an 'ambitious range of activities' that often aims to perform well.

My underlying justification for undertaking this project is connected to the premise that in order to understand the challenges of food security, the structural causes of hunger, and the roots of food insecurity, it is important to understand the missing dimensions of *stateness* that include the strength of state institutions, the scope of state functions, and the like. Hence, in the course of examining the politics of food security in Bangladesh, the core of my attention will lie in investigating the role of the state with special reference to the process of policymaking. In particular, I am interested in the interactions between various (political) actors. After identifying the politics of policymaking, I then draw my attention to exploring its implementation mechanisms to understand the state's capacity to promote food security. At the very outset of dealing with the policymaking process, a series of sub-questions are raised. These are: 'What is the nature of the state that formulates policy?', 'Is the state responsive to demands from within the society?', 'Has the state the capacity to formulate a better policy to promote food security?', 'What is the nature of Bangladeshi politics that shape and/or re-shape the state mechanism?', 'How is the policy formulated?', 'Who is making the policy?', 'Are food issues on the agenda of policy-makers?', 'Who are the beneficiaries of the policy outcome?', 'Who participates in policy-making in Bangladesh?', 'Who is included and excluded?'. I argue that it is imperative to deal with these critical issues as outlined above, and to examine the politics of food, as all these issues are linked to the state capacity of a particular nation state, in particular, the Bangladesh state.

Throughout this study, I critically engage the capability of the state's policymaking process and implementation mechanisms with regard to food security. In other words, in order to understand factors and conditions that prevent food from being distributed throughout society from a welfare perspective and to seek reasons for market failure focussing on patronage politics, my main concern is to critically review the politics of policymaking and policy implementation. In doing so, however, it is worthwhile to note that instead of a narrow understanding through a 'good governance' lens, my study endeavours to examine the issue critically and in a broader sense using a new analytical framework which include five elements: rent-seeking behaviour, public corruption, partial reform syndrome, weak state capacity, and poor governance.

It is important to note that this book is a revised version of my doctoral thesis entitled 'The Politics of Food Security in Bangladesh' approved by the University of New South Wales, Australia. In December 2012, I was awarded the degree of Doctor of Philosophy and since then I have published several research articles using various sections of the thesis in various international academic journals.

In preparation of this book, I received many helpful and constructive comments from many people. First of all, I am deeply grateful to Professor Marc Williams for his patient and thoughtful advice, support and valuable insights on my thesis writing process. I have been especially fortunate to work under his close supervision and I am grateful to him for his helpful assistance, critical evaluation and appreciation of my work throughout the course of the research process. I am also grateful to Dr Duncan McDuie-Ra, my co-supervisor, for his generosity in sharing his knowledge and providing me with outstanding advice and constructive suggestions.

I have also benefited from the discussions with other faculty members and colleagues, too many to be named here, at the University of New South Wales (UNSW) whose discussions, comments, criticisms, suggestions, and intellectual exchange enriched both my personal and professional life. However, I would like to single out Associate Professor Dr Ursula Rao, Tamara Nair, Rabia Ali and Ian Michael Zucker for special thanks.

During my fieldwork in Bangladesh, a great many people helped me a lot. They are too numerous to thank individually.

I deeply remember and would like to express my heartfelt gratitude to the three most wonderful people that I have ever met who had/have great influence on my critical understanding of society and politics in the sense of the welfare of human beings: my father, late Abdus Samad, my uncle, late Abdul Hamid, and Abdus Sabur. With deep respect and gratitude, I also remember my mother,

Habiba Khatun: she has been incredibly understanding and supportive of what I aspire to do.

My hearty thanks go to Shaila Solaiman. During the book writing process, she has always provided me with enormous support in various ways: nevertheless, her unconditional love, friendship, and support were unwavering.

This study was conducted under the scholarship of the University International Postgraduate Award, UNSW. My deep acknowledgment also goes to the Graduate Research School, UNSW for providing me with the financial assistance to conduct this research in Australia.

Finally, I would like to thank all those who have inspired me to somehow accomplish this book.

Dhaka MOHAMMAD MOZAHIDUL ISLAM
December 2021

CHAPTER 1

Introduction

Historical evidence suggests that in almost every year prior to Independence in 1971, today's Bangladesh experienced a general scarcity of foodgrains if measured by any objective norms. The fact is that the low foodgrain intake status was one of the general characteristics of Bengal (Alamgir 1980: 108). In addition to this scarcity of foodgrain, the adverse impact of natural disasters, widespread poverty and income inequality has always been underlying features of Bangladeshi society, and these can be seen as dominant factors causing hunger and starvation. After Independence, Bangladesh experienced another devastating famine in 1974 and the country is still one of the most poverty-stricken societies where hunger, food insecurity and inequality are common phenomena. It is to be noted that the magnitude of the food crisis of Bengal was academically disseminated to the wider world by the famous work of Amartya Sen (1981). He examined the Bengal famine of 1943 and the Bangladesh famine of 1974. The Bengal famine of 1943 killed about three million people and was arguably the greatest famine of the twentieth century (Sen 1981).

Akin to the pre-Independence period, hunger is still prevalent in today's Bangladesh. For political reasons, although successive governments attempt to hide the presence of hunger, available data indicates a different scenario. For instance, according to a recent study, 52 million people in Bangladesh remained moderately or severely food insecure between 2018 and 2020 (FAO 2021: 148). A study of the Food Security Nutritional Surveillance Program (FSNSP)[1] shows the prevalence of food insecurity in Bangladesh during our study period. According to the first round of the study, 45 per cent of the population was food-insecure based on the Household Food Insecurity Access Scale (HFIAS). By comparison, the fourth round of surveillance found that over 75 per cent of households with children under the age of five were food insecure, an increase of 69 per cent (FSNSP 2011: 2). With regard to undernutrition, recent FAO data shows that a little more than one in every four (26 per cent) people of Bangladesh was undernourished in the period of 2006-8 (see FAO 2011). In addition, in 2011, using the Household Hunger Scale (HHS), the fourth-round data of FSNPS surveillance indicates that 31 per cent of households exhibited behaviours that indicated hunger (FSNSP 2011: 3).

On two recent occasions—in 1973-4 and in 2007-8—the surge in food prices, especially those of staples such as rice and wheat, generated catastrophic sociopolitical impacts throughout the world. As a consequence, in recent times, the number of hungry people has increased dramatically. Not surprisingly, as a net food importing country, Bangladesh suffered the most from the global food crisis of 2007-8 as in 1973-4. While the 1973-4 food crises led to sky-rocketing price hikes which resulted in famine in Bangladesh, the impact of the more recent global food crisis (2007-8) was also enormous: Bangladesh's poor were the hardest hit. According to a study, because of the sudden sharp price hike in 2007-8, an additional 7.5 million people have joined the ranks of the hungry, bringing the number of people who consume less than 2,122 kcal/person/day to 65.3 million (see FAO/WFP 2008: 7) out of the total 150 million people. Although this phenomenon gained currency on a grand scale, the fact is that hunger and food insecurity in Bangladesh is neither a new phenomenon nor is it only associated with global food price hikes. Oddly enough, hunger and starvation has never gained popular attention unless it amounts to devastating famine.

Although the data noted above provides information on the food and nutrition situation in Bangladesh, a critical observation of 'the political economy of statistics' of Bangladesh reminds us that no one knows the exact number of hungry people. This is also true of the number of global malnourished people. However, without mentioning any specific figures, the fact Hartmann and Boyce

(1990: 11) stated two decades ago which still holds true: 'today Bangladesh is a land of hunger'. My objective in this thesis is to understand why the Bangladesh state does not follow a policy that could feed its people. Why has Bangladesh always been an extremely vulnerable country in the world in relation to food insecurity? Why could Bangladesh not avoid the impact of the global food crisis? Why do a large number of people go hungry in Bangladesh? This thesis aims to critically investigate these questions.

The food security of a nation state has a multidimensional aspect which involves national and international politics. However, the focus of this study is that the role of the state is still central in shaping and reshaping national food policies and in order to promote food security. This is because national governments adopt policies that ultimately influence and/or eliminate hunger. In this age of globalization, the emerging global food network remains over-dependent on policies which are, in turn, driven by external actors. This issue is complemented by regimes which neglect the need for proactive food security governance, thereby posing major challenges for many nation states to provide resources to overcome the existing labyrinth of hunger-related problems.[2]

In this book, I endeavour to provide a detailed empirical study of the state's role in promoting food security in Bangladesh, focussing on two important aspects: food availability and food accessibility. In doing so, my aim is to examine the state capacity of Bangladesh in promoting food security, and this will be accompanied by a discussion of the components and logic of different approaches and an explanation designed to enhance understanding of the social and political organization and relationships between actors. With regard to the food security issue, I am particularly keen to explicate the politics of development, global governance, and patronage politics, and their impact on the nation state.

THE ARGUMENT OF THE BOOK

The central claim of this book is that the root cause of food insecurity is deeply embedded in the nature of the Bangladesh state itself and the political institutions that link the state and society.

Millions of people go hungry in Bangladesh not because it is a resource-poor country, but rather, because of the nature of the state. Because of its foundation in neopatrimonial politics which systematically weakens the state capacity, promotes patronage politics and results in poor governance, the state has failed to plan and execute sound policies and to enforce laws cleanly and transparently. This has adversely affected governmental markets and non-market based policies. In a neopatrimonial state, on the one hand, the state fails to provide entitlements for the very poor segments of the population. On the other hand, the state fails to regulate and to allow for the flourishing of markets which, in turn, causes an increase in food prices. This central hypothesis then fosters several different assumptions to explain different aspects of food security.

First, drawing on the neopatrimonial tendencies of the Bangladesh state, I assess the extent to which the state is capable to plan and execute sound policies which are essential for promoting development, including food security. I posit that the neopatrimonial Bangladesh state has a lack of administrative capacity, effective institutions and coherent ideology, and thus, is unable to carry out developmental as well as economic goals. In other words, as a consequence of loss of state capacity, the state's ability to define and pursue basic services has declined over the years and been rendered incapable or rarely capable to provide basic services to its citizens. Most importantly, the neopatrimonial regimes of Bangladesh survive based on patronage politics, where personalized exchanges are the mechanisms of the government. Thus, the neopatrimonial regime is the antithesis of good governance as well as the antithesis of development.

Second, this thesis will unpack the challenges of the neopatrimonial Bangladesh state to promote food availability essential for ensuring food security. It is argued that, because the nature of the state implies a weak connection between state and society, its weak capacity, and patronage politics, it is difficult for the Bangladesh state to ensure food availability. In order to understand the complexities in promoting food availability, a deep understanding in the role of the state in propelling agricultural growth, its trade mechanisms, and other means of the steady supply of food grain is important. I will show that all of these complex issues are linked with the political culture of the state, where political elites have been using state resources to generate benefits for themselves rather than the society. As a result, the state's failure is evident in promoting food availability through domestic production and by trade, mainly, because of the failure to execute economic management. In the process, state elites depend on food aid, which further jeopardizes food availability, as there is no guarantee that the Bangladesh state will receive food aid when it is required.

Third, similar to the challenges of food availability, it is also difficult for the neopatrimonial state to promote food accessibility which is essential to ensure food security. My discussion will show that policies taken by a neopatrimonial state are politically motivated, and therefore, projects and programmes designed to promote food accessibility have failed to reach the vulnerable sections of the poor. Because of patronage politics, the policy formulation mechanisms predominantly fall within the interests of the small ruling elite. Therefore, the state initiatives fail to carry out any meaningful projects or programmes that can promote food accessibility.

WHY THIS BOOK

In this book, by providing an historical and political analysis of the state's role in promoting food security, my primary goal is to contribute to three areas of scholarly inquiry which is evidenced through the development of the argument within the chapters.

The first contribution I claim is that this study is the first systematic detailed empirical study of the state's role in promoting food security in Bangladesh. In doing so, the main focus of this study is to draw attention to political and institutional factors such as structural causes of food insecurity. It is important to note that this research is neither a study in public policy, nor does it aim to provide an economic analysis of food security. The fact is that comprehensive literature on food security in Bangladesh is scant and the existing literature either entails policy prescriptions or economic analyses. My approach involves an analysis of political economy. However, it is to be noted that I do not seek to undermine or dismiss the previous literature. I only argue that these studies do not adequately address the problem of food security in Bangladesh. In fact, in this regard, in order to identify and explain the politics of food security this study is the first of its kind in that it attempts to provide a detailed empirical analysis and document key discourses on the food security mechanisms during the period, 1975 to 2010.[3] In doing so, I apply qualitative methods in which interviews and documentary analyses were used.

In my second contribution, I claim that this thesis is the first of its kind as it seeks to provide a political explanation of the complex issues of food insecurity in Bangladesh. By examining the nature of the state, state capacity and institutional effectiveness, the central purpose of this study is to investigate the politics of food security in Bangladesh. I argue that it is imperative to examine the nature of the state in order to understand its responses in its attempt to eliminate hunger and promote food security. In other words, I argue that the food security of nations is greatly dependent on the nature of a state. Similarly, while most of the studies focus on policy failure, this study examines the politics of policymaking and execution and, therefore, reveals a new window to allow one to grasp some new dimensions of food security. In order to examine food security of nations, researchers mainly focus on governance, corruption, rent-seeking and so on, which mostly fail to capture the intrinsic weaknesses of the policy issues as these analyses only tell us what actors do but never tell us why actors take certain actions in certain ways. For instance, conventional research has typically identified specific rent-seeking groups but does not adequately tell us about the politics behind rent-seeking. Similarly, analysis tells us the story of policy failure but does not critically explore the detail. In order to gain further insight and to analyse food policy critically, I not only use the issue of governance, corruption, rent-seeking and the like, but also use the concept of patronage politics to identify the inherent weaknesses of policymaking and implementation. In the process, this study attempts to tackle the issue of politics which lies at the forefront of food security literature in

Bangladesh, noting that political contexts contribute to policymaking as well as execution mechanisms which affect all aspects of national food security.

My third claim to originality is that this book provides a distinctive framework in analysing food security in Bangladesh. To do so, this thesis employs the concept of neopatrimonialism to explore the Bangladesh political system. In this regard, my contribution that this thesis provides is twofold: it involves an empirical application of the notion of neopatrimonialism in the context of Bangladesh as well as a theoretical contribution to the concept.

The application of the notion of neopatrimonialism in Bangladesh politics provides us with a framework for understanding elite beliefs, patronage politics, and the root causes of the failure of policymaking and policy implementation. In order to establish a framework for analysing the politics of food security in a neopatrimonial state like Bangladesh, I employ five concepts under the umbrella of neopatrimonialism: rent-seeking, public corruption, the partial reform syndrome, weak state capacity and poor governance. I argue that the combination of all five generates inevitable outcomes of neopatrimonial regimes which, in turn, provide us with a clearer basis for understanding the politics of food security.

On the other hand, drawing on the Bangladesh case, I propose a special variant of the neopatrimonial state, which I suggest is a bipolar neopatrimonialism; thereby contributing to the literature on neopatrimonialism. Although neopatrimonialism is a single concept for comparative politics, there are clear variations in existing neopatrimonial themes. In other words, it is not true that all neopatrimonial regimes govern in identical ways. Considering the fact that the regime variants are neither rigid nor immutable (Bratton & Van de Walle 1994: 472), I suggest another variant of the regime: a competitive bipolar neopatrimonialism.

By introducing a new framework to investigate the politics of food security, I fill in an important research gap in current debates on the food security of Bangladesh and thereby claim that this thesis makes a substantial contribution to original empirical research.

STRUCTURE OF THE BOOK

My research draws heavily on political and institutional factors in examining the politics of food security in Bangladesh. I was particularly keen to investigate some structural dimensions that weaken state capacity and how that impedes various state-led development programmes including food security.

The next chapter (Chapter 2) of the thesis discusses two vital key concepts used in this study: food security and the state. Considering the fact that this study draws heavily and builds upon recent Global Political Economy (GPE), International Relations (IR), and political science scholarship on food security, institutional effectiveness of development focussing on the state, state capacity, state-society relationship, interaction between political actors, in this chapter, I attempt to highlight several caveats that require preliminary clarification in relation to their use throughout this thesis. In doing so, I first critically examine the notion of food security which is followed by the key approaches used in the food security literature relating to Bangladesh. I then critically examine the degree of state intervention in promoting growth and development, and the nature of the Bangladesh state.

Chapter 3 examines the nature of political power of Bangladesh with special reference to the concept of neopatrimonialism, the personalization of state power and its impact on democratic governance. This chapter is broadly divided into two sections. The first section of the chapter seeks to explore the nature of the Bangladesh state and highlight the neopatrimonial character of the relationships underpinning it. It shows that since Independence, successive governments and political leaders always attempt to monopolize state power in various ways. The patron-client society of Bangladesh helps political leaders to personalize the state power they possess. It sheds light on the way in which the political elite of Bangladesh create networks and alliances, relying upon *exchanges* to meet their objectives. In this regard, the state elite use elements of the state and political system to mediate these exchanges. In the second section of this chapter, I develop an analytical framework to be employed throughout this study. In doing so, I investigate the costs and impacts of the neopatrimonial regimes in Bangladesh by using five political economy concepts—rent-seeking, public corruption, partial reform syndrome, weak state capacity and poor governance.

Chapter 4 aims to document the challenges of food security in Bangladesh with particular reference to the issue of food availability and accessibility. It seeks to set up a framework through which the empirical discussion can be drawn in Chapters 5 and 6. While the purpose of Chapter 3 is to establish a framework of the political system of the Bangladesh state in the light of neopatrimonialism, this chapter attempts to formulate its framework using the entitlement approach of Sen (1981) and the right to food approach. This chapter, thus, examines the challenges of food security in Bangladesh by focussing on three major issues: key discourses of food security in Bangladesh; contemporary as well as future challenges of food availability and accessibility; and the problems of food accessibility in Bangladesh focussing on the vulnerable section of population. Examining the entitlement theory, the discussion demonstrates several major challenges of food accessibility in Bangladesh which include poverty, increasing number of urban poverty, intra-household disparity of food, and the impact of sudden price hike.

Chapter 5 endeavours to examine the way in which the Bangladesh state has attempted to ensure that food is available for all people at all time. The chapter critically examines all three components of food availability: domestic production, international trade, and food aid. The discussion attempts to unpack the way in which the state has attempted to ensure food availability through propelling agricultural growth, facilitating scope for steady supply of food grains when it is needed by international trade and/or food aid. I attempt to investigate how rent-seeking, corruption and partial reforms impede food availability. Moreover, throughout the chapter, I seek to examine how other weaknesses relating to weak state capacity and poor governance impede food availability in Bangladesh. In other words, in order to understand the impacts in the making of state's agricultural development policy and implementation, this chapter utilizes five concepts: rent-seeking, public corruption, partial reform syndrome, poor governance and weak state capacity. Moreover, this chapter addresses the major challenges of effective imports of foodgrain in Bangladesh in order to promote food availability by means of international trade, and also questions the importance of food aid as means of food availability in the present context of Bangladesh.

Chapter 6 examines whether the state has attempted to ensure that vulnerable sections of the population have access to food. This chapter, in particular, examines two major aspects of food accessibility in Bangladesh: the political dynamics of market regulation as well as state sponsored entitlement generation mechanism through the Public Food Distribution System (PFDS). In order to investigate the role of the state in entitlement generation, this chapter examines the historical evolution of the PFDS in Bangladesh. In particular, it examines how the PFDS of Bangladesh has developed, multiplied and diversified with special reference to its 'target errors' and 'leakage errors'. In order to examine the 'target errors' and 'leakage errors', this chapter seeks the linkages between interest politics, patronage politics, and distribution of state resources for 'regime survival' rather than promoting food security. On the other hand, considering the impact of the sudden price hike as an important impediment of food accessibility to the poor, this chapter seeks to explore the state mechanisms of market regulation necessary for price stabilization. In other words, given the neopatrimonial nature of the state, this chapter aims to investigate the challenges of food accessibility in Bangladesh in relation to the market, market failure, and market interventions.

Chapter 7 concludes the thesis. It first revisits the objectives of the thesis in brief and then summarizes the key stages of the argument, and the main findings of the thesis. It finally places the implications of the study and provides direction for additional research.

NOTES

1. The Food Security Nutritional Surveillance Program (FSNSP) is a joint five-year project between James P. Grant School of Public Health, BRAC University (JGSPH), and Helen Keller International, Bangladesh (HKI),

with funding provided by the European Commission. This project provides up to date, seasonal information on the food and nutrition situation in Bangladesh. In addition to BRAC University and HKI, the Bangladesh Bureau of Statistics is also one of the strategic partners of FSNSP.

2. Here it is important to note that, although I emphasise that the national governments make policies that determine food security and insecurity, I do not suggest that external agencies do not play significant role in shaping and reshaping national policies through 'conditionality' or other forms of influence (s). In fact, I have argued earlier that food security in Bangladesh has a multidimensional aspect which involves national and international politics. I further clarified that this thesis will only deal with the state capacity of Bangladesh. Hence, here I do not discuss the role of external actors.
3. It is to be noted that the beginning of the period of study, 1975, was chosen as it was the important turning point in the history of the development strategy of Bangladesh. Until 1975, the development strategy of Bangladesh emphasized 'socialist' principles of distributive justice. In order to achieve the long range goal of a socialistic economy, effective steps were taken, which includes nationalization of all industrial enterprises, banking, insurance and all units in the jute, cotton textiles, sugar industries, and so forth. The aim of this policy was to extend the scope and sphere of state participation in production activities (Ahamed 1978: 1168). In contrast, the end of Mujib's regime (1972-5) ushered in fresh ideas and new development policies. The new regime of Ziaur Rahman (1975-81) marked a decisive break in the country's economic policies: a massive policy shift towards privatization and promotion of the public sector took place. Following the footsteps of Zia, in the mid 1980s, market-based liberalizing policy reforms were initiated with the support of the IMF and the World Bank, and have been followed through since then in various phases. Consequently, today, Bangladesh has attained a largely liberalized import regime, a much-reduced public sector, very limited input subsidies for the agricultural sector and the area of manufacturing and a much-reduced public sector where virtually no new investment has taken place in the last two decades. The market-oriented economic reforms also marked a decisive break in the country's food policy, which began since the end of 1975. The year 2010 was chosen as the end period of this study because the field data collect was carried out from June 2010 to December 2010. Again, Bangladesh suffered in both the global food crises that occured in 1973-4 and 2007-8. Coincidently, the study period of this book, 1975 and 2010, is linked with two global food crises.

CHAPTER 2

Food Security, the State and Institutional Effectiveness

INTRODUCTION

My central postulate of this study, as noted earlier, is that the root cause of food insecurity is deeply embedded in the nature of the Bangladesh state itself and the political institutions that link the state and society. Hence, in the course of examining the politics of food security in Bangladesh, the core of my attention will lie in investigating the role of the state with special reference to the process of policymaking and implementation. In other words, I am interested in investigating the institutional effectiveness for promoting development with a particular focus on food security. Thus, as can be seen in the following discussion, this study draws heavily and builds upon recent Global Political Economy (GPE), International Relations (IR), and political science scholarship on food security, institutional effectiveness of development focussing on the state, state capacity, the state-society relationship, interaction between actors, etc. It is to be noted that as my key objective is to examine the role of the state in promoting food security, several caveats require preliminary clarification in relation to their use throughout this thesis. Hence, the purpose of this chapter is to draw the conceptual framework of two important keywords of this study: food security and the state. In doing so, I first critically examine the notion of food security which is then followed by the key approaches that deal with the food security in Bangladesh. I then critically examine the degree of state intervention in promoting growth and development, and the nature of the Bangladesh state. And finally I attempt to recount conventional accounts of the Bangladesh state. However, before beginning the discussion of the role of the state with special reference to its institutional capacity for promoting growth and development, I firstly, attempt to illustrate my understanding of the state.

A CRITICAL ANALYSIS OF FOOD SECURITY

The World Bank's definition of food security continues to dominate the literature. It defines food security as 'access by all people at all times to sufficient food for an active, healthy life' (World Bank 1986: 1). This frequently/commonly cited definition has suffered from a serious deficiency in that it lacks a dimension which was later modified by the definition provided by the Food and Agriculture Organization (FAO). This new definition suggests that '[f]ood security exists when all people, at all times, have physical, social and economic access to sufficient, *safe and nutritious food* that meets their dietary needs and food preferences for an active and healthy life' (FAO 2010: 8; emphasis added). In addition to basic definitions of food security some authors have focussed on the key dimensions (or pillars) of food security. For example, the FAO (2006b) identified four main dimensions of food security—availability, access, utilization and stability. And Barrett (2011: 825) argues that food security is commonly conceptualized as resting on three pillars—availability, access and utilization. In order to understand the definition of food security, I examined 40 recognized definitions published from 1975 to 2010 (adapted from Maxwell's appendix of 32 definitions of food security and insecurity, 1975-91; Maxwell 1996). I found four key recurring terms from these definitions: access, availability, utilization, and vulnerability.[1] My conceptualisation of food security is, therefore, similar to that of the FAO and entails one dimension omitted by Barrett. Thus the comprehension of the term 'food security' can be determined by these keywords although each captures different, but overlapping, dimensions of the phenomenon. I realized that one of the key aspects of food security is *food safety and quality* which is ignored in mainstream literature with regard to food security definitions. However, the definition by the FAO (originally in 2009; and also see 2010) fills this important gap by including the aspect of *safe and nutritious food.* Thus, I propose five recurring key terms of the definition of food security: access, availability, utilization, vulnerability, and quality (safe and nutritious food).

Although Chapter 4 provides a detailed explanation of my understanding of food accessibility, here it is important to provide a brief introduction to my use of the concept. I have argued that in the contemporary food security literature, *accessibility* of food refers to the ability of individuals and households to obtain food necessary for maintaining healthy and active lives through purchase, produce or by trade, and failure to do so is considered a major constraint to food security. Barrett (2011) suggests that access reflects the demand side of food security, as manifested in uneven inter- and intra-household food distribution and in the sociocultural limits on what foods are consistent with prevailing tastes and values within a community. Access also accentuates problems in responding to adverse shocks such as unemployment spells, price spikes or the loss of livelihood-producing assets. Through the access lens, food security's close relationship to poverty and to social, economic and political disenfranchisement comes into clearer focus. But because access is an inherently multidimensional concept, measurement is more difficult than the related concept of availability.

The concept of food security involves rigorous examinations of a variety of social, economic, political and ecological factors to identify the choices and challenges that determine various aspects of food availability, accessibility, utilization, vulnerability and quality. In doing so, research has focussed on multiple levels of analysis: individual, household or community, national, international, and global (for example, see Sen 1982, 1999; Pottier 1999; Smil 2000, 2004; Alston, Pardey & Taylor 2001; Devereux & Maxwell 2001; Webb & Weinberger 2001; Fogel 2004; Federico 2005; Clapp & Fuchs 2009; McDonald 2010; Clapp 2012). Considering the importance of various actors (i.e. Government, Non-governmental Organizations (NGOs), Inter-Governmental Organizations (IGOs), Trans-National Corporations (TNCs), Multilateral Economic Institutions (MEIs), etc., in the web of food security mechanisms, in this thesis,

I argue that food security in nations has a multidimensional aspect which involves national and international politics. However, this project focusses in particular on the state capacity of Bangladesh and, therefore, this study is basically a 'national level analysis'. In order to examine food security in the context of a national level analysis, my research exclusively focusses on two key issues relating to food security: food availability and accessibility.

Here, two further clarifications are required and, therefore, I seek to answer two corresponding questions: Why a national level analysis? Why only analyse food availability and accessibility? In response to the first question, a national level analysis of food security in the context of the present research is important for at least three reasons. First, as noted earlier, the role of the state is still predominant in shaping and reshaping national food policies and promoting food security; national government's adopt policies that ultimately influence and/or eliminate hunger. My discussion in the following section will show that the state is central to development; it needs to ensure food security to the hungry poor by generating entitlements and by emerging as a guardian, partner, facilitator, and even as a direct provider of growth. Although many international institutions such as the World Bank, World Trade Organization (WTO), International Monetary Fund (IMF), etc., overtly attempt to influence domestic policies in a global effort to eliminate hunger and undernutrition, the fact is that policy implementation mechanisms remain within the domain of the abilities of the nation state. Within a nation state, state policies play pivotal roles in shaping agricultural reform and ensuring the well-being of small peasants and landless farmers, the urban poor, etc. Second, the idea of global food governance has not yet emerged, nor has it been successful although global institutions, such as the FAO, World Food Programme (WFP), etc., play roles in promoting global food security. The recent global food crisis of 2007-8 and the most recent famine in the Horn of Africa illustrate the importance of the nation state in ensuring food security. In other words, recent experiences confirm that the success or failure of nation states in promoting food security ultimately depends on the capacity, wealth and power of the nation state. Third, I have found considerable research gaps in the context of Bangladesh food security literature as there was no systematic, politically transparent scheme. Hence, I argue that, in order to understand the complex issue of food security in Bangladesh, national-level analysis demands further investigation.

Although it is not my aim to claim that other aspects of food security are less important, from the perspective of this thesis the two most important components of food security are food availability and food accessibility. First, as this thesis attempts to examine the role of the state in promoting food security in Bangladesh, it is obvious that food availability and accessibility are most in control of the institutions of the state. In other words, the state has more influence over availability and access dimensions rather than other dimensions of food security. Second, as the aim of this study is to examine the politics of food security in Bangladesh, it is rational to discuss the two most important political factors of the food security literature. Although the term 'politics of food' denotes a range of issues such as food security, social inequality, nutrition policy, and agricultural policies (Lien 2004: 1), there is no denying that the issue of food security is the most vital issue in the global politics of food and, within the food security debate, food availability and accessibility are the most vital components of the politics of food security. Third, it is beyond the scope of this thesis to discuss every aspect of food security and, therefore, I had to prioritize various aspects with regard to Bangladesh's unique situation. The fact is that, although every aspect of food security is important, it is still worthwhile to analyse the components of food security in order of priority. Fourth, both food availability and accessibility, and particularly the latter, are still major challenges for the Bangladesh state.

It is imperative to note that throughout this study, 'food insecurity' refers to the absence of food security and also to a state in which people do not have adequate physical, social or economic access to food for an active and healthy life. Additionally, 'hunger' (often referred to as 'undernourishment') denotes a situation in which caloric intake is below the Minimum Dietary Energy Requirement (MDER) which is required for light activity and to maintain a minimum acceptable weight for attained height. As noted in

Chapter 1, a recent study of the Food Security Nutritional Surveillance Programme (FSNSP) clearly shows the prevalence of food insecurity in Bangladesh and also indicates that a significant number of households exhibited behaviours that indicated hunger (see FSNSP 2011: 3). The fact is that, as McDonald (2010: 3-4) argues, the most important problem is the classical food security challenge of malnutrition which remains a significant and widespread form of food insecurity. Although many conceptualized this as hunger, Pinstrup-Andersen (2007; as cited in McDonald 2010) suggests that malnutrition is actually a set of three distinctive problems (often described as the 'triple burden of malnutrition'): energy deficiencies, nutrient deficiencies and excessive net energy intake. With regard to this study, however, it is important to note that my aim is not to draw on the nutritional aspects of food security.

In my understanding of food security which will be employed throughout this study, I believe that one additional clarification is needed. Differing from a conventional analysis of the mainstream economics of food security, I view food security and hunger as important and emergency issues. The general perception is that poverty is the principal cause of hunger. A report of the World Bank similarly suggests that 'hunger is the most deplorable manifestation of poverty' (World Bank 1995: 1). In view of this 'unsatisfying' argument, many argue that success in poverty reduction through market-driven economic development would automatically resolve the problem of hunger. On the contrary, I argue that poverty reduction is a very important means of eliminating hunger but it is not the only means. Poverty is one of many sources of hunger, which include conflict, natural calamities, social practices, harmful economic systems, etc. Hunger is a vicious cycle which can lead to greater poverty which, in turn, causes greater hunger. In this vein, I acknowledge that poverty reduction is a very important factor contributing to food insecurity, but targeting it is not the only avenue to ensuring food security. Accordingly, the question of priority must be considered to eliminate hunger. Strategies for reducing poverty and hunger, therefore, cannot be addressed collectively as the rate of change in the former is far slower than for the latter. Accordingly, this research aims to address urgent strategies for reducing food insecurity.

A related but different approach to the issue of food insecurity and the poor has been made by those who use the concept of food sovereignty. The concept of food sovereignty was developed by *La Via Campesina,* or the International Peasant Movement, and brought to public attention at the World Food Summit in 1996. It represents an alternative to neoliberal policies (*Via Campesina* 2012). *La Via Campesina* offers the following definition of food sovereignty:

Food sovereignty is the peoples', countries' or state unions' RIGHT to define their agricultural and food policy, without any dumping vis-à-vis third countries. Food sovereignty includes:

1. prioritizing local agricultural production in order to feed the people and access of peasants and landless people to land, water, seeds and credit—hence the need for land reforms, for fighting against Genetically Modified Organisms (GMOs), for free access to seeds, and for safeguarding water as a public good to be sustainably distributed;
2. the right of farmers, peasants to produce food and the right of consumers to be able to decide what they consume, and how and by whom it is produced;
3. the right of countries to protect themselves from too low priced agricultural and food imports;
4. agricultural prices linked to production costs: they can be achieved if the countries or unions of states are entitled to impose taxes on excessively cheap imports, if they commit themselves in favour of a sustainable farm production, and if they control production on the inner market so as to avoid structural surpluses;
5. the populations taking part in the agricultural policy choices; and
6. the recognition of women farmers' rights, who play a major role in agricultural production and in food (ibid.).

Approaching the Food Security of Bangladesh in the Literature

Under the auspices of the National Food Policy Capacity Strengthening Programme (NFPCSP) of the Government of Bangladesh, Rao (2007) surveyed the literature on food security in Bangladesh which includes an ample bibliography of 1,441 titles from 1975 to 2007, incorporates reviews of research conducted in and outside of Bangladesh and covers all the main dimensions and cross-cutting dimensions of food security. It seeks to achieve a minimal thematic coherence for the dimension of food security as a whole. The survey result categorized the food security literature in Bangladesh in the following four dimensions:

- The Production and Availability dimension which includes internal market integration; comparative advantage and external market integration; the global food market structure and imbalance; agricultural liberalization and the poor; the economics of dynamic advances; and access to inputs including public services.
- The Physical and Social Access dimension which includes access via government safety nets and other food security interventions; and shocks, seasonality and stability of access.
- The Economic Access dimension which is represented by the clusters of ultra-poverty, poverty, inequality and exclusion; incomes, access to assets, employment and factor markets; and food prices, purchasing power, pricing policies and food markets.
- The final main dimension of Utilization of Food for Nutrition which is structured under the clusters of food safety and food quality; dietary patterns, food composition and nutrition standards, and a residual cluster of miscellaneous issues related to utilization.

In addition, a further cross-cutting dimension includes governance and institutions, infrastructure, environment, and women and other disadvantaged groups. However, a closer look at this survey result clearly shows that there is a lack of historical-political analysis of the food security problem in Bangladesh.

In order to understand the politics of food security in Bangladesh, I first began my research with the above-mentioned benchmark food security literature survey by Rao (2007) and then attempted to understand the existing literature with a particular focus on the post-2007 period. A critical look at the food security literature of

Bangladesh suggests that much of what has been done so far and continues to be done about Bangladesh food security shows the following major characteristics:

1. Much of the work which has been written is mainly research/project reports funded by the donors, particularly the World Bank, USAID, International Food Policy Research Institute (IFPRI), etc., (e.g. see World Bank 1977, 1979, 1992, 2004, 2006; Ahmed et al. 2004, 2007). Thus, some suggest that donors, particularly USAID and the World Bank, are the key architects of the food policy reforms of Bangladesh (Montgomery 1983; Shahadat Ullah 1988; IFPRI 1993; Adams 1998; Chowdhury & Haggblade 2000).
2. Almost all but a few studies are highly dominated by the field of economics which provides an economic explanation of food security in Bangladesh (e.g. see Ahmed, Quisumbing & Hoddinott 2007; Ali et al. 2008; Hossain & Deb 2009; Chowdhury, Farid & Roy 2010; Hossain 2010; Shahabuddin 2010).
3. Much of the literature has a strong lack of a multidisciplinary approach and, therefore, has often failed to grasp the deeper understanding of the food security problem.
4. There is little emphasis laid on the nutritional and household aspects of food security. Only a few research studies attempt to examine the nutritional and household aspects of food security (e.g. Ahmed, F. et al. 1993; Ali, A. 2005; Kimmons et al. 2005; Eckhardt 2006; Coates et al. 2010; Mallick & Rafi 2010).

The literature which deals with cross-cutting dimensions such as governance and institutions has mainly attempted to examine 'target' and 'leakage' errors of the food security mechanism in Bangladesh (e.g. see Ahmed et al. 2004, 2007; World Bank 2004, 2006; Mugai & Zaidi 2005; BRAC 2006; Bode 2007; BRAC 2010). Many of these studies do not adequately explain the causes of institutional failure or the nature of institutions. The fact is that very little attempt has been made to examine the food security of Bangladesh by using a historical-political analysis. Only two studies, namely *Politics of Food Aid: Case of Bangladesh* (Molla 1990) and *Bangladesh, the First Decade* (Franda 1982) use political approaches to the food issues of Bangladesh: these studies are now nearly three decades old and, therefore, out of date. Again, there is no academic research work which has undertaken a state-centric analysis of the politics of food security using a historical-political approach.

THE STATE, INSTITUTIONS, AND DEVELOPMENT

Considering the fact that the state is an important actor in this study, here I first attempt to outline my understanding of the state. In other words, here my aim is not to define the state but rather to show my understanding of the state which I will be employing throughout this study. I then critically examine the degree of state intervention in promoting growth and development, and the nature of the Bangladesh state. And finally, I attempt to recount conventional accounts of the Bangladesh state.

My current understanding of the state has been profoundly influenced by a variety of intellectual debates. By far, Max Weber offered the most influential definition of the modern state. He defines the state as a human community that (successfully) claims the *monopoly of the legitimate use of physical force* within a given territory. As he suggests (1978: 54), 'a compulsory political organization with continuous operations will be called a "state" insofar as its administrative staff successfully upholds the claim to the monopoly of the legitimate use of physical force in the enforcement of its order'. Hay and Lister (2006) rightly observed that two aspects of this definition are particularly important. Firstly, the state for Weber is a set of institutions with dedicated personnel. And secondly, Weber regards the modern state as wielding a monopoly of authoritative rule-making within a specific territory. Thus, this definition provides, the basis and/or point of departure for much contemporary reflection on the state (ibid.). Drawing heavily on Weber's idea, many scholars have tended to emphasize the state's institutional character (as an organization or set of organizations), its functions (especially regarding the making of rules), and its recourse to coercion ('monopoly of the legitimate use of physical force') (see Migdal 1994: 11). In this view, '[t]he essence of stateness is', in the words of Fukuyama (2004: 8), '*enforcement*:

the ultimate ability to send someone with a uniform and a gun to force people to comply with the state's laws'. Reusch-meyer and Evans (1985: 46-7) argue 'the state to be a set of organizations invested with authority to make binding decisions for people and organizations juridically located in a particular territory and to implement these decisions using, if necessary, force'. Mann (1986a: 26) sees the state as a power organization that engages in 'centralized, industrialized, territorialized regulation of many aspects of social relation'. Here 'power' denotes what Mann suggests is infrastructural power: 'the capacity of the state actually to penetrate civil society, and to implement logistically political decisions throughout the realm' (ibid. 1986b: 113; as cited in Migdal 1994: 11-12).

In his *Strong Society and Weak States: State-Society Relations and State Capabilities in the Third World*, Migdal (1988) discusses the capabilities of states for achieving the kinds of changes in society that their leaders have sought through state planning, policies and actions. Migdal (ibid.: 4-5) argues that 'capabilities include the capacities to *penetrate* society, *regulate* social relationships, *extract* resources, and *appropriate* or use resources in determined ways. Strong states are those with high capabilities to complete these tasks, while weak states are on the low end of a spectrum of capabilities'. Society can be understood as 'a melange of social organizations' made up of heterogeneous groups organizing social control, meaning that social control overall is disbursed (White 1999: 319). Therefore, the state is simply one set of institutions amongst others which seeks to exercise control, operating in an 'environment of conflict' (Migdal 1988: 28-9; White 1999: 319). Migdal (1988: 33) points out that '[t]he strength of the state organization in an environment of conflict has depended, in large part, on the social control it has exercised. The more currency—that is, compliance, participation, and legitimation—available to state leaders, the higher the level of social control to achieve state goals'. In the sense of institutional capabilities, Fukuyama (2004: 12) shows the strength of a state to include the ability: to formulate and carry out policies and enact laws; to administrate efficiently and with a minimum of bureaucracy; to control graft, corruption, and bribery; to maintain a high level of transparency and accountability in government institutions; and, most importantly, to *enforce* laws.

The Degree of State Intervention in Promoting Growth and Development

At the risk of generalization, it can be argued that the size, functions, and scope of states have been the subject of debate since the beginning of the modern state system. However, this debate has gained currency in recent years, mainly, because of the challenges of economic globalization. As McGrew (1992: 92) suggests, globalization is 'compromising the authority, the autonomy, the nature and the competence of the modern nation state'. Despite the state's greater subservience to globalization, Pierson (2004: 104) shows that 'in most of the developed world, the state remains the single largest and most decisive economic actor'. In response to the challenges of economic globalization, I cite Cox (1993: 260) who suggests that 'states must become the instruments for adjusting national economic activities to the exigencies of the global economy'.

While the role of the state in the developed world remains the most dominant, a strong emphasis on diminishing the role of the state in every sphere of activity is a key feature of the developing world. In the 1980s and early 1990s, as a result of the rise of neoliberalism, the size of the state sector throughout the 'Third World' was reduced or was obligated to be reduced as imposed by Multilateral Economic Institutions (MEIs) such as the World Bank, International Financial Institutions (IFIs), the International Monetary Fund (IMF) and the US government. Under the auspices of neoliberalism, a package known as the 'Washington Consensus' dictated the degree of state intervention in economic affairs which significantly reduced the role of the state. Following the impact of this, and coupled with the fact that thousands of anti-globalization protesters emerged, many prominent academics persistently attacked the Washington Consensus. For example, Stiglitz not only documented the impact of the Washington Consensus (see Stiglitz 1989, 2002, 2006) but advocated for a more interventionist role for the state in the economy, using the strategic levers of regulatory institutions, social insurance programmes, and fiscal and monetary policies above and beyond the mere ensuring of free market conditions through protecting private property rights and the rule of law.

In response to the neoliberal emphasis on the 'minimal state', another important change took place in the history of economic thought. The New Institutional Economics (NIE) emerged as a school of thought based on two major propositions. Firstly, 'institutions do matter'; and secondly, 'the determinants of institutions are susceptible to analysis by the tools of economic theory' (Matthews, as cited in Williamson 2000: 595). In their famous article 'Institutions Rule', Rodrik, Subramanian, and Trebbi (2004) argued that the quality of institutions 'trumps' everything else. Similarly, a number of studies also linked the direct and/or indirect relationship between the quality of institutions and economic growth and/or socio-economic development (Knack & Keefer 1995; Aron 2000; Persson, Roland & Tabellini 2000; Acemoglu Johnson & Robinson 2000, 2002; Persson 2002; Persson & Tabellini 2003; Rodrik & Subramanian 2003; Bates et al. 2004; Persson & Tabellini 2004; Kaufmann, Kraay & Mastruzzi 2005; Alesina, Ardagna & Trebbi 2006; Chhibber, Peters & Hale 2006).

In their influential work, *Why Nations Fail: The Origin of Power, Prosperity, and Poverty*, Acemoglu and Robinson (2012) persuasively show that it is manmade political and economic institutions that underlie economic success or the lack of it. Drawing on the example of the city of Nogales which is divided by the fence between two different countries, Arizona, USA and Sonora, Mexico, the authors argue that:

> The reason that Nogales, Arizona [USA] is much richer than Nogales, Sonora [Mexico] is simple: it is because of the very different institutions on the two sides of the border, which create very different incentives for the inhabitants of Nogales, Arizona, versus Nogales, Sonora.

Likewise, they provide a number of fascinating examples which include North and South Korea, and the former East and West Germany. For example, they argue that Korea is one of the most homogeneous nations in the world, yet the people of North Korea are among the poorest while the people of South Korea are among the richest. It is nothing but the politics that have created completely different institutions that promote development in South Korea. By examining a number of case studies and historical narratives, Acemoglu and Robinson (2012) raise a question as to why nations fail today. For them, the answer is: 'institutions, institutions, institutions'.

On the other hand, throughout the 1970s, 1980s, and 1990s, a number of neoclassical economists and political economists advocated that the state was the single most important impediment to economic development. Extensive state intervention, in the form of regulatory mechanisms, parastatal industries, investment, etc., was seen as central to explaining economic stagnation. In the 1980s, a new orthodoxy of market liberalism saw state intervention in markets as a logical outcome of a close alliance between rent-seeking public officials and rent-seeking economic interests. This radically diminished the size and scope of state intervention and was considered as the only solution to end rent-seeking and to promote more dynamic economies (see Grindle 1996).

In contrast, welfare economics or the 'market failure' approach views state intervention as necessary for economic growth. State intervention is seen to be important mainly because of the inability of decentralised agents, in their pursuit of self-interest, to produce outcomes which would fulfil the 'efficiency' conditions of a competitive equilibrium (Chang 2003: 47). When a market 'fails', the state can emerge as a guardian, partner, facilitator, even as a direct provider of growth by means of public production, subsidies, reallocation of property rights, etc. However, with the rise of neoliberalism, this view has been the subject of severe criticism (ibid.).

More recently, as Kohli (2003: 3) suggests, 'there is a continuing recognition of the importance of macroeconomic stability and getting some prices right, such as exchange rate and food prices'. However, today the role of the state in economic development has been seen in the context of the 'effectiveness of the state' (e.g. see World Bank 1997; Fukuyama 2004). According to the *World*

Development Report 1997, 'the state is central to economic and social development . . . as a partner, catalyst, and facilitator' (World Bank 1997: 1). However, this statement is conditional on a certain interpretation of 'effectiveness': this study further states that 'an *effective state* is vital for the provision of the goods and services—and the rules and institutions—that allow markets to flourish and people to lead healthier, happier lives. Without it, sustainable development, both economic and social, is impossible' (ibid.; emphasis added). Similarly, with regard to the contested role of the state, Fukuyama (2004: 7) argues that '[t]he problem lay in a basic conceptual failure to unpack the different dimensions of *stateness* and to understand how they related to economic development'. Here, two points are vital: the state is central to development, but that must be an effective state. In other words, quality of state intervention is required rather than its quantity with a view that states and markets need to work together to promote growth, not to compete with each other.

I agree that 'the state is central to economic and social development' and the willingness and effective mechanisms of the state 'allow markets to flourish and people to lead healthier, happier lives'. With regard to 'effectiveness', I contend that the effectiveness of the state needs to be seen in the context of the differential abilities of different countries with due regard given to the socio-political culture of a particular state. Throughout this study, I will, therefore, expose the underlying limitations of the unregulated market system in Bangladesh and the resultant need to protect the consumer, small businesses and the hungry poor. Hence, the need for a stronger role of the state shall be evidenced. I contend that the state is not only an important and active economic and social development actor, but it is also important because the state is the fundamental actor seeking to protect its citizens by providing goods and services, and using the economic resources of its own societies, which in turn allows markets to flourish via rules and institutions. My research views food security in a welfare context in general whilst employing a rights-based development approach (see Pinstrup-Andersen & Sandoe 2007; particularly Eide 2007). Thus, in order to promote food security, the state needs to ensure food accessibility to the hungry poor by generating state-sponsored entitlements. In other words, in this thesis, the state is seen as a source of entitlement. To that end, in order to promote development and to eradicate poverty and hunger, I finally place an emphasis on institutions which are the outcome of the political system of a particular nation state.

The Nature of the State: A Weak State or A Neopatrimonial State?

Throughout this study, I question the scope of state functions (e.g. education, health, food, etc.) and the strengths of the state institutions of the Bangladesh state in terms of their capacity to effectively carry out state functions and to pursue development programmes for its citizens. I frequently refer to state failure. Thus, according to conventional studies, this state needs to be labelled as a weak state.[2] However, in contrast with conventional analysis, although I question the state's ability, I do not term it to be a 'weak state', but rather, a neopatrimonial state. What causes this distinction? Weak states are most frequently cited and accepted as states which do not have 'capacities to penetrate society, regulate social relationships, extract resources, and appropriate or use resources in determined ways' (Migdal 1988: 4). I will discuss in Chapter 3 the point that the Bangladesh state neither has the capacity to penetrate society, nor does it regulate social relationships or extract resources. It also cannot appropriate or use resources in resource-determined ways. On the other hand, the neopatrimonial state is different from what Kohli (2007) terms as a 'cohesive-capitalist state' and/or a 'fragmented-multiclass state'. The neopatrimonial state refers to a type of state where the simultaneous operation of the Weberian ideals of 'patrimonial' and 'legal-rational' domination exist (for details, see Chapter 3). Despite the façade of a modern state, the notion of the *personalization of power* or personal rule is the key characteristic of the neopatrimonial state because the state, in neopatrimonial regimes, is treated as an extension of the property of the leader, and the leader rules with the help of clients who receive pay-offs for their support. Kohli (ibid.: 9) suggests that 'these [neopatrimonial states] are, therefore, not really modern, rational-legal states'. Here, my first argument is that when a type of state is different from other modern states, it is illogical to compare them. I, therefore, reject the approach of the 'Failed States Index'[3] for the purposes of studying the Bangladesh context. Here, it is important to note that although *Foreign Policy* and the Fund for Peace use a perception-based method of assessing state failure known as the Failed States Index, the fact that a state is a 'weak state' does not necessarily mean that it is a failed state. Paul (2010: 6-7) identified four types of weak state in the South Asian region: failed states, very weak states, weak states, and strong-weak states. This is more eloquently expressed by Patrick (2011: 19-20) who argues that:

> Over the past decade, 'failed states' have gained unprecedented attention in both official policy and popular discourse. . . . Despite this unprecedented recent attention, the concept of the 'failed state' remains vague and imprecise. Analytical shortcomings include the absence of clear criteria to measure weakness or define 'failure,' and an inattention to the specific histories, trajectories, and regimes of the countries so designated. The concept of the 'failed state' also raises troubling normative questions, implicitly placing the blame entirely on developing countries for their current circumstances, and (at least potentially) privileging the preservation of domestic order over the pursuit of justice.

My second argument is that, while a weak state is a state that fails to perform a number of activities as mentioned earlier, the failure to perform is a determined and intended outcome of regimes in the neopatrimonial Bangladesh state. For example, the ability of the state to extract resources such as through tax collection, is one of the most important pillars of measuring state weakness. Because of patronage politics, as well as 'pay-off' or exchange-based rules, regimes 'do not' extract resources (this is not to be mistaken with regimes which 'cannot' extract resources). It is the rich, particularly those linked with governmental regimes, who do not pay tax in Bangladesh: that Members of Parliaments (MPs) import luxury cars without paying tax is widely known in Bangladesh. Another point is that they do not pay income tax against their salary which is permitted via the patronage of the Prime Minister. Similarly, in a pyramidal structure of a patron-client society, state élites offer remedies for their clients to avoid tax and punishment for wrong-doing, etc.

A third reason for labelling the Bangladesh state as a neopatrimonial state rather than a weak state also lies in a distinctive analytical framework which will be proposed in Chapter 3. I will show that the Bangladesh state exhibits neopatrimonial tendencies, and argue that the costs and impacts of a neopatrimonial state can be unpacked by using several explanatory concepts. In the context of the present research, I will use five concepts: rent-seeking, public corruption, partial reform syndrome, weak state capacity, and poor governance. I contend that the concept of the weak state only partially explains the nature of the Bangladesh state while the neopatrimonial character of the state provides further explanatory tools.

Throughout this thesis, I refer to the Bangladesh state as a neopatrimonial state to indicate its weaknesses and statelessness. However, it is important to keep in mind that this weakness denotes the purposeful weakness which is associated with patronage politics. In other words, I contend that the inability of the state to perform well in regulating the market and the inability to carry out activities necessary for promoting food security are linked with the political will of the state elites. I argue that if there are problems, they are related more to patronage politics than to administrative incapacity or economic power.

Conventional Accounts of the Bangladeshi State

Bangladesh is one of the poorest countries of the world. Using economic indicators, however, some suggest that the country made considerable progress and, therefore, is often depicted as a 'development surprise' (Mahmud 2008; Mahmud, Ahmed & Mahajan 2008; Devarajan 2005; Ahluwalia & Mahmud 2004) which Banerjee and Duflo (2011: 267) describe as a 'small miracle'. Sen (2011: 44) also compared its impressive gains, focussing on social indicators, compared to India. However, Mahmud (2008: 96) rightly observed that 'the country has recovered from its image of being prone to famines and disasters, only to be perceived as one of the most corrupt and ill-governed countries'. In explaining the origin, nature and impacts of this corrupt and ill-governed country, a plethora of literature, most of which are historical narratives, attempts to map out the institutional, political, and cultural transformations that have shaped the contemporary Bangladesh state (e.g. see Riaz 2004, 2008; Milam 2009; Van Schendel 2009; Ali 2010). Several studies, for example, by Kochanek (1993, 1996, 2000) show the highly-centralized and personalized decision-making process in Bangladesh. Kochanek clearly demonstrates the recurring tendency of the state towards 'centralization' and brings two important aspects of the Bangladesh polity to the forefront: 'patronage politics' and the 'patron-client nature of politics'. However, most conventional studies point out the successive governments' legitimacy crises, civilian autocracy, the burden of military rule, and the civilization process and its consequences in democratic governance (Khan 1976; Lifschultz 1979; Bertocci 1982; Franda 1982; Zaman 1984; Ahmad 1988, 2004; Hossain 1988; Ziring 1992; Alam 1995; Jalal 1995; Jahan 2000, 2005; Evans 2001; Ahmed 2003; Maniruzzaman 2003; Kukreja 2008; Milam 2009). Some suggest that most of these conventional studies are uncritical and basically provide a straightforward narrative of history. For example, in the words of Siddiki (2011: 7), '[c]onventional accounts of the country's politics tend to take regime histories as their points of departure'. Similarly, Alam (1995) criticizes two most influential and widely-read scholars on Bangladesh politics. He (ibid.: xxii) suggests that, while analysing the politics and the state in Bangladesh, many prominent scholars such as Jahan (1972) and Maniruzzaman (1980) compiled episodes, events, facts, and 'objective' data without a context. The basic limitation of this kind of work is that it does not allow a theoretically-informed reading and interpretation of the social and political processes of a historically-constituted society (Alam 1995: xxii). Therefore, I have rigorously reviewed the literature which takes a more critical approach in examining the Bangladesh state.

In contrast, most of the critical literature demonstrates that the state that today's Bangladesh has inherited from its colonial past was simultaneously modern and 'limited'.[4] In the words of Siddiki (2011), the Bangladesh state inherited a colonial structure which was alienated from society and remained so well after Independence and the post-1990 'democratic' era. But then this alienated state also remained highly *governmentalized* since its very inception in 1971 which originated from both the colonial and 'internal colonial' rule of Pakistan: in the process, neither the practice of rendering *governmental policy* (the cause of the contention) nor the culture of *policing the people* (the cause of the action) were removed (see Ahmed 2001; emphasis original). Drawing the case of post-colonial Bangladesh and the Pakistan state, Alavi (1972) suggests that colonialism resulted in an 'overdeveloped' state relative to the comparatively underdeveloped local bourgeoisie. This overdeveloped nature of the state helped foster and preserve the interests of local élites.

The post-colonial state of Bangladesh, in the words of Alam (1995), has failed to achieve any reasonable rate of economic growth, and the development of an industrial bourgeoisie, the main concern of economic development since 1975, remains unattainable. He suggests that the centre of this problem lies in the nature of the post-colonial state of Bangladesh. He shows that since the prerequisites for internal capital formation, like viable land reform, infrastructural development, price control and the creation of a strong internal market, were never developed, the state became perpetually dependent on foreign aid. Anu Muhammad (2006) examined this failure of the state in view of the power and ownership aspects of the globalization process. He argued that, as a peripheral economy, Bangladesh has become more marketized, more globalized, and more urbanized; and in the process it now has a larger number of super-rich people and an increasing number of uprooted poor people. It is to be noted that the process of the integration of Bangladesh with the global economy has evolved and developed under the mechanism of what Sobhan (2010) calls 'unjust governance' in South Asia. With a particular focus on the Bangladesh state, in his *Challenging the Injustice of Poverty: Agendas for Inclusive Development in South Asia*, Sobhan (ibid.: 8) states that:

> [t]his inequitable and unjust social and economic universe is compounded by a system of unjust governance in South Asia, which discriminates against the excluded and effectively disenfranchises them from the political benefits of a democratic process. The excluded, whether they tend to be women, the resource-poor or minorities, remain excluded from the policy concerns of the ruling elite, voiceless in the institutions of governance and, hence, underserved by available public services. Where such services are at all accessible to the excluded, they pay high transaction costs for these services. The agencies of law enforcement insufficiently protect the excluded and frequently oppress them for personal gain as well as on behalf of the elite.

In the 'centralized' state of Bangladesh, neither the judicial system nor the institutions of democracy are responsive to the needs of the 'excluded'. The excluded of Bangladesh remain tyrannized by the state as well as by money power and have to seek the protection of their oppressors within a system of patron-client relationships, which perpetuates the prevailing hierarchies of power (Sobhan 2010: 8). Although the poor and voiceless are trapped by the state as well as by money power, the benefits of democracy remain the privilege of the elite supported by small collectives of sectoral power in an inequitable and politically unjust environment like Bangladesh (ibid.: 9). The fact is that the state remains dependent on particular social classes and, particularly, on the emerging economic elite (Sobhan 2000). Here, it is imperative to understand the following: why don't the benefits of democracy reach the poor? Why do they only remain for the privileged? In order to understand these questions, one needs to look at the existing political culture and political system of Bangladesh.

Several key concepts have been widely used by scholars in explaining the Bangladesh polity, which include: criminalization of politics, confrontational politics, eroded governance, massive corruption, lack of accountability and transparency and the absence of the rule of law (e.g. see Kochanek 1996, 2000; Khan 2000a; Zafrullah & Haque 2001; Zafarullah 2003; Sobhan 2004; Sarker & Rahman 2006; Sarker 2008; Khan 2010). The general impression of today's Bangladeshi society is that 'Bangladeshis now live in an environment in which politics has been criminalized while crime itself has been politicized' (Siddiki 2011: 17). Sobhan (2004) demonstrates how political leaders and the nature of political parties and political culture systematically criminalize politics in Bangladesh. He argues that political leaders now increasingly use *mastaans* or hoodlums as a political resource in their contention for political office and use state patronage to access public resources. Politically-patronised *mastaan* culture has institutionalized itself over successive regimes. This extra-legal activity is now an integral part in the election system and in securing a support base in particular areas (ibid.). As a result, as one observer suggests, the country is now caught in an economic trap of criminalization (Barakat 2003; as cited in Siddiki 2011: 17).

The strong bipolar system of the polity is extremely confrontational in nature. Since 1990, the almost equal strength of the two major political parties has contributed to the emergence of a duopoly over the national political system. This *winner-take-all* power game in Bangladesh is not the outcome of class difference nor is it based on ideological difference but, rather, it is based on power sharing over the state's resources. This power sharing is concerned with job sharing, the acquisition of property and business licences and tenders, etc. (see Sobhan 2004; Mohsin & Guha-Thakurta 2007; Siddiki 2011). The nature of this takeover of power resembles, in the words of Mohsin and Guha-Thakurta (2007: 50), the politics of *char dokhol* (the occupation of *char* lands), which is more typical of a thriving peasantry than a burgeoning bourgeois democracy. The competition's zero-sum nature raises stakes, helping to institutionalize violence as an instrument of political pursuits (see Peiris 1998; Datta 2005; Maniruzzaman 2009; Ali 2010; for a general overview of political violence, see Islam 2011). In this political culture, the rest of the society is forced to go with the more powerful party if they wish to participate in and receive benefits from the system. Force and patronage politics trump ideology and political predilections in this instance (Siddiki 2011: 15).

The rapid erosion in governance is another important feature of the Bangladesh polity. As Kochanek (2000) notes, '[d]espite large amounts of aid, the World Bank and Western donors argue that poor governance and weak institutions in Bangladesh have acted as significant constraints on development'. In explaining the state, a considerable number of studies have focussed on the governance issues of Bangladesh (Kochanek 2000; Zafrullah & Haque 2001; Khan 2003, 2010; Sobhan 2004; Roy 2006; Sarker 2008). The main argument of these studies is that, as a result of the rapid erosion in governance, the political system remains fragile and unstable, the economy in disarray, and social services are practically non-existent. For example, Khan (2003) notes that the state of governance in Bangladesh is in dismal shape: social, political and economic governance suffer from stagnation and show little sign of progress. In fact, political governance in Bangladesh is a problem and political institutions are becoming increasingly dysfunctional due to the imperfections prevailing in political markets (Roy 2006: 16). On the other hand, Mahmud (2008) highlights Bangladesh's impressive record of economic growth despite what he calls 'apparently poor governance'. Khan (2010) rightly points out that 'economic growth and indices of governance in Bangladesh tend to move in dissimilar directions'. He further argues that the deeply-entrenched illiberal democracy could not suppress the flowering of her people's creativity in agriculture, microcredit for the ultra-poor, innovative programmes of NGOs in primary health and education, and the vibrancy of civil society.

CONCLUSION

In this chapter, my aim was twofold. First, I sought to sketch the operational definition of food security so that this definition could be employed throughout this thesis, and also to explore the different approaches of the food security literature in Bangladesh. And second, I critically examined the degree of state intervention in promoting growth and development, the institutional capacity of the state in promoting development, and the nature of the Bangladesh state. By examining 40 recognized definitions published from 1975 to 2010, although I propose that there are five recurring key terms of the definition of food security (access, availability, utilization, vulnerability, and food safety and quality), it is important to note that, throughout the thesis, I will only examine two aspects of food security, namely food availability and accessibility. By analysing these two aspects of food security, that is, food availability and accessibility, I attempt to make a national-level analysis of the politics of food security in Bangladesh. A rigorous review of Bangladesh's food security literature shows that there is a significant gap of academic research relating to state-centric and national-level analysis of the politics of food security in Bangladesh. On the other hand, by examining the state, its institutional capacity, and development, I assert the argument of NIE which suggests that the 'institutions do matter'. In the light of the study by Acemoglu and Robinson (2012), as noted earlier, I contend that the origin of power, prosperity and poverty of nations very much depends on its institutions. Therefore, in order to provide basic services to the citizens, the state institutions need to be effective. In this study, by employing the framework of the state as presented in this chapter, I will, therefore, particularly focus on the underlying limitations of the unregulated market system in Bangladesh and the resultant need to protect the consumer, the small businesses and the hungry poor. It is to be noted that, throughout this thesis, by considering state weakness as the result of patronage politics, I refer to the Bangladesh state as a neopatrimonial state to indicate its weaknesses and statelessness instead of taking the conventional approach of it being a 'weak state'. Finally, I concluded this chapter by illustrating the conventional literature of the Bangladesh state, and I link my work with existing critical scholarship and seek to extend what has already been written.

NOTES

1. According to C.R. Løvendal, M. Knowles & N. Horii (2004), vulnerability refers to people's propensity to fall, or stay, below a predetermined food security threshold. Vulnerability is a function of people's exposure to risks and of their resilience to these. By risks we understand events or trends that create a measure of instability which may have a negative impact on people's welfare. Resilience is determined by the potential effectiveness of risk management strategies (prevention, mitigation and coping) in maintaining a person above a minimum welfare threshold or in preventing that person from falling into an even deeper state of ill-being as the result of a negative

event or trend. In the words of FOA (2008), utilization is commonly understood as the way the body makes the most of various nutrients in food. Sufficient energy and nutrient intake by individuals is the result of good care and feeding practices, food preparation, diversity of the diet and intra-household distribution of food. Combined with good biological utilization of food consumed, this determines the nutritional status of individuals. See, Chapter 4 for details concerning food availability and accessibility.

2. Considering the scope and function of modern state as noted earlier, unlike the Western states, the Bangladesh state is very weak as it does not have a plethora of enforcement agencies to enforce anything from traffic rules to commercial law. For example, the United States has a system of limited government that has historically restricted the scope of state activity. Within that scope, its ability to create and enforce laws and policies is very strong (Fukuyama 2004: 9). On the other hand, the ability to create and enforce laws and policies is very weak in Bangladesh compared to the United States or any other Western democratic state. On the contrary, some see the state as a power organization that engages in 'centralized, industrialized, territorialized regulation of many aspects of social relation' (Mann 1986: 26). Mann suggests that 'the capacity of the state actually to penetrate civil society, and to implement logistically political decisions throughout the realm' (ibid. 1986b: 113; quoted in Migdal 1994: 11-12). In this respect too, Bangladesh is not a very strong state as its civil society is highly fragmented and often works based on patronage in carrying out the distribution of state resources. Grindle (1996) suggests that capable states ought to have: 'institutional capacity', 'technical capacity', 'administrative capacity', and 'political capacity'. Theoretically as well as practically, none of these elements of a capable state is strong in the Bangladesh state.
3. According to the Failed States Index 2011, Bangladesh ranks 25 (in danger category) and scores 94.4.
4. I borrowed this argument from Kohli (2007: 228) who argues by drawing on the case of India. According to Kohli (ibid.), 'The state that sovereign India inherited from its colonial past was simultaneously modern and "limited". It was modern in at least two senses. First, the state was centralized. It held a monopoly over the use of coercion in the territory it governed. And, at least at the apex, it was relatively bureaucratized on the basis of a clear separation between the public and various personal realms. And second, it was increasingly constitutional, with elements of a parliamentary government. But then this state was also quite limited: First, the colonial state had by design been essentially laissez-faire. Second, and less obviously but of more

profound importance, the British entered into a variety of ruling alliances with traditional Indian elites, limiting the state's downward reach. And third, Indian nationalist leaders mobilized various social classes into politics, which pushed a limited colonial state into a reactive mode. This modern but limited state was India's fragmented-multiclass state in the making, the product of both colonial state construction and pressures from Indians, especially the nationalist elites'.

CHAPTER 3

The Political Origin of Hunger in Bangladesh

INTRODUCTION

To understand the political dimensions of food security in Bangladesh, this book focusses on the nature of the state, the institutional effectiveness, and the state capacity of Bangladesh. To do so, in this chapter, I endeavour to investigate the nature of the Bangladesh state and highlight the neopatrimonial character of the relationships underpinning it. This chapter is broadly divided into two parts. The first section seeks to examine the empirical evidence on the personalization of power and the development of clientelism, and attempts to show why the concept of neopatrimonialism is helpful in explaining politics in Bangladesh. Here I am particularly interested in examining whether the Bangladesh state is a special variant of the neopatrimonial state. I seek to examine how successive governments and political leaders have always attempted to monopolize state power in various ways since Independence. I posit that the patron-client society of Bangladesh indeed helps political leaders to personalize the state power they possess. To monopolize state power, the political elites of Bangladesh create networks and alliances, relying on *exchanges* to meet their objectives. In this regard, state elites use elements of the state and political system to mediate these exchanges.

The aim of the second section is to develop and explain an analytical framework with five central explanatory concepts—rent-seeking, public corruption, partial reform syndrome, weak state and poor governance—to be used throughout the study. In this section, I attempt to examine the costs and impacts of the neopatrimonial regimes/politics in Bangladesh. I seek to investigate whether neopatrimonial regimes in Bangladesh survive based on patronage politics where personalized exchanges are the mechanism of the government. I explore the way in which the personalization of state power undermines democratic governance in various ways: whether it protects the vice of corruption or works as a catalyst in rent-seeking, it deters the reform mechanism necessary for good governance. I also attempt to examine the linkage between patronage politics, the systematic regression of the state capacity, and the poor governance of Bangladesh. Here, it is noteworthy to point out that many see fragile bureaucratic capacity rent-seeking and corruption, uncoordinated public management, politicization and political interference in civil administration, etc., as factors impairing state capacity (Zafarullah & Rahman 2008). I attempt to examine how these factors are an inseparable part of neopatrimonial regimes and how patronage politics, which is the outcome of neopatrimonial regimes, further weakens those factors. I contend that in contemporary Bangladesh politics, the goals and skills of state leaders largely determine the capacity of the other institutions of the state such as civil administration and are thus the key determinant factor of the state capacity.

THE POLITICS OF CLIENTELISM AND PERSONALIZATION OF POWER IN BANGLADESH

In order to examine whether the Bangladesh state is a special variant of the neopatrimonial state, which I suggest to be a bipolar neopatrimonialism, in this section, I seek to examine how successive governments and political leaders have always attempted to monopolize state power in various ways. Throughout this section, I endeavour to explain Bangladesh politics in light of the concept of neopatrimonialism, with special reference to the personalization of state power. I begin this discussion by conceptualizing neopatrimonialism in theory and practice. I then draw on the historical background of Bangladesh in order to understand the origin of the patron-client relationship which characterizes this society. Then, I seek to explore how various regimes have attempted to monopolize state power, which is followed by an analysis of contemporary politics with special reference to party politics in Bangladesh. I then address the tools and mechanisms that function as catalysts to consolidate power in the hands of the leader. The chapter finally concludes with the argument that Bangladesh is a special variant of the neopatrimonial state.

Neopatrimonialism in Theory and Practice: Conceptual Framework

Before conceptualizing the term 'neopatrimonialism', it is imperative to begin this discussion by defining patrimonialism because the term denotes the simultaneous operation of the Weberian ideals of 'patrimonial' and 'legal-rational' domination (Medard 1982, as quoted in Clapham 1985: 48; Bratton & Van de Walle 1997: 62). According to Weber (1978: 1041), a patrimonial state is one in which '[p]ractically everything depends explicitly upon personal considerations: Upon the attitude towards the concrete applicant and his concrete request and upon purely personal connections, favours, promises, and privileges' (as cited in Marcus 2010: 17). Under this system, where the exchange of resources occurs between political officials and their associates, policies tend to be particularistic rather than universalistic in nature, the rule of law is secondary to the 'rule of man' or 'rule of woman' and political officials tend to blur the boundaries between the public and private realms (Eisenstadt 1973; Callaghy 1984; Budd 2004). In other words, the right to rule is ascribed to a person rather than an office (Weber 1978; Theobold 1982; Braton & Van de Walle 1994: 458), and the allegiance to a leader is based on personal loyalty and customary legitimacy and not on legal-rational legitimacy. On the contrary, at least in principle, both the organization and the legitimacy of the post-colonial state rest on what Weber described as legal-rational authority. Therefore, patrimonial rule in post-colonial developing countries relies upon modern forms of exchange between patrons and clients rather than customary legitimacy. Because of this contradiction between the Weberian ideal of patrimonial rule and the political nature of modern developing countries, Eisenstadt (1973), Medard (1982, 2002), Clapham (1982, 1985) and others have developed the analysis of neo-patrimonialism. With the emergence of 'democracy' in the 1990s, it became difficult for leaders to gain enough legitimacy through patrimonial relations to maintain power (Marcus 2010: 117). With this changing context, most developing countries' leaders seek to maintain their power by employing various new strategies which can be better understood by reference to neopatrimonialism.

Neopatrimonialism has commonly been conceptualized as a form of organization in which relationships of a broadly patrimonial type pervade a political and administrative system which is formally constructed on legal-rational lines (Medard, as cited in Clapham 1985: 48). In other words, it is a combination of two types of political domination: patrimonial and legal-rational bureaucratic domination. In neopatrimonial regimes, the chief executive exercises unlimited and incalculable powers as far as it can, as a form not of public service but of private property through personal patronage rather than through ideology or law. Relationships with others likewise fall into the patrimonial pattern of vassal and lord, rather than the rational-legal one of subordinate and superior, and behaviour is correspondingly calculated to reflect personal status, rather than to perform an official function (ibid.). Unlike social practice which is often personal and informal, public norms under these types of regimes are formal and rational. Therefore, neopatrimonial regimes are intimately linked to informality and formality with each other, in various ways and by varying degrees (Bratton & Van de Walle 1994; Marcus 2010: 117).

The notion of the *personalization of power* is the key characteristic of the neopatrimonial state because the state, in neopatrimonial regimes, is treated as an extension of the property of the leader, and the leader rules with the help of clients who get a pay-off for their support. There are diverse examples of neopatrimonialism indicating that the basis of this new form of rule is the ability of leaders to personalize their power and avoid accountability (Khan 2005: 714). Regimes often use various means to personalize state power as patronage alone is often not enough to achieve this end. For instance, once civil society is considered a threat to the regime's authority, neopatrimonial rule will undercut it, thus weakening the foundation for anti-systemic change and setting about weakening all independent centres of power (Bratton & Van de Walle 1994: 462). Migdal (1988) shows how fear of rivals drives dictators to emasculate the very state institutions that could institutionalize their rule (as cited in Bratton & Van de Walle 1994: 462).

Although many scholars use the concept of clientelism or neopatrimonialism to characterize an entire political system of a particular nation, often focussing in particular upon African and Latin American politics, this does not necessarily imply that this form of rule takes place only in non-democratic countries. As noted earlier, a number of studies suggest that neopatrimonial behaviour can coexist with democratic norms in countries such as Russia, Uzbekistan, Nigeria, Venezuela, and Cote d'Ivoire (for details, see Marcus 2010: 117). In insecure political and economic environments, according to Migdal (1988), clientelism is a fertile breeding ground and is integral to the 'politics of survival' for both patron and client. Here it is imperative to clarify that the patron-client relationship or clientelism is indeed an application of the principles of neopatrimonialism to relationships between superiors and inferiors (Clapham 1985: 55). This is a complex network and an alliance of personal bonds between superiors (patrons) and inferiors (clients or followers) which relies on mutual exchanges for parties to meet their objectives. In this form of exchange, the patron provides protection and/or all forms of benefits including resources such as money, employment, etc., to dependents and accomplices by using political power; conversely, the client provides their support and cooperation (votes, attendance at rallies) in return.

Thus, in brief, in a patrimonial system, the rule of law is secondary to the 'rule of man' or 'rule of woman' and political officials tend to blur the boundaries between the public and private realms. In other words, the right to rule is attributed to a person rather than an office, and the allegiance to a leader is based on personal loyalty and customary legitimacy and not on legal-rational legitimacy. In contrast, neopatrimonialism is a form of organization which is a combination of two types of political domination: patrimonial and legal-rational bureaucratic domination.

Nature of The Social Stratification and Patron-Client Relationships in Bangladesh

In order to examine Bangladesh politics in the light of neopatrimonialism, I firstly examine the social stratification of contemporary Bangladesh society in its historical context. Here, my premise is that although traditional social stratification has changed dramatically over the years, it still maintains the same patron-client relationship[1] which can be likened to 'old wine in a new bottle'. This has paved the way for successive regimes to personalize state power.

Historically, Bangladeshi society has become increasingly based on a subtle and intense network of interpersonal patron-client relations. In particular, rural society is highly fragmented and hierarchically structured based on miniscule distinctions in rank and status (Kochanek 1993: 44). Traditionally, the social stratification system of Bengal was very strong: Hindu society was built along caste lines which later patterned Muslim social stratification. However, during the colonial period, initially as a result of the 'Permanent Settlement' in 1793 and, subsequently, due to emerging business, politics and other forms of elite formations, class identities of the upper classes began to change. Subsequent land policy in the colonial period caused a highly stratified society to come about based on land interests. As a result, the following agrarian classes and groups were found to constitute rural society with hierarchical status and prestige: landlords/capitalist farmers, rich peasants, middle-class peasants, poor/marginal peasants, and landless labourers. This hierarchical structure of society essentially created a patron-client network.

Despite the above noted changes, patron-client relationships were reinforced in rural Bangladesh throughout the colonial and post-colonial period, by mainly economic factors such as the scarcity of credit, scarcity of land, tenancy contracts and employment opportunities as well as by political factors, such as the need for protection. The strength of the patron network makes it difficult to develop horizontal relationships and larger corporate ties (ibid.). Although each household is responsible for itself, typologies of relationships which are based on dependency continue to exist in society. This relationship is based on reciprocal exchanges where one group of people acts as a patron and another group is treated as a client. While the patrons are accorded the right to extract labour, services, and respect from people of lower ranks, clients, in turn, can expect material and other forms of support from their patrons. A very basic service of the state (e.g. filing a general diary in a police station) is not accessible to a poor villager without the help of the 'powerful' local elite. Thus, this is the way a mutual interdependence based on hierarchical structure works. Kochanek (ibid.) suggests that the very strength of the patron-client network inhibits the development of corporate units based on kinship, politics or geography, and strengthens a system of individual customary patrimonial leadership based on charisma, patronage and corruption.

Although there is no direct comparability in urban society to the rural structure, the nature of the patron-client relationship also dominates urban social life in various ways and in various forms. A common local saying, *chacha-mama chara chakri hoy na* (you won't get a job unless you have an uncle or a maternal uncle), demonstrates the necessity of a 'connection' to gain anything in society, ranging from a business opportunity to obtaining employment, or a promotion to job security, or very basic social justice. The very fact that, as Sobhan (2010: 8) notes, '. . . the excluded of South Asia remain tyrannised by state as well as money power and have to seek the protection of their oppressors, within a system of patron-client relationship, which perpetuates the prevailing hierarchies of power'. Over the years, although the democratic process has been renewed after long episodes of autocratic rule, the excluded in such a social universe are still denied adequate access to office in political parties or representation in the systems of democratic governance from the local to the national level (ibid.).

The contemporary democracy of Bangladesh further strengthens the power of a handful of the political elite. In the words of Sobhan (ibid.: 8-9), '[r]epresentative institutions tend to be monopolized by the affluent and socially powerful, who then use their electoral office to enhance their wealth and thereby perpetuate their hold over power'.

The nature of the patron-client relationship in Bangladesh is that individuals acquire their prosperity from a higher authority that is legitimized by the individuals' feeling that they have a moral right to command food and subsistence, and abstract goods from those who are well-placed (Maloney 1986: 41; Kochanek 2000: 548). Individuals who command resources (including wealth, education or *tadbir*, i.e. help through political or administrative connections) are expected to distribute them to clients and, in return, those in command expect to be both feared and obeyed. The nature of this society causes leaders to be authoritarian and authority becomes highly personalized rule (ibid.). According to Kochanek (ibid.), 'the very texture of Bangladesh society and the general pattern of interpersonal relations contribute to the problem of institutional weakness, organizational development and effectiveness, and the absence of consensus. This pattern of behavior is reflected in Bangladesh political parties, governmental institutions, and civil society at large'. In an interview, a prominent civil society member, rights activist and Bangladeshi author argues that 'we are citizens of an independent country on paper only, in practice we are still subjects (*proja*) of the state'.

Thus, clientelism, a form of political contact, has permeated Bangladesh society from top to bottom. It has established a whole chain of patron-client relationship. In a pyramidal structure, this web connects the prime minister, through numerous links down the system, to the lowly peasant. Each client uses the resources received from the patron above them to build their own patronage empire. Individuals, therefore, simultaneously act as a client of a superior and as a patron to those below them.

Personalization of State Power: Return to Multi-Party 'Democracy', The Rise of Neopatrimonial Rule, and Personalized Decision Making

While in Western nation states, representative, accountable and efficient governments usually distribute political power to the various organs of the state so that no one area could become hegemonic, in Bangladesh, political leadership struggles to personalize state power. For instance, since Independence, successive governments of

Bangladesh have continuously tried to control the judiciary under the executive. Every government of Bangladesh has wanted to accumulate power in specific core offices of the state, and usually within the executive branch. In other words, a monopoly over all formal political power is sought by the leaders. With respect to the accumulation of power, and despite rule by whichever party or the military, the basic character of leadership remains the same. A plethora of studies (e.g. Khan 1976; Zaman 1984; Ziring 1992; Kochanek 1993; Alam 1995; Jalal 1995; Ahmed 2004; Kukreja 2008; Milam 2009; Ali 2010) shows the historical trend of power accumulation as well as the personalized decision-making trend in Bangladesh.

In the following section, I examine four regimes in Bangladesh in which two leaders held office, in order to understand the nature and similarity of power accumulation by the successive leaders of Bangladesh since the return of 'pluralistic democracy' in 1991. I argue that regime change in Bangladesh only affects a small group of elites and it does not bring any significant change to these state mechanisms and society.

After the return of multi-party democracy in 1991, the Bangladesh polity switched from a presidential rule to a parliamentary system. Although the presidential system switched to the parliamentary system, in the words of Muhith (2006: 5), 'the switch did not bring about collective responsibility of cabinet or the end of the arbitrary rule of the head of government. The presidential secretariat was just converted into the Prime Minister's Office (PMO) and it retained the same absolute control over all ministers'. This parliamentary democracy has strong competitive dynastic politics and is what I call a 'hybrid system' consisting of an amalgamation of presidential and parliamentary democracy—this is a uniquely Bangladeshi type of democracy somewhat removed from the Westminster system. Like many other Western democracies, this 'one-day democracy' (personal interview, IvCS6) has also formally defined power, but regimes under this system exercise power informally as long as they can. In the following part of this discussion, I will examine the nature of regimes under this hybrid parliamentary democracy.

Theoretically, 'in "neopatrimonial regimes" political leaders may represent no more than a tiny coterie of clients and may be unable to build a political consensus around any intra-elite agreement. The emerging political parties and civic organizations typically lack traditions, experience and funds, and find it difficult to escape factionalism' (Bratton & Van de Walle 1994: 465). In Bangladesh, with a strong political background in the anti-Ershad movement, Khaleda Zia had no administrative experience. However, her leadership was unchallenged and power was accumulated extraordinarily in both her party and office. During her regimes (in both 1991-6 and 2001-6) she was increasingly surrounded by a coterie of inexperienced advisors (clients) who were previously advisors of President Zia: some of them had also advised President Ershad. Fragmentation within these elites is always so prevalent that the only remaining challenge for a party leader is to appoint his/her deputy, a position every group member wants. As a result, as Kochanek (2000: 534) argues, during Khaleda's office in 1991-6, she practised a 'slow, highly centralized, and highly personalized decision making' style of government. In a personal interview, a very close observer of her second tenure also suggested that decision making was slow, highly centralized, and personalized (IvGOB8). A leaked US embassy cable sent by former Ambassador, Harry K. Thomas sheds light on the 'dysfunctional decision making' process of Bangladesh under Khaleda Zia (2001-6) and its control by a handful of individuals. Thomas notes that:

> Loyalty, proximity, and length of service to PM Zia still count for far more than title or institutional position, but for Zia loyalty is a two-way street. Many insiders have a close relationship with her son and heir apparent, Tariq Rahman. The good news is the USG has productive relationships with 12 of the 17 insiders. . . . The bad news is that very few of them have the ability or the interest to pressure Zia's basic outlook on politics or governance (Wikileaks 2011a).

Similarly, recalling Sheikh Hasina's first tenure as Prime Minister, Kochanek (2000: 536; also personal interview, IvGOB8) points out that 'power within the [Awami] League has been highly centralized and personalized and decision making has been surrounded by secrecy. There is a total absence of prior consultation. Formal institutions including the cabinet play only a minor role, and decisions are made on the advice of a very small group of Hasina's relatives and personal advisors'. In her second tenure (2009-current), according to an official note of the US diplomatic mission in Bangladesh, '. . . Hasina relies on a small circle of trusted relatives, family friends, and time-tested devoted advisers while sidelining individuals she perceives as disloyal. Hasina's sister and son who reside abroad, are among her closest confidantes'. Although there is a small circle of trusted people, this report further emphasized that '[u]ltimately, however, Hasina trusts close family relations to carry out her most sensitive agenda' (Wikileaks 2011b). The nature of the regime shows all the symptoms of personal rule.[2] An article published in *The Economist* ([London], 30 July 2011) suggests that her regime 'is becoming increasingly autocratic'.[3] I will further discuss her immense inclination towards power accumulation and its strategies below.

A critical investigation of the successive regimes suggests that the basic character of leadership in Bangladesh since Independence remains the same. The basic goal of all the political leaders is to achieve centralized power by any means. In generating the personalization of power, every regime has focussed on the centralization of state power rather than decentralization. Political leaders show no interest in the concept of a 'separation of powers' between various branches of the state such as the executive and the judiciary; powers are also never dispersed between the state and civil society. A common practice is that different regimes always take initiatives to monopolize the political process in various state institutions, with initiatives being taken to render parliament ineffective. Thus, while power was concentrated by the Mujib regime through constitutional means (i.e. by introducing a one-party system), military regimes utilizing coercion in the absence of pluralism are now dangerously concentrated by the state's various strategies.

To personalize power in the centralized state of Bangladesh, regimes effectively formed patron-client relationships with various groups and associations such as student branches of political parties, labour unions, professional groups and even the civil bureaucracy of the nation. In this process, civil society leaders received direct patronage and in return only served one higher authority. Since Independence, every regime has operated the same way: after a regime changes, it is a common phenomenon in Bangladesh that all institutions see a change in the office chief. For example, considering educational institutions, such as universities, as potential threats to the government, the incumbent regime forces the vice-chancellor to resign and then appoints a more obedient one based on 'connections'; student wings of the incumbent political party also occupy and control university campuses with the support of the police and paramilitary forces. Unlike other societies, such as in Africa where the centralization process can be completed effectively, in Bangladesh it is a never-ending process because some challenges to the personalization of state power always remain. This threat of challenge further encourages governments to continually monopolize power and enforce stronger clientelist politics.

Political Parties, Political Culture and Clientelism: Power Accumulation Through Dynastic Politics

Neopatrimonial rule in Bangladesh is not based on customary legitimacy but rather on modern forms of exchange between patrons and clients. However, this complex web of clientelism is not only practised in the state apparatus but also appears in the internal political structure of major political parties in Bangladesh. Although many suggest that there are some differences between major political parties based on ideological orientations and the origins of the party, the fact is that over the years the ideological distinctions between parties have been reduced dramatically. Rather, the major political parties of Bangladesh now share some common characteristics the most notable of which is the clientelistic political system. While many argue that hereditary politics and the lack of internal democracy are main characteristics of the political culture, I argue that these are only tools of clientelistic politics. These tools only strengthen power accumulation in the hands of the party chief which is then further entrenched in the pyramidal structure of a patron-client network. I suggest two major features of the party politics of Bangladesh: (a) strong competitive bipolar dynastic politics; and (b) patron-client politics.

A COMPETITIVE BIPOLAR POLITICAL SYSTEM

The principal characteristic of the democratic political tradition in Bangladesh is a competitive two-party system. National politics is divided between two major political parties: the Awami League and the Bangladesh Nationalist Party (BNP), each of whom forms a polarity with small political parties to further strengthen their power. Each party has held office and demonstrated that it can win elections and has the ability to challenge any attempt by a ruling party to impose its will on the national polity (Sobhan 2004). Although the strength of such a bipolar political system is well known in modern democracy, it has contributed to the confrontational style of polarity in Bangladesh.

Over the years, the Bangladesh polity has become sharply polarized and people are now more divided than ever before. In other words, the strong bipolar political competition has effectively been forging two separate 'tribes' in a homogeneous society, which I call the politics of tribalization. A winner-takes-all power game can be used to describe the political polarity in Bangladesh. Mohsin and Guha-Thakurta (2007: 50) suggest that 'the polarization . . . did not reflect class differences. Conflicts between the Awami League and BNP were more about power sharing than anything else—namely, they were concerned with job sharing, the acquisition of property and business licences and tenders, as has been clearly demonstrated in open disputes between the two student branches of mainstream parties in various university campuses'. I compare Bangladesh to one kingdom with two dynasties where 'incumbent and opposing leaders are usually so polarized as a result of the *winner-takes-all power struggles* that there is slim potential for moderate factions from either side to negotiate an agreement' (Bratton & Van de Walle 1994: 465; emphasis added). Some ingredients of this sharp polarization include: 'Bengali vs. Bangladeshi' nationalism, 'pro-Pakistan vs. anti-Pakistan', 'pro-Indian vs. anti-Indian', 'secularism vs. Islamist', 'Mujib vs. Zia' (a competition of national heroes) and using or misusing the past, particularly the heroes' roles in the Independence war of 1971. As a result of *winner-takes-all power struggles* and the possibility of being vanquished if power struggles fail, political elites see the personalization of state power as the only way to survive in an insecure political and economic environment. As a result, Bangladeshi politics offer a very special type of neopatrimonial character.

PATRON-CLIENT POLITICS

The basic feature of Bangladesh's politics is its patron-client structure. Some other distinct political features include a lack of internal democracy, hereditary dynastic politics, etc., which are simultaneously, the tools and by-products of the clientelistic politics.

As noted earlier, a number of studies suggest that the nature of Bangladesh politics is patrimonial. A key argument of conventional studies is that the relationship between the party loyalist and the leaders is unmistakably a patron-client relationship (Riaz 2008: 23). In fact, political parties in Bangladesh are multi-class organizations that bring together a large number of patron-client networks in a pyramidal structure (Khan 2000a: 17). Looking from the top down, political party leaders at the national level look around for local leaders who command appropriate support within their own areas. They offer the local leader a place in the party via nomination as the Member of Parliament (MP) in his home constituency or local party leadership, or both. It has been observed in Bangladesh that the decision of the party chief is final regarding nominations for MP candidates although 'eyewash' attempts are undertaken by each party through a committee. However, the local leader manages to garner the votes essentially through his own contacts and authority, and delivers it to the national party. The national party, in turn, assuming that it will come into power, delivers benefits to its local representative either in the form of economic allocations from the centre to the constituency or through a purely personal pay-off or of central government support in local political conflicts. On the other hand, looking from the bottom up, according to Khan (ibid.), '. . . the basic component of any party or coalition, however large, is a pyramid of basic patron-client factions. Each of these is organized around a single or small group of leaders. These basic patron-client factions are ubiquitous and range from neighbourhood groups led by petty *mafia* bosses known in Bangladesh as *mastans* to village factions led by somewhat more respectable *matabbars, dalals* and *upazilla* chairman [a present Member of Parliament (MP)]'. However, the above-mentioned patron-client politics are sustained by two other basic features of Bangladesh politics, namely, (i) hereditary dynastic politics, and (ii) a lack of internal democracy within party politics. In the following section, I show how these mechanisms only strengthen the patron-client politics of Bangladesh.

Presently, the leadership of the two major political parties, the BNP and the Awami League, is hereditary. In the past 20 years, it has been proven that there is no place for any leadership if that entails a challenge to the dynastic leadership authority of Hasina of the Awami League, the daughter of Sheik Mujib, and Khaleda Zia of BNP, the widow of late President General Ziaur Rahman. In the contemporary party politics of Bangladesh, the top leadership has never been challenged as clients would risk losing out entirely if they challenged their existing patrons. Within the party culture, these hereditary dynastic politics are not only unchallenged, but there is also huge competition among party followers or clients to further strengthen the existing dynasty.

On the other hand, many political observers identify that major political parties in Bangladesh are constitutionally undemocratic, and that the party activities such as policymaking, decision-making, and committee structuring are centered on the cult of the leader (Barman et al. 2001: 44). Leaders of these political parties accumulated patrimonial rights to control the parties. These patrimonial rights are not only a matter of practice, but are also incorporated in the party constitutions. For example, the constitution of BNP entrusts absolute authority to the party chairman, and its chief holds all the executive powers of the party. The chairman will determine the posts, positions, responsibilities and authority of various office-bearers of the office' (Karim 2004).

The general perception of the society, in relation to the unprecedented power of the party chief in both the BNP and the AL, is that 'leaders and activists of both the parties are apparently highly obedient and they say *yes* when their party chairman or president says *yes* and they say *no* when their chief says *no*' (ibid. 2004). As a consequence of this power, the party chief can easily accumulate her/his power through patronage and coercion (which entails expulsion from the party). In the process, many top level party leaders have been expelled when they lost the trust of the chairperson and, overnight, many ordinary leaders became very powerful by dint of gaining personal trust.

Elsewhere, I (see Islam 2013) have examined how various organs of the state such as parliaments, local governments, the bureaucracy, the judiciary and other institutions became subordinate to the executive. Here it is important to note that in contemporary Bangladesh politics, as the political leaders occupy the highest offices of the state, the politicians and political parties stand at the centre of a complex set of relationships and exercise state power. Thus, politicians determine and influence the careers of individual members of the bureaucracy or military (Alavi 1972: 62). Thus, unlike the military-bureaucracy oligarchy during the period of military rule in 1976-90, the contemporary elite club is a conglomeration of a political-military-bureaucratic-business oligarchy where politicians play the central role. However, if individual members of the bureaucracy or military gain the trust of the government through the practice of clientelism, he/she can secure maximum power in his/her domain.

TROUBLES OF A NEOPATRIMONIAL STATE: RENT-SEEKING, PUBLIC CORRUPTION, PARTIAL REFORM SYNDROME, WEAK STATE CAPACITY AND POOR GOVERNANCE

While the purpose of the previous discussion was to suggest that Bangladesh is a neopatrimonial state, the aim of this section is to establish an analytical framework which I will employ throughout this thesis. In doing so, I investigate the costs and impacts of the neopatrimonial regimes/politics in Bangladesh. The analysis utilizes five key concepts: rent-seeking activity, public corruption, partial reform syndrome, poor governance, and weak state capacity. In other words, in order to establish a framework for analysing the politics of food security in a neopatrimonial state like Bangladesh, here I attempt to capture how these concepts pose a challenge to development in a neopatrimonial state. I posit that the aim of the personalization of state power undermines democratic governance in various ways: it protects the vice of corruption, works as a catalyst in rent-seeking, erodes state capacity, challenges the rule of law, and seeks reforms only for the sake of regime survival. I then suggest that there is a strong relationship between politics, business and corruption in Bangladesh. To monopolize state power, the political elites of Bangladesh create networks and these alliances rely on *exchanges* to meet their objectives. In this regard, state elites use elements of the state and political system to mediate these exchanges. These exchange-based bonds of relationships between politics, business and corruption are not only procrastinating reforms for improving governance but also impede the institutional development for ensuring good governance.

Rent-seeking Activity

My purpose in this section is twofold. First, I attempt to examine rent-seeking activity in the context of a neopatrimonial Bangladesh state. Second, by examining the degree and nature of rent-seeking in Bangladesh, I intend to deploy it as a framework in subsequent chapters of this thesis in order to capture the politics of food security in Bangladesh. My argument is that if the rent-seeking activity is an inseparable part of the successive regimes of Bangladesh, then it will do much to explain the challenges of food availability and accessibility as a development outcome of the state.

Rent-seeking is widespread in politics. It is particularly widespread in patron-client systems as they tend to have fewer countervailing powers or 'agents of restraint' (Collier & Pattillo 2000) to check the insiders as they use their contacts to pursue self-serving government policies (Brinkerhoff & Goldsmith 2002: 12). Rent-seeking can be broadly interpreted as activities which seek to create, maintain or change the rights and institutions on which particular rents are based (Khan 2000b: 6). In other words, economic rents are simply windfall gains that would be absent in competitive markets: these include occupational licences, franchises, permits, special tax breaks, business subsidies and tariffs (Brinkerhoff & Goldsmith 2002: 12). As noted earlier, the key characteristic of the patron-client politics of Bangladesh is the politics of patronage. All patronage goes from patron to client through channels such as occupational licences, franchises, permits, special tax breaks, business subsidies, tariffs, etc.

Rent-seeking is widespread in every regime in Bangladesh. Rent-seeking activity is nothing new in contemporary Bangladesh politics. As a legacy of colonial and Pakistani rule, since Bangladesh's birth as a nation state, rent-seeking has been an integral part of every regime although the degree of patronage varies from government to government. For instance, rent-seeking was widespread in the first administration of Bangladesh after Independence.[4]

Similarly, during the military regime in Pakistan, as Alavi (1983: 66) points out, from the 1960s, many army officers became deeply involved with the business community and some generals emerged (as did some senior bureaucrats) as some of the biggest businessmen in the country. After Bangladesh's Independence, in a move mimicking the Pakistan military, many army officers under the military regime of Zia and Ershad, together with their civil bureaucrat partners, became deeply involved with the business community. Many were given prestigious and profitable places on boards of companies on their retirement and others, still in service, could look forward to similar rewards, and cultivated contracts for that purpose. Similar ties were also established with large foreign business concerns in Bangladesh.

Because of rent-seeking, during the regime of the military-bureaucracy oligarchy in Bangladesh (1975-90), as noted earlier, an entrepreneur with good political connections could easily set up a plant without contributing any financial investment of his own (Alam 1995: 93). It is argued that 'rapid growth and government policy have created a large class of "briefcase" businessmen and indenters who make huge profits by taking advantage of the system without producing anything. They secure immense bank loans which they do not repay,[5] create phantom factories that do not produce, and earn large commissions for doing very little' (Kochanek 1993: 198). During this period, 'most of the new entrepreneurs grew very fast and were highly dependent upon government patronage in the form of contracts, loans, and credits' (ibid. 1996: 713). According to Sobhan, businessmen in Bangladesh are nothing but a non-productive class of touts (quoted in ibid. 1993: 199) and the emergence of this business class is the result of state patronage through rent-seeking channels.

After the return of a pluralistic democracy, the business-politics nexus is still a major ramification of the corruption of Bangladesh. As stated by Ghulam Rahman, Chairman of the Anti-Corruption Commission (ACC) of Bangladesh, 'the nexus between politics and business is a major factor behind corruption at the upper class of the society' (*The Daily Star*, 7 April 2010). The nexus between business and politics can provide a meaningful explanation of the rent-seeking activity in Bangladesh.

Business-politics nexus: the cocoon of rent-seeking in Bangladesh? Throughout the world, the business-politics relationship is highly reciprocal. However, the reciprocity of the business-politics nexus in a patron-client society is hugely different from that of Western democracy. As stated earlier, because of the lack of 'agents of restraint' to check the insiders as they use their contacts to pursue self-serving government policies, rent-seeking may become unrestrained in a neopatrimonial regime. In Bangladesh, the business-politics nexus is the cocoon of rent-seeking.

After the return of multi-party democracy in 1991, the presence of a business elite in major political parties has expanded dramatically. It has been evident that, by joining political parties just before an election, a growing number of wealthy businessmen are becoming Members of Parliament (MPs). The proportion of MPs listing business as their primary or main profession has hovered between 50 per cent and 60 per cent of the total number in the democratic period. In addition, MPs defining themselves as businessmen have overwhelmingly dominated parliament since the 1990s (IGS 2006: 14). In his article in *The Daily Star*, to explain the growing relationship between business and politics, Majumdar

(2006: 14) suggests that 'politics is now practised largely without politicians and it is increasingly turning into a highly profitable business'. In 2003, the then country director of the World Bank suggested that in the existing electoral system of Bangladesh,

> Candidates spend huge amounts of money to get elected, and if they win, many use their offices to recoup their investments, with profit. The election system generates the demand for bribes. Candidates from the major political parties violate the campaign spending limitation, and when the winners become MPs, one of their first acts is to lie, by certifying they did not exceed the campaign expenditure limit. One motive for running is . . . to gain the protection that being an MP provides from being prosecuted, especially for loan default (ibid.).

Similarly, many believe that 'entering politics is a business investment. It assures access to state resources, gives a competitive edge over business rivals and establishes influence over the policy process (for example, policies made against loan defaulters). Businessmen involved in big infrastructure contracts may also choose to affiliate with an incoming ruling party to protect against the fallout from involvement in corrupt deals with the past regime' (IGS 2000: 15). Kochanek (1996: 714) also points out that 'the leaders of the new industrial elite are active in politics and business associations, and although the size and character of the elite are still highly fluid and depend heavily on an individual's political connections with the regime of the day, it is clear that the most successful are those who have been able to maintain significant connections despite changes in regime'. Today, many political-business elite establish joint venture business institutions such as private banks with the opposition political-business elite so that a regime change will not hamper government patronage.

In a political environment like Bangladesh where the election outcome is heavily dependent on muscle, miscreants and 'black money', the business-politics relationship is not only a common phenomenon but also highly reciprocal. On the one hand, some businessmen come to the government to join politics for their personal gain. According to a former cabinet minister, on the other hand, 'the political parties prefer successful businessmen to join their party because they do not have to fund their election expenses. . . .' (IGS 2006: 14). As money and muscle are the main elements of elections in Bangladesh, political parties are always keen to generate strong funds for this purpose. All political parties claim that their funds come from party members and well-wishers. However, in practice, most of the party funds come from businessmen. For example, in the words of Kochanek (1993: 226), the BNP attracted strong support from the old industrial elite and from the new class of entrepreneurs which it had created with state patronage. In a move mimicking the BNP's relationship with business elites, the Awami League (AL) is also reportedly embracing big business' (as cited in IGS 2006: 14). In return, through rent-seeking, the Bangladeshi business elites gain more than they invest.

Since Independence, the politics of patronage in the form of rent-seeking and corruption have plagued every government in Bangladesh. However, almost all observers agree that the situation is deteriorating under every government (see Kochanek 1993: 258). Since 1991, the two major political parties, the BNP and the AL, have formed governments one after another. Neither has completed two successive tenures. It is widely believed that every regime is more corrupt than the previous regime, even after they broke the record from their previous tenure. Under the politics of patronage, every regime produces new business elites.

It is not only the top-level businessmen who are involved in rent-seeking in Bangladesh. Rather, this practice can be noticed throughout the society. Maloney (as cited in ibid.) suggests that 'Bangladesh society is a highly complex network involving reciprocal favours and obligations'. As a result, he further adds, pay-off 'is the life blood of the country'. In every sector such as health, education, food, etc., the practice of rent-seeking is a common phenomenon. For example, a study by Killingsworth et al. (1999) showed that the widespread collection of unofficial fees at health facilities is a common form of rent-seeking behaviour in Bangladesh. Adams (1998) examined the operation of the food subsidy system in Bangladesh from 1980 to 1995 from a political economy perspective using the concepts: rent-seeking lobbies and rent-seeking bureaucrats/agents. He argued that:

From the perspective of Bangladesh food subsidies, the concept of rent-seeking bureaucrats/agents is useful because it focusses attention on the powers that *some*—but certainly not all—government bureaucrats hold in implementing government policy. By offering people preferential—and illegal—access to scarce public goods, government officials in certain ministries and their agents in the outside world can decisively alter both the character and intent of public policy. In Bangladesh, for example, officials in the ministry of food can 'cut deals' with private rice millers in such a way so that these two groups—and not the poor—receive the bulk of the benefits of food subsidies. (Adams 1998: 71)

Based on the above-mentioned discussion, it is evident that patronage politics under the neopatrimonial regimes in Bangladesh have undermined economic development and promoted the nexus between politics and business, producing a cocoon of rent-seeking activity. While corruption and rent-seeking activity are widespread at the top level, small-scale rent-seeking such as unofficial fees in various service sectors occurs in every sector of the country. In this way, the pyramidal structure of patron-client networks spreads rent-seeking in the pyramidal model as well.

Public Corruption

While the previous section dealt with the politics of neopatrimonialism and its impact on rent-seeking activities in Bangladesh, this section deals with public corruption. So, it is imperative to clarify that 'rent-seeking' and 'processes such as corruption and patron-client exchanges' which have long attracted the attention of political scientists often demonstrate a similar meaning. The resources spent on corruption, or spent within patron-client networks, are sometimes, but not always, expended to capture rents which expenditures too are variants of rent-seeking (Khan 2000b: 6). In the following section, I endeavour to analyze the relationship between corruption and patron-client politics in Bangladesh. Here, I posit that public corruption is the inevitable outcome of patronage politics in Bangladesh. If that is the case, I contend, this would be very useful in explaining leakages of the Public Food Distribution System in Bangladesh, the challenges of agri-governance, etc.

The cost of corruption. Corruption is typically defined as the misuse of public office and responsibility for private benefit. Almost all international organizations view corruption as inimical to every aspect of development—economic, social and political—and especially damaging to the interests of the poor. Corruption hurts the poor via its damaging consequences for economic growth and public services as well as its direct costs (Smith 2007: 176-8). Corruption is, in some ways, injurious to or destructive of the public interest (Szeftel 1983: 164, quoted in Harris 2003: 5). The IMF (2002) emphasizes the economic and public financial aspects of corruption, and its harmful effects on both taxation and public expenditure which lead to greater income inequality (quoted in Smith 2007: 176-8). Similarly, the Organisation for Economic Co-operation and Development (OECD) sees corruption as a major hindrance to economic development. Empirical literature which aimed to quantify the consequences of corruption was pioneered by Mauro (1995) who observed a significant negative relationship between corruption and investment that extended to growth. Later, Mauro's (ibid.) results were reinforced by Mo (2001) who introduced a new perspective on the role of corruption in economic growth and provided quantitative estimates of the impact of corruption on the growth and importance of the transmission channels. The most important channel through which corruption affects economic growth is political instability, which accounts for about 53 per cent of the total effect (ibid.). The analyses of Wei (2000) and Lambsdorff (2003), of many such studies, also extended to other macroeconomic variables such as foreign direct investment and productivity, respectively.

Corruption in Bangladesh. 'Bangladesh presents a typical case where corruption has found a remarkably fertile ground, despite the 'existence' of several mechanisms, albeit ineffective, for tackling it' (Zafarullah & Siddique 2001: 466). Available data indicates that Bangladesh is one of the most corrupt countries in the world. According to the annual Corruption Perception Index (CPI) of Transparency International (TI) in 2006, on a scale of 0-10, Bangladesh scored 2.0 compared to 1.7 last year. After staying at the bottom of the list for five consecutive years from 2001-5, in

2006 Bangladesh was ranked third from the bottom together with Chad, Democratic Republic of Congo, Sudan and Guinea who scored the same number of points. It was further revealed from the CPI (2006) that, in fact, Bangladesh was mentioned together with Myanmar and Cambodia among Asian countries where the lack of political will to strengthen anti-corruption institutions has perpetuated rampant corruption, undermining improvements in the quality of life for the poorest citizens. Moreover, within the country, a number of surveys over the decades unmistakably demonstrate widespread corruption in Bangladesh (Khan 2003: 398).

It is imperative to note that a number of questions arise in relation to the methodology of various studies, mainly by the World Bank and Transparency International, which like to rank countries by their degree of corruption. It is argued that cultural differences between countries undermine the legitimacy of such rankings, which are, after all, based on surveys of the public (Bhagwati 2010). However, without even mentioning the endemic corruption in Bangladesh based on the above-mentioned studies, corruption remains an inescapable fact of life in Bangladesh. While, in the past, only a few departments were known for corrupt officials and practices, the vice has now spread throughout the governmental structure and no public agency is spared from its influence (Zafarullah & Siddique 2001: 466). In other words, in contemporary Bangladesh, there is no public sector where there is no corruption. For instance, a TIB study (2005) provides information on the incidence of corruption as a consequence of weak public institutions. It shows that an average Bangladeshi paid Tk 485 per year as bribes. The bribes paid by households for 25 service categories within the nine sectors (education, health, land administration, police, judiciary, electricity, taxation, local government-*shalish* and relief, and pension) are Tk 6,796 crore. Considering the degree of corruption in Bangladesh, it is fair to say that corruption is everywhere in the society, from the cradle to the grave.

Linkage between corruption and neopatrimonialism in Bangladesh. Empirical evidence suggests that corruption is a widespread phenomenon and indeed a fertile ground in any neopatrimonial regime. The state officials, who include ministers, party officials, members of parliament, bureaucrats, military officers, etc., generally avoid the legal-rational practices and thus secure personal gain. Theoretically, in contemporary neopatrimonialism, relationships of loyalty and dependence pervade a formal political and administrative system and leaders occupy bureaucratic offices less to perform public service than to acquire personal wealth and status. The distinction between private and public interests is purposely blurred. The essence of neopatrimonialism is the award by public officials of personal favours, both within the state (notably public sector jobs) and in society (for instance, licences, contracts, and projects). In return for material rewards, clients mobilize political support and refer all decisions upward as a mark of deference to patrons (Bratton & Van de Walle 1994: 458).

The fact is that the main mechanism in neopatrimonial regimes is patronage and, therefore, I suggest, neopatrimonialism is widely associated with corruption. In a patron-client network, 'once the system had taken root, corruption percolated downward, from senior bureaucrats and politicians, who could be bribed [to] do what they were not supposed to do, to lower-level bureaucrats, who would not do what there [they] were supposed to do unless bribed' (Bhagwati 2010). However, to examine the linkage between corruption and neopatrimonial regimes, political analysts mainly focus on African regimes. In Africa, 'it [corruption] is a habitual part of everyday life, an expected element of every social transaction' (Chabal & Daloz 1999: 99). Again, it is in Africa where, despite the variants of regimes, patrimonial and neopatrimonial regimes have been a dominant feature of the politics over the past three decades. Patronage through a patron-client network is the underlying nature of these regimes. Thus, many suggest that neopatrimonial politics provide a fundamental explanation of the widespread corruption in Africa. Similarly, I argue that the nature of the Bangladesh state is neopatrimonial and, therefore, public offices and political parties run through patronage. As a result, corruption is also widespread in every institution in the state.

Corruption in Bangladesh is the outcome of the clientelistic politics of the country. As a result of personal rule in a neopatrimonial state, the rule of law of whichever party comes to power tends to become the 'ruling party's law'. Under the patronage of the incumbent government, a new elite emerges who are allowed to do whatever they wish including corruption. The politics of patronage under the personal rule of the incumbent government works as a safeguard to a coalition of the elite linked to the chief executive. As some argue that increasingly 'people are joining politics to make money or stay out of jail' (Khan 2009), all kinds of people benefit through state patronage. Soban (2004: 4105) suggests that the resultant nexus between politicians, business, the *mastaans* and the law enforcement agencies is now embedded into the social structure of Bangladesh. In the past four decades, closer investigation has revealed that the ruling party is always responsible for all types of unlawful activities including land-grabbing, extortion, bribery, etc., party members and government officials disobeyed the rule of law if something went against them. I discussed in the previous section how the ruling party rescued its followers when they breached the rule of law.

As Bhagwati (2010) suggests, the cost of corruption has been particularly high in India and Indonesia where policies created monopolies that charged low rents, which were then allocated to officials' family members. Such 'rent-creating' corruption is quite expensive and corrosive to growth. In Bangladesh, similarly, the practice of such 'rent-creating' corruption is a very common phenomenon. For example, according to a report of *The Daily Prothom-alo* (30 October 2009), in the last eight years, four state-owned banks of Bangladesh exempted Tk 3,644 crore worth of bank interest, most of which was enjoyed by a group of political leaders of both the BNP and the AL as well as some influential businessmen. This exemption is a kind of abandonment of legal-rational practices by officials and is designed to secure personal gains. In other words, public resources were distributed to an elite group. A number of studies suggest that the number of wilful defaulters have increased over the years, virtually crippling government financial institutions (see Quadir 2000; Akram 2005a; Akram 2005b; Sarker 2008). These defaulters are directly or indirectly involved in political party activities and receive political favours by dodging their loan payments to financial institutions (Sarker 2008: 1429). In addition to getting indirect favours from the ruling party, many of the defaulters are now sitting in parliament. Thus, they have the capacity to bring their concerns directly before the legislators (see ibid.). As a result, the most crippling problem of the financial sector in Bangladesh is loan defaults. In 1989, classified loans stood at 29 per cent of all outstanding loans. By the end of 1998, it rose to over 39 per cent (Chowdhury 2002).

The patron-client networks of Bangladesh promote the practices of corruption in various ways, overtly or covertly. First, it promotes corruption through special arrangements. Second, the state fosters corruption through a special form of patronage which works as a major hindrance in preventing corruption. For example, towards the end of 2009, President Zillur Rahman granted mercy to Shahdab Akbar who was sentenced to 18 years' imprisonment in four graft cases (*The Daily Star*, 3 January 2010). He is the son of Syeda Sajeda Chowdhury, the influential presidium member of the Awami League and the deputy leader of the parliament. Third, every political government in Bangladesh intentionally paralyses the Anti-Corruption Commission as well as some other law enforcement institutions to protect party leaders, ministers and activists.

Partial Reform Syndrome

In Bangladesh, like many African neopatrimonial regimes, as was noted by Mwenda and Tangri (2005: 455) in the context of Uganda, 'political leaders . . . have for many years been using public service institutions to generate the benefits and patronage needed to fashion patron-client linkages of support for themselves'. As noted earlier, in order to strengthen personal rule, successive regimes have always attempted to weaken the institutional capacity by various means. The fact is that any public sector reform that can challenge personal rule and patronage politics is the antithesis of neopatrimonial regimes. With this in mind, in this section, I aim to examine the political economy of public sector reform in Bangladesh. I contend that, as a result of neopatrimonial rule, Bangladesh is a typical case of 'partial reform syndrome'. In this process, the only reforms implemented are those necessary for the interests of various political actors and which will not endanger the interests of the neopatrimonial regime. Hence, reforms are rarely capable of pursuing development goals. This discussion is useful in analysing the politics of food in Bangladesh as over the past two or more decades, Bangladesh's food policy, agriculture sector and trade policy have all gone through a number of reforms. I contend that the nature of reforms in a neopatrimonial state such as Bangladesh sheds light on why reforms relating to food and/or the agriculture sector do not promote development.

The political economy of reform in Bangladesh. In his *African Economics and Politics of Permanent Crisis, 1979-1999*, Van de Walle (2001: 60) argues that '[t]hese three domestic factors—clientelism, low capacity, and elite beliefs—have interacted with the international aid system to drag out the process of reform for several decades'. As a result, the reforms fail to bring any positive outcome and donors are regularly frustrated by the way aid-receiving countries fail to follow through on promised economic, sectoral and governance reforms. This can be called the 'partial reform syndrome' (Hellman 1998). Using the framework of the 'partial reform syndrome' as used in the African context by Van de Walle (2001), I argue that neopatrimonial regimes in Bangladesh lead to a significant gap between espoused and real commitment to reform. As a result, without strong political commitment of successive governments, reforms in Bangladesh resemble a 'sisyphean task' as a reform is rarely completed (Khan 2010: 28). As with African politics, in Bangladesh three domestic factors—clientelism, low capacity and elite beliefs—have played a vital role in dragging out the process of reform for several years or have caused complete failure. However, I particularly emphasize two factors: clientelism and elite beliefs. I contend that neopatrimonial regimes and low capacity are interlinked and significantly influence each other: neopatrimonial regimes inevitably weaken the state capacity and development outcome. It is important to note that in using the term, partial reform syndrome, I do not mean to imply that reform is an ad hoc sporadic rearrangement dealing with specific situations.

In addition to market-based reforms in Bangladesh throughout the 1980s and onwards, 'the World Bank and Western donors argue that poor governance and weak institutions in Bangladesh have acted as significant constraints on development. The donors have, therefore, embarked upon a set of major programmes designed to strengthen political institutions in Bangladesh and ensure good governance based on transparency, accountability, and responsibility' (Kochanek 2000: 530).[6] Here, I will examine the politics and progress of the reform agenda which has been initiated by the donors. The fact is that in the past two decades (1991-2010), only five out of 25 priority structural reforms were fully implemented and three were significantly implemented (Khan 2010: 28). Why is reform in Bangladesh proceeding at snail's pace? According to a note from the Independent Evaluation Group (IEG) of the World Bank, '. . . a core constraint in the development process in Bangladesh was the government itself and its unwillingness to enforce the needed public sector reforms' (IEG 2010). Another study of the World Bank (2002: 11) suggested why the government was not willing to implement reforms: '[w]ith elections every five years, short run election calculations have dominated decision-making. To date the political leadership has clearly perceived the short run political costs of reforms as outweighing the longer term welfare benefits'. In other words, this study basically suggests the J-curve analysis which is based on an assumption about the distribution of costs and benefits of reform (see Hellman 1998). It can be 'simply stated, reforms are expected to make things worse before they get better' (ibid.). However, these studies of the World Bank only partially explain, or rarely explain, the politics of reforms in Bangladesh. I raise these questions: if the government is aware of the 'short run political costs of reforms' then why do they need to make attempts at reforms? Why were some structural reforms fully implemented while others were only partially implemented and many failed entirely? In answering these questions, I use the notion of clientelism and 'elite beliefs' in Bangladesh.

Not surprisingly, this reform agenda provided an opportunity for the ruling elite, both military and civil, to consolidate their power. Initially, by accepting the donors' reform agenda, military regimes were rewarded with considerable foreign aid and gained international legitimacy/acceptance. Later, strong competitive bipolar neopatrimonial politics compelled successive governments to accept various reform agendas imposed by the donors. In addition, as Quadir (2000) argues in relation to economic reforms, successive regimes treated market reforms as an instrument to build and maintain political coalitions, in particular with traders and industrialists. In other words, successive regimes of Bangladesh accepted the donors' reform agenda, solely in order to consolidate their regimes. In doing so, neither good governance nor development was the goal of the state elites. Rather, reforms which could jeopardize the personal rule of the neopatrimonial regime have never been implemented while reforms that are necessary in the interests of the regime's survival, such as the 'process of globalization', have been implemented. For example, out of the five implemented reforms, four related to exchange rates, external debt management, and exchange and payment restrictions. The other implemented reform was privatization of agricultural inputs and equipment to farmers. On the other hand, Bangladesh's performance in implementing important governance reforms such as civil service reforms, judicial reforms, police reforms, decentralization, people's participation, etc., was much more disappointing (Khan 2010: 30).

As Khan (ibid.: 30-1) notes, despite incessant pressure from development partners, no government in Bangladesh initiated any meaningful step to reform the Bangladesh administration that was riddled with inefficiency, corruption and anachronisms. It is imperative to note that many reforms necessary for better governance such as civil service reforms, judicial reforms, police reforms, decentralization, people's participation, etc., are not only on the agenda of MEIs but are also societal demands. There is increasing domestic demand to curtail the unbridled power of the executive which is mainly the outcome of the traditional state apparatus inherited from colonial and Pakistani dictatorial rule. Under the pressure of both civil society and donors, the neopatrimonial regimes of Bangladesh declare their intention to reform public institutions and its mechanism but the reality is that no reform agenda has so far been implemented that can challenge the state power of the neopatrimonial regime such as judiciary reforms or establishing an effective anti-corruption commission.

By employing this notion of the partial reform syndrome, I attempt to examine the state initiatives in making and implementing agricultural policies, trade policies, and other policies, such as a Public Food Distribution System. I am also keen to show that, because of the partial reform syndrome, many reforms necessary for food and agricultural governance are not implemented and policies which are implemented are mostly not for societal interests but rather only to ensure the interests of the elite.

Weak State Capacity

Here, my premise is that the 'state capacity' approach is one of the most important concept for best explaining the politics of food security. Policy making, policy implementation, and the nature of policy—all are subject to the state capacity of a particular state that aims to promote food security. In order to deploy weak state capacity as a framework for understanding the politics of food security, here I focus on two particular issues. These are whether Bangladesh is a weak state, and which capacities of the state are weak and might affect Bangladesh's food security.

Throughout this study, I question the scope of state functions (e.g. education, health, food, etc.) and the strengths of state institutions of the Bangladesh state for effectively carrying out state functions and pursuing a development programme for its citizens. State weakness in Bangladesh hinders the implementation of some basic functions that the state needs to carry out. In order to understand whether Bangladesh is a weak state, here it is imperative to firstly define state capacity. Paul (2011: 5) argues that state capacity is 'the ability of a state to develop and implement policies in order to provide collective goods such as security, order, and welfare to its citizens in a legitimate and effective manner untrammeled by internal and external actors'. State capacity, in the words of Burkle Jr (2006: 246) is 'the capability of a government to protect its citizens from the consequence of a crisis'. The existing scholarship on the subject suggests that some basic capacities which are required for a well-functioning state are: capacities to penetrate society, regulate social relationships, extract resources, and appropriate or use resources in determined ways, monopolize the legitimate use of force, shape national identity and mobilize consent, regulate the economy and provide internal coherence of state institutions. Hence, a weak state is a state that does not have these (aforementioned) basic capacities necessary for a well-functioning state. In this regard, the Bangladesh state is a weak state as it neither has the capacities to penetrate society, nor does it regulate social relationships, nor can it extract resources, and it also cannot appropriate or use resources in determined ways. Thus, according to conventional studies, the Bangladesh state needs to be labelled as a weak state. However, it is a subject of academic debate whether or not Bangladesh is a weak state (e.g. see Riaz 2010).

The fact is that, with the colonial legacy, and since its birth as a nation state, patronage politics, a centralized decision-making process, and employment of various state institutions for promoting the interests of the state elites have slowly eroded the above-mentioned capacity of the Bangladesh state and thus weakened the state capacity. On the one hand, 'the overdeveloped state' (Alavi 1972) which was endowed with an unusually strong bureaucratic and military apparatus, hindered the state initially in penetrating society and addressing societal interests; on the other hand, further striking erosions of state capacity have been brought about through patronage politics by successive regimes. For instance, considering administrative reforms as a potential threat for patronage politics, regimes successfully avoided reforms and/or have been procrastinating in implementing them. As a consequence, despite 'democratic rule', the state capacity has not been strengthened since 1991.

Administrative capacity is necessary for state capacity which is denoted as 'the ability of states to deliver goods and services such as public health and education, provide physical infrastructure, and carry out the normal administrative functions of government, such as revenue collection, necessary economic regulation, and information management' (Grindle 1996: 10). The fact is 'administrative capacity is essential to state strength: one cannot delegate policymaking authority to skilled bureaucrats, or implement the policies they make, if one does not have them in sufficient number' (Rapley 2007: 164). While a sufficient bureaucracy size is important, that is not everything: the state also needs an efficient bureaucracy for policymaking. I have argued elsewhere (Islam 2012) that as with some other neopatrimonial regimes, Bangladeshi bureaucrats are recruited and promoted as a reward for personal connections with political leaders, and can be dismissed without any reason. Traditionally, the bureaucracy of Bangladesh inherited a mindset which was a hangover from the colonial legacy and which separated them from the rest of society. In post-colonial Bangladesh, along with this colonial mindset, the politicization of the bureaucracy has further weakened its administrative capacity.[7] In a similar vein with regard to African bureaucracies, the Bangladesh civil service is characterized by pervasive absenteeism, endemic corruption, politicization, declining legitimacy, and low morale (for the African context, see Van de Walle 2001; for Bangladesh, personal interviews, IvGOB8 and also IvGOB9).

The current bureaucratic system and culture of Bangladesh is the legacy of the past: nearly 190 years of British colonial rule and 25 years of Pakistani rule. Thus, Jamil (2007) rightly points out that the bureaucracy in Bangladesh is characterized somewhat more by traditional than by modern norms. While traditional bureaucracy had many weaknesses as well as malpractices, the magnitude of bureaucratic corruption and politization of the administration and the service delivery system has increased manifold in post-Independence Bangladesh (Sarker 2004). Many analysts suggest that the bureaucracy in contemporary Bangladesh is often accused of inefficiency, corruption, nepotism, lack of accountability and an assortment of other ailments. It is sometimes portrayed as standing in the way of development rather than stimulating it (see Jamil 2007).

The declining nature of bureaucratic performance questions whether the bureaucracy has the ability to design, implement, monitor, and evaluate the policy necessary for social development, particularly promoting food security. This systematic regression of state capacity is the result of the historical and political experience of the country. The above-noted discussion clearly shows that because of the sectoral interests, state elites did not take any meaningful initiatives to strengthen state institutions which could have enhanced state capacity. In order to monopolize state power in the hands of the state elites, the neopatrimonial politics of Bangladesh systemically weaken administrative capacity and, therefore, state capacity.

The cost of the declining administrative capacity is huge in Bangladesh: a malfunctioning administrative capacity can interrupt the essentials of an effective state such as penetrating society, regulating social relationships, extracting resources, etc. For instance, extracting resources is one of the most essential functions of an effective state: without the availability of resources, the state cannot carry out any programmes/tasks necessary for its national purpose. Available studies suggest that 'the tax raising powers of the Bangladesh state are notoriously weak, and the "leakage" of resources to purposes other than those for which they were intended seems almost more the rule than the exception' (White 1999: 319). The World Bank Development Report (2009) shows that tax/GDP ratio in Bangladesh is 10.3 per cent whereas the weighted global average tax-revenue ratio is 26.8 per cent and the South Asian average is 13.5 per cent, about 31 per cent higher than that of Bangladesh. According to a study of the Ministry of Finance, the financial losses of state-owned enterprises during the period 2006-7 to 2008-9 stood at one per cent of GDP and their total arrears on loans from the government amounted to about 12 per cent of GDP in 2008-9 (see Khan 2010: 33).

As a consequence of the steady loss of state capacity, the state's ability to deliver basic services such as education, health, food, etc., has also gradually declined. For example, the justice system in Bangladesh was rated by investors as the worst among the countries surveyed by the World Bank in 2005 (see ibid.: 159). Drawing on the cases of the successive failure of measures to prohibit dowries, enforce minimum ages of marriage, effectively redistribute *Khas* (government) land or, indeed, provide an independent judicial system. White (1999: 319) shows the inability of the Bangladesh state to regulate relationships. In the subsequent chapters, I will show the signs of the progressive loss of state capacity in Bangladesh to promote food security which points out the failure of the state to efficiently redistribute resources, 'the authoritative allocation of scarce resources among different social groups' (Wang 2003: 38).

Over the years, it has been seen that the state has clearly failed to 'penetrate' society effectively. After making a critical analysis between the periods of 1958-85, Blair (1985) summarized his arguments:

> . . . four successive regimes in Bangladesh have felt reluctantly compelled to set up structures for local participation in government. Each found it had to reach out beyond the support of urban and rural elites and the military if it was to move beyond mere stability to real development of the country. Despite many problems, most notably local an elite takeover at the local level and military coup at the national level, there is considerable evidence, particularly from neighbouring India, to suggest that local participatory institutions can be successful over the longer term in promoting development for the middle and the poorer rural classes.

After the return of the multi-party democracy in 1991, despite plentiful promises, successive regimes failed to set up effective structures for local participation. The failure to reorganize the local administration in order to penetrate society in Bangladesh caused a weak link between the state and the society. The ramifications of this weak relationship are multifaceted: no shared political culture between the state and society, an unaccountable state, the erosion of legitimacy, etc. The fact is that, as a result of this weak link, the state cannot be responsive to citizens' desires nor be more effective in service delivery.

A statistical service is essential for scientific analysis of state policy. Over the years, the ability of the contemporary Bangladesh state to provide statistical data for basic national accounts has been in question: it is either unavailable or of increasingly suspect quality. For instance, the preliminary findings of the latest census of Bangladesh (BBS 2011) that put the country's population at 142.3 million generated huge controversy. With regard to the criticism of the census, the Finance Minister stated that '[t]he complaint is every house was not covered. Even the House of the Agriculture

Minister was not covered' (*The Daily Star*, 25 July 2011). As someone who was an exclusion in the census, Agriculture Minister, Matia Chowdhury, argued that 'I can say the preliminary findings are at best unrealistic. There is a big gap between the census outcome and the reality' (*The Daily Star*, 19 July 2011).

Using this framework, in Chapters 5 and 6, I will seek to reveal how various indicators of state capacity such as the administrative capacity, statistical service, etc., impede or promote food security in Bangladesh. In other words, this framework will provide an insightful pathway for understanding the role of the state in making and implementing policies with regard to food availability and accessibility.

Poor Governance

Although many factors such as weather, war, terrorism, conflict, overpopulation, environmental degradation, corruption and faulty policies have been identified as causes of food insecurity (Foster 1992), it is the concept of governance without which it is almost impossible to deeply dig into the politics of food security. This is particularly important in understanding the politics of food security in Bangladesh where the state of governance is in dismal shape. Here, I first define governance and then discuss the state of governance in Bangladesh in order to develop a framework to be employed in Chapters 5 and 6 to examine the politics of food security.

Government, in general, is portrayed by 'its ability to make decisions and its capacity to enforce them': it is 'the formal and institutional processes which operate at the level of the nation state to maintain public order and facilitate collective action' (Stoker 1998: 17). The term 'governance' is not a synonym for the word 'government' although it is still often used as a virtual synonym for government. Rather, governance denotes 'a change in the meaning of government, referring to a new process of governing; or a changed condition of ordered rule; or the new method by which society is governed' (Rhodes 1996: 652-3). In the 1990s, governance as a concept was preceded by discussions based on the 'new institutionalism'. The concept of governance gained currency and came to the forefront as policy analysts found that the formal organizational system of government did not adequately describe the patterns of interaction they found in policy formulation and implementation (Bogason & Zolner 2007: 4). Initially, the term 'governance' seemed to have wide currency in the field of economic development, with widespread advocacy by international development agencies and Western governments of 'good governance' as a necessary component of effective economic modernization (Hirst 2000: 14). However, the most frequently cited definition of governance broadly is as: 'the exercise of authority through formal and informal traditions and institutions for the common good, thus encompassing: (1) the process of selecting, monitoring and replacing governments; (2) the capacity to formulate and implement sound policies and deliver public services; and (3) the respect of citizens and the state for the institutions that govern economic and social interactions among them' (Kaufmann 2003: 5).

Rapid erosion in governance is one of the important features of the Bangladesh polity. The Worldwide Governance Indicators project constructs aggregate indicators of six broad dimensions of governance which show relatively very poor perceptions of governance in Bangladesh. For instance, in the most recent governance dataset released by the World Bank for 2011, Bangladesh's ranking among 212 countries varies from the bottom 9th to the 38th percentile in the 6 indicators. These are: 9.9 for political stability, 21.5 for government effectiveness, 21.5 for regulatory quality, 16.2 for control of corruption, 26.5 for rule of law, and 38.3 for voice and accountability (see World Bank 2011).[8]

As a consequence of this poor governance and as Kochanek (2000: 530) notes, '[d]espite large amounts of aid, the World Bank and Western donors argue that poor governance and weak institutions in Bangladesh have acted as significant constraints on development'. A considerable number of studies have focused on the state of governance in Bangladesh (e.g. see Kochanek 1993, 1996, 2000; Sobhan 1998, 2004; Zafarullah & Haque 2001; Khan 2003, 2010; Zafarullah 2003; Roy 2006; Sarker & Rahman 2006; Sarker 2008; Zafarullah & Rahman 2008). The main argument of this literature is that, as a result of rapid erosion in governance, the political system remains fragile and unstable, the economy in disarray, and social services are practically non-existent. For example, Khan (2003) notes that the state of governance in Bangladesh is in dismal shape: social, political and economic governance suffer from stagnation and show little sign of progress. According to Sobhan (1998: 13), the basic argument about the role of governance in development holds that weak governance originates as a result of the sequential failure of the state to:

(a) project a developmental vision.
(b) demonstrate a commitment to realise this vision, through putting in place policies and programmes, as well as calibrating its allocative priorities to realise this vision.
(c) develop a capacity to fulfil its commitments. This includes administrative and technical capacity as well as political capacity to mobilise necessary support both within civil society as well as in the political arena to translate the vision into reality.

The concept of governance is worth employing in exploring both food availability and accessibility in Bangladesh. By using the lens of poor governance, I will attempt to analyse food production, distribution, and market regulation. In particular, this concept will provide valuable insight into grasping two important dimensions of food security in Bangladesh, namely, agricultural governance which is vital for food production and 'leakage errors' of public food distribution in Bangladesh which is the key discourse of the neoliberal food policy.

CONCLUSION

Considering the fact that regime variants are neither rigid nor immutable in contemporary neopatrimonial literature, in this chapter, I first suggest that the Bangladesh state is a competitive bipolar neopatrimonial state. As a result of the competitive bipolar nature of the polity, a winner-takes-all power game is the dominant feature of the state. Under the nature of this polity, regimes survive through patronage based on personal rule. Not surprisingly, although regime change is more frequent and no party has been able to continue rule since 1991 for longer than five years at a time, the nature of the polity remains unchanged under the new regime. In other words, with the emergence of a new personal ruler, a new regime with a new group of elites practises the existing political, administrative and other mechanisms through patronage in a patron-client society. Therefore, the state policy remains unchanged.

This chapter further demonstrates that in order to personalize state power through patronage politics and personalized exchanges, regimes intentionally weaken the various state apparatus necessary for good governance such as the bureaucracy, judiciary, etc. So, on the one hand, the neopatrimonial state promotes personal and sectional interests through patronage politics, while on the other hand, in doing so, regimes intentionally weaken the ability of the state to provide basic services. As a consequence, the neopatrimonial regimes/politics of Bangladesh have caused damaging impacts on democratic governance and thereby impeded development outcomes. This chapter shows five different impacts which are linked with a neopatrimonial regime, patronage politics, and the underdevelopment of Bangladesh. These are widespread rent-seeking, public corruption, poor governance, weak state capacity, and a partial reform syndrome which only serves the interest of the state elite.

NOTES

1. According to Scott (1972: 92), 'The patron-client relationship—an exchange relationship between roles—may be defined as a special case of dyadic (two-person) ties involving a largely instrumental friendship in which an individual of higher socioeconomic status (patron) uses his own influence and resources to provide protection or benefits, or both, for a person of lower status (client) who, for his part, reciprocates, by offering general support and assistance, including personal services, to the patron'.
2. Many argue that the regime does not tolerate any opposition or criticism. For instance, according to Ahmed, 'any criticism provoked sharp response on the part of the government' (interview with *The Daily Prothom-alo*,

13 November 2011). Out of many reports, this report of *The Daily Star* (6 September 2011, Dhaka) shows the nature of the regime: 'In a weekly cabinet meeting, Prime Minister Sheikh Hasina came down heavily on those who recently arranged a sit-in programme at the Central Shaheed Minar on Eid day, to press home a seven-point demand on road safety and resignation of the communications minister. Hasina directed intelligence agencies to gather details of the organizers of the sit-in. The PM wanted to know whether those among the programme organizers, who drive their own cars, had their driving licence issued following proper procedure and whether their drivers are educated and have valid driving licences. She also 'instructed the intelligence agencies to collect information about the houses and cars the protesters own.' 'Find out whether they pay taxes and how lavish their houses are', she instructed to the intelligence agencies.

3. According to *The Economist* (30 July 2011), '. . . Sheikh Hasina . . . is becoming increasingly autocratic. Opposition boycotts of parliament and general strikes are run-of-the-mill. Corruption flourishes at levels astonishing even by South Asian standards. A June decision to rewrite the Constitution looks to be a blunt power grab, letting the government run the next general election by scrapping a 'caretaker' arrangement. Sheikh Hasina is building a personality cult around her murdered father, 'the greatest Bengali of the millennium', says the propaganda. Elsewhere, the hounding of Muhammad Yunus, a Nobel laureate and founder of the Grameen Bank who briefly flirted with politics, was vindictive. Similarly, war-crimes trials over the events of 1971 are to start in a few weeks. They are being used less as a path to justice than to crush an opposition Islamic party, Jamaat-e-Islami'.
4. To understand the rent-seeking activity during the Mujib regime, it is worthwhile quoting Maniruzzaman (1975: 118): 'In most of the nationalized industries, the administrators appointed by the government were AL supporters who had no knowledge of either a socialist or a capitalist system. The administrators grew rich overnight by smuggling machinery and raw materials to India. While the government nationalized 85 per cent of the industries and 90 per cent of the foreign trade, the distribution of home produced and imported goods was carried on by 'dealers' who were issued 'permits' and 'licences'. The major portion of permits and licences were given to AL workers who sold their licences to professional traders. This provided them with 'unearned income,' most of which was not invested in productive enterprises'.
5. In the words of a foreign donor, 'Bangladesh cannot afford a private sector.

They don't pay taxes; they do not repay their bank loans; and they do not pay their utility bills' (as cited in Kochanek 1993: 199).

6. 'These programmes include, among other things, improving the performance and effectiveness of the bureaucracy, the judiciary, and the legislature; strengthening local government; developing public awareness and civil society advocacy; and enhancing the research and policy development capabilities of political parties. The fundamental dilemma faced by the donors, however, is whether foreign-funded institutional and technical fixes can genuinely address problems of governance that are deeply rooted in the country's historical experience and the behaviour and values of the Bangladeshi elite' (Kochanek 2000: 530).
7. After Independence, 'about 6,000 government employees including nine former CSP officers lost their jobs on charges of "collaboration" with the Pakistani military regime' (Maniruzzaman 1979: 48), which can be seen as the first step of the weakening administrative capacity. In addition, all new appointments were based on patronage, mainly 'reserved for the members of the *Mukti Bahini* (Liberation Army)'. In previous discussion, I have shown how successive regimes followed the footsteps of the Mujib regime and have gradually eroded administrative capacity by creating a partisan bureaucracy.
8. Percentile rank among all countries ranges from zero (lowest) to 100 (highest) ranks.

CHAPTER 4

The Problems of Food Availability and Accessibility

INTRODUCTION

The purpose of this chapter is to problematize the challenges of food security in the context of Bangladesh, with special reference to the issue of food availability and accessibility. In doing so, this chapter attempts to understand the state policy and mechanisms in dealing with food availability and accessibility focussing on the 'entitlement approach' of Sen (1981) and the 'right to food' concept. This chapter seeks to address three interrelated issues: first, the central discourse of food security in Bangladesh; second, the problems and key mechanisms that are used to generate food availability and the empirical evidence relating to food availability; and third, the problems and key mechanisms that are used to generate food accessibility and the empirical evidence relating to food accessibility. This chapter attempts to understand both short-term as well as long-term challenges of food security which include environmental challenges, rapid urbanization and the like. In doing so, throughout the chapter, I raise two key questions: whether the important source of food availability in Bangladesh such as domestic production and timely import is under threat; and what are the state mechanisms that are used to generate food availability and accessibility as well as how well the state is doing in order to generate entitlement in promoting food accessibility to the very poor segments of the population considering the prevalence of poverty.

This chapter is divided into four main sections. The next section attempts to conceptualize the two keywords of this thesis, food availability and food accessibility in the context of Bangladesh.

The chapter begins with the discourse of food security in Bangladesh, where I endeavour to examine how different actors see the issue of food. In this section my discussion particularly focusses on the centrality of food security in Bangladeshi politics with particular emphasis on electoral politics and the way in which food security is framed in Bangladesh with its key images and narratives. I then explore the challenges of food availability in Bangladesh. This section begins with discussion of consumption patterns of food in Bangladesh and then discusses the domestic production of foodgrains as a source of food availability, its uncertainty, and future challenges. It then examines the challenges of food accessibility. The last section of this chapter summarizes and discusses the findings of the chapter.

FOOD AVAILABILITY AND FOOD ACCESSIBILITY

In order to examine the politics of food security, this chapter seeks to establish a framework to understand the challenges of food availability and accessibility. In doing so, I first attempt to conceptualize these two keywords in the light of the central hypothesis of this study. In chapter 2, five recurring key terms relating to food security were outlined: access, availability, utilization, vulnerability, and *food safety and quality*. Comprehension of the term, 'food security', can be determined by these keywords although each captures different, but overlapping, dimensions of the phenomenon. However, the endeavour of this book in general, and this chapter in particular, is to address two major elements of food security: availability and accessibility.

Historically, at the time of World Food Conference of 1974, food security was widely viewed as a problem of insufficient and unstable production (FAO 1974; UN 1974; Wiess & Jordan 1976). In other words, aggregate food availability was considered as the determinant factor of food security. Since the early 1980s, both the concept of food security and the policy of food security have evolved, developed, multiplied and diversified, which Barrett (2002: 15) classified in three different generations: the first generation focussed on aggregate food availability; the second generation emphasized individual and household level access to food; and the third generation conceptualization places food security in a broader framework of individual behaviour in the face of uncertainty, irreversibilities and binding constraints on choice. He asserts (p. 16) that the third generation's view of food security builds on food availability and entitlements as a summary of food access. The character of the food system and the nature of food policy are both changing as urbanization, technical change and the industrialization of the food system transform the way food is produced, marketed and consumed in developing countries (Maxwell & Slater 2003). In the changing nature of the food system, where the entitlement approach of Sen (1981) is seen as the breakthrough, national food security is not to be understood merely as national food self-sufficiency or food availability but, rather, whether the people on the whole, has the accessibility of food.

In the context of national level food security, the term *food availability* refers to the availability of sufficient food in a particular country from domestic production and/or international trade and/or food aid or a combination of all of these, which needs to be always available to individuals or within their reach in any circumstances without any sort of interruption. At the national level, the constraint of food availability generally depends on public policy of a particular nation. Although it is the individual or a household who goes hungry, national policy is the determinant factor of the state of food availability and, of course, in most of the cases many factors are beyond the control of individuals to ensure food availability. For example, food availability in any country depends on agricultural production, which is the result of appropriate agricultural technologies, knowledge and its implementation or practices; and appropriate market management, which includes economic policies, including pricing, marketing, tax and tariff policies. Food availability can be further complicated due to the lack of foreign exchange, inadequate agricultural inputs, an ineffective private sector, population growth rates, and poor marketing and transportation systems. Moreover, the inability of the state to predict, assess and cope with emergency situations can seriously interrupt food supplies; and the role of the political elite and, therefore, political choice on the part of the government is very vital in relation to the food availability of any nation (for constraints of food availability, see USAID 1992). Therefore, in any particular country, the concept of food availability must be seen in the context of public policy as well as its execution. In other words, food availability in the context of the national level is the outcome of state policy. Thus, food availability or 'food supply is a matter of factual investigation' (Sen 1981: 1) which demands critical review of the political nature, elite behaviour and the public policy of a nation state.

On the other hand, in the contemporary literature of food security, *accessibility* of food, referring to the ability of individuals and households to obtain necessary foods for maintaining healthy and active lives, through purchase, produce or by trade, is considered the major constraint to food security. In other words, *accessibility* can be defined as: *access* by households and individuals to adequate resources to acquire appropriate foods for a nutritious diet (USAID 1992). In the light of the entitlement theory of Sen (1981), *accessibility* of food can be defined as the ability of individuals or households to acquire adequate foods through the legal means available in society, including the use of production possibilities, trade opportunities, entitlement vis-à-vis the state, and other means. Similar to food availability, the nature of the public policy, its implementation mechanisms and the outcome of the policy significantly affect the accessibility of food to millions of people at the national level. For example, if economic growth is not pro-poor and fails to create adequate training opportunities and/or job skills for the poor; if the state does not create adequate direct entitlements for poor and vulnerable people and so forth, then accessing food can be challenging to the poorer segments of the society. In brief, poverty, inequality, impact of natural disasters and sudden price hikes of foodgrains are often seen as the main obstacles of food accessibility.

In the context of the food availability and accessibility in Bangladesh, it is imperative to examine the distinction between chronic and transitory food insecurity. Sudden high food prices, the impact of natural disasters, etc., are major causes of transitory food insecurity. Barrett (2002: 12) outlines three distinct types of transitory food insecurity: periodic, regular, and conjunctural. Many poor people lose their minimum access of food for several basic reasons: sudden price hikes, lean seasons (hungry seasons) and during times of natural disaster. The lean season in particular reduces the people's access to income, which is a shock to their food security. In the north-western part of Bangladesh, seasonal food insecurity caused by unemployment and income deficit is generally known as *monga* (famine like situation), which can be termed as periodic food insecurity. Barrett (ibid.) notes that '[r]egular food insecurity is associated with repeated but a- or quasi-periodic events'. In Bangladesh, climate extremes such as floods, cyclones, droughts, and other natural disasters that often occur are the principal sources of regular food insecurity. Finally, conjunctural food insecurity is associated with the conjuncture of periodic or regular food insecurity with irregular disasters, most importantly and commonly, civil unrest and war (ibid.). Famines, the worst realization of transitory food insecurity, commonly stem from conjunctural food insecurity, especially associated with severe socio-political disruptions (Sen 1981; Foster 1992; Devereux 1993; Webb & von Braun 1994; Barrett 2002). The Great Bengal Famine in 1943 and the Bangladesh Famine of 1974 are two examples of the most devastating transitory food insecurity. After the Bangladesh Famine of 1974, although famine has not occurred again, the threat of transitory food insecurity is still a major challenge. On the other hand, in addition to the threat of transitory food insecurity, a huge number of the population in Bangladesh is still too poor to afford enough food to sustain a healthy and productive life, and this group suffers from chronic food insecurity.

Moreover, it is not easy to formulate a simple food policy to ensure food security in a country like Bangladesh, where food insecure people are both: 'peasants' and 'rural and urban poor'. On the one hand, a large majority of the poor people in Bangladesh depend on markets for access to food. Adverse movements in terms of trade between purchased food and the goods or services they produce and sell (including wage labour) can cause entitlements failure (Barrett 2002: 17). Sen (1981) demonstrates that the Bangladesh famine of 1974 occurred because of entitlement failure. In Bangladesh in 2007-8, as noted earlier, an additional 7.5 million people joined the ranks of the hungry because of high food prices. Many net food sellers are poor themselves, and the decline in relative food prices has hurt them, too (Barrett 2002: 17). Like many other good harvest years, for example in 2009 and 2011, many poor farmers were adversely affected because of bumper rice production as the low prices of rice did not return their investment. Here is the 'food price dilemma' (Timmer, Falcon & Pearson 1983; quoted in Barrett 2002: 17): higher food prices are necessary to induce increased local food production and to increase the incomes of poor, net seller food producers, yet high food prices threaten the food security of low income countries like Bangladesh. Mellor (1978), Weber et al. (1988) and Barrett & Dorosh (1996) suggest that a large proportion of small holder food producers are net food buyers (as cited in Barrett 2002: 17). Hence the food price dilemma results in a further complicated scenario in attaining both food availability and accessibility, particularly in Bangladesh.

THE DISCOURSE OF FOOD SECURITY IN BANGLADESH

This section deals with the discourses of food security in Bangladesh. The purpose of this section is to examine how different actors see the issue of food in Bangladesh. More particularly, I examine: (a) the centrality of food security in Bangladeshi politics focussing on electoral politics, and also attempt to explicate whether there is consensus on the issue among various actors in Bangladesh; (b) the way in which food security is framed in Bangladesh, and its key images and narratives. I begin this section by addressing the actors that play vital roles in the making of the food policy discourse. I then seek to explore how different actors such as the state, political parties, civil society, focussing on NGOs, see the issue of food security. And finally I will seek the policy discourse in Bangladesh in the context of food security.

There are six key actors which play vital roles in the making of food policy discourse in Bangladesh. First, the state itself is a discourse creator. Its constitutional commitments, policy papers and promises of successive regimes generate discourse with regard to food security. Second, political parties create discourse, particularly the political opposition, which criticizes the government and demands the taking of measures to reduce the unbearable burden of price hikes, in the process, generating a special type of food policy discourse. Third, a number of research institutes, such as Bangladesh Institute of Development Studies (BIDS) and Centre for Policy Dialogue (CPD), prepare occasional papers, including policy papers. Fourth, external agencies such as the World Bank, USAID and IFPRI carry out research and provide research support to the government (see Chapter 6 for a general discussion on the influence of external agencies in making and shaping food policy in Bangladesh). Fifth, the media plays an important role with particular focus on food crises. The nature of discourse portrayed by the media is of mainly three types: (a) price hikes of daily essentials; (b) political debates over the food crisis; and (c) drawing of attention to the chronic and seasonal hunger, such as *monga* (famine-like situation). And finally, NGOs are another important actor in the food policy discourse in Bangladesh.

The State as a Discourse Creator

Food security in Bangladesh is framed as legally binding. Article 15 (a) of the Constitution of the People's Republic of Bangladesh explicitly states that providing food shall be a fundamental responsibility of the state. According to the *National Food Policy, 2006*, '[t]he first and foremost responsibility of the state is to ensure an uninterrupted supply of food to all people at all time' (NFP 2006: 1). Moreover, Bangladesh is a signatory country of many international declarations which ensure the commitment of the nation to implement the right to development, human rights and, especially, promoting food security. By ratifying the *International Covenant on Economic, Social and Cultural Rights* in 1998, the country has made a legally binding commitment to implementing the right to development. Article 11 (2) of the Covenant declares that '[t]he State Parties to the present Covenant, recognizing the fundamental right of everyone to be free from hunger, shall take, individually and through international cooperation, the measures, including specific programmes' (OHCHR 2011). Thus, food is a constitutional right of every citizen and it is a fundamental responsibility of the government to provide it; and as a signatory nation of various international covenants it is a global commitment of the nation to respect, protect and fulfil the right to food of its citizens.

The Food Planning and Monitoring Unit (FPMU) of the Ministry of Food and Disaster Management, which is the government unit responsible for monitoring the food security situation in Bangladesh and the implementation of related policies, is a key actor in food policymaking. Moreover, this government wing is also involved in collecting, storing and disseminating information for food security analysis and policy formulation, and delivering evidence-based policy advice to the government on issues relevant to food security—on its own initiative or on demand by the Government of Bangladesh (NFPCSP 2011).

Political Parties, Political System, and the Discourse of Food Security

The key narratives of food security in Bangladesh come from the lessons of famine in 1974, which made it imperative for successive governments to organize swift relief, import foodgrains to stabilize rice prices and to work hard to prevent famine. As a result, it has been observed that while famine became a recurrent feature in some parts of Africa in the 1970s, 1980s and 1990s, Bangladesh has successfully avoided a recurrence of famine since 1974. As Sobhan (2010: 215) states, 'the government is conscious of the political fallout from a possible famine situation developing and is willing to make a sizeable fiscal investment to avert such a possibility'. In contrast, currently, just over every one in four (26 per cent) Bangladeshis have been suffering from chronic hunger (FAO 2011). Despite its magnitude of hunger and malnutrition, some suggest that it is neither an issue of parliamentary debate nor street agitation nor has it given rise to buzzwords in the media (IvCSPol10). Although nationwide *hartal* (general strike) is a common practice in Bangladeshi politics, which often occurs for the purpose of pushing very silly political demands, there is no history of *hartal* for ensuring the right to food. Sometimes, the issue of price hikes of daily essentials is the subject matter of political campaigns against the government, but the purpose of this issue is to gain the attention of the middle and lower middle classes, not the ultra-poor. No mainstream political party in Bangladesh has ever arranged any protest for putting pressure on the government to increase budgetary allocation for Public Food Distribution Systems (PFDS) or introducing and/or increasing food rationing. Throughout the 1980s and 1990s, when the government was downsizing the PFDS including rural rationing, no protests were observed from the mainstream opposition or the civil society. While the present political system in Bangladesh is ready to avert famine by any means, it is still not on their political agenda to ensure an uninterrupted supply of food for all people at all times.

One particular feature of the politics of food security in Bangladesh is that although every government is highly sensitized for famine and related issues, they perceive it as a discredit for the government to make it public that there is a food crisis. For example, in an interview with the daily *Prothom-alo* (10 October 2010) Hossain Z. Rahman, a former advisor (Cabinet Minister) of the caretaker government of Bangladesh, notes that '[in a meeting,] in making of the Poverty Reduction Strategy Paper (PRSP) in 2004, even though I raised the issue of *monga* [seasonal food insecurity], the then policy makers of the government showed their strong apathy to the issue. Considering it to be an embarrassing issue for the government, many of the policy makers were not interested in including such an issue in a government policy paper'. The fact is that for political reasons, every regime wants to show that they are successfully tackling any food crisis, including *monga*. In response to the 2005 *monga* situation, the governmental National News Agency of Bangladesh (BSS) quoted official sources as saying that 'adequate steps taken by the government [in form of an] adequate supply of food grains helped the people to overcome the *monga* in all the districts of greater Rangpur . . . *So-called* 'monga' *exists only in the media reports now-a-days*' (as cited in Zug 2006: 13; emphasis added). Yet the opposition regularly blames the government for not taking sufficient steps to address *monga* (ibid.).

It is true that the issue of food has gained importance as a political agenda in society, which is evident in every national election in Bangladesh. The food security and agricultural issues in the election manifesto of the two major political parties in the 2008 election. Not surprisingly, both parties' manifestos are similar in nature. Mechanisms such as state regulation, state intervention and state support in production, import and distribution are promised in order to ensure food security. Most importantly, the policies, in general, are very vague and, therefore, sound merely like political rhetoric. Interestingly, while the Awami League did not make any promise with regard to the distribution of food free of cost, some political observers finds the BNP's policy 'an empty promise' or 'political rhetoric' (Ahmed & Khan 2008). With regard to an article in *The Daily Star* (15 December 2008), about a proposition of the BNP, Ahmed and Khan (2008) note that:

> . . . its pragmatism and practicality is that the party wants to distribute food free of cost among the destitute, helpless, elderly and the unemployed. This certainly looks like an impossible proposition. There are at least 25 per cent of the population falling below the poverty line, another 9 per cent above the age of 55, and another 4.2 per cent unemployed. So in total, at least five to six crore people will need to be fed free of cost, the resource needed for which will be enormous and certainly beyond any government's capability. Is this an empty promise then, or a political rhetoric? The proposal for extending the programme of assured jobs for 100 days is, however, well received, and promises good results in *monga*-prone areas.

Considering the nature of the election manifestos of the major political parties, in a personal interview, one political observer suggested that this election manifesto is nothing but a campaign that is only for the purpose of electoral gain. In other words, the purpose is solely to win the election (IvCSPol10). The issue of food, particularly price hikes of 'daily essentials', is not only the major agenda of election manifestors of all the political parties; it is also the major agenda of the election campaign. It is imperative to bear in mind that 'daily essentials' includes a number of luxury items that are not important in reducing hunger. In other words, while importance is given for a broad agenda that covers a big list of daily essentials, it is difficult to pay attention to the basic food items for the hungry poor.

It is important to bear in mind that the major political parties of Bangladesh have never been concerned about a targeted pro-poor distribution system of Bangladesh nor do they have any specific policy in relation to food security. Although political parties, particularly in the opposition, repeatedly raise issues relating to the high price hike of daily essentials including foodgrains, none of the political parties ever presented a full-fledged policy paper. Rather, the purpose of the food policy issues and its uses in the election manifesto of the major political parties is nothing but a tactic to win the election and to form the government (ibid.).

Competing or Consensus: How is Food Security Framed in Bangladesh?

The degree of state involvement in promoting food security is the central issue of the food policy debate in Bangladesh. In order to ensure an uninterrupted supply of food to all people at all times, Bangladesh's food policy has undergone major changes throughout the 1980s and, particularly, in the 1990s. The key feature of this policy shift is that by reducing a large-scale public intervention Bangladesh moved into a more market-oriented system, reduced food subsidy bills by downsizing Public Food Distribution Systems and allocated more resources to development and anti-poverty projects (Ali et al. 2008; Chowdhury, Farid & Roy 2010). This notable policy shift happened largely with consensus among the main political parties of Bangladesh. All major political parties, which include the Awami League, the BNP, the Jatiya Party and Jamaat-e-Islami were either directly, or as coalition partners of the government, involved in this policy shift. In the zero-sum game politics of Bangladesh, although the BNP and Awami League are very hostile to each other and almost always oppose each other on every issue, each wholeheartedly welcomed the market-oriented liberalizing policy reforms which were initiated with the support of the IMF and the World Bank and which have been followed through since then in various phases. Food policy and agricultural policy changes are a part of these market-based reforms.

Because of the nature of the policymaking process (as discussed in Chapter 3), there were no challenges of policy shift within the government or the party of the incumbent government. The fact is that, as one observer suggests 'food policy is never a subject of parliamentary discussion, nor is it a subject matter of discussion in the cabinet' (IvCSPol10). Rather, as Chowdhury, Farid and Roy (2010: 26) suggests, 'the World Bank produced an important document, *Food Policy Issues* (World Bank 1979), that framed all major policy and analytical issues in managing Bangladesh's food sector'. Moreover, there is a general consensus in the food security literature in Bangladesh that donors, particularly USAID and the World Bank, are the key architects of the food policy reforms of Bangladesh (Montgomery 1983; Shahadat Ullah 1988; IFPRI 1993; Adams 1998; Chowdhury & Haggblade 2000). The reason why the Bangladesh state needs the support of external agencies is because it is incapable of or disinclined towards making a comprehensive food policy. For example, Franda (1982: 201) suggests that throughout the 1970s, Bangladesh never had a coherent food policy. The story of the making of the *National Food Policy 2006* also shows the elite beliefs in promoting food security in Bangladesh. Interestingly, before 1999, without the recommendation of donors the state elite of Bangladesh did not realize the need to adopt a comprehensive food security policy. The fact is that 'following the 1999 Development Forum held in Paris which emphasized the need to adopt a comprehensive food security policy, the Government of Bangladesh established a task force of nine ministries' (NFPPA 2008: 21). In other words, while a comprehensive food policy is essential for ensuring an uninterrupted supply of food to all people at all times, the Bangladesh state did not even feel the importance of formulating it. Hence, it would not be wrong to conclude that although political parties engage in some rhetoric in their election manifestos and electoral campaigns, the truth is that the origin of the food policy of Bangladesh has been shaped, developed and evolved by external agencies.

Debate continues over the degree of state intervention in the food security discourse of Bangladesh. As noted earlier, there is a commitment of the major political parties to provide free food to the poor and to provide subsidies to the agricultural industry in order to support production. In practice, available data indicates that in the last three decades all major political parties downsized PFDS while each of them held office, and reduced large-scale public intervention in both the agriculture and food sectors (for details see Chapter 5 and 6). However, controversy exists over a number of issues concerning the food and agricultural policy of Bangladesh.

The first question is whether the country should discontinue the strategy of self-reliance[1] and move to self-sufficiency[2] in promoting national level food availability. The chronology of food policy of Bangladesh suggests that until the early 1990s, the Bangladesh state aimed to achieve food availability by following a policy of self-sufficiency. Since 1993, the policy was changed to one of self-reliance (Deb, Hossain & Jones 2009). Until the global food crisis of 2007-8 which hit Bangladesh severely, there was no policy debate about the strategy of self-reliance as 'the strategy of self-reliance worked well' (Deb, Hossain & Jones 2009). However, after the 2007-8 food crises in Bangladesh, the question of the strategy of self-reliance was revisited. A study by Deb, Hossain and Jones (ibid.) suggests that Bangladesh should target self-sufficiency in rice production, which will satisfy domestic demand in normal production years. Similarly, in the dialogue of a conference titled *Food Security and Containing Price Inflation*, held on 28 March 2009 in Dhaka, leading food policy experts and policy makers unanimously agreed that the most important thing to attain sustainable food security in Bangladesh is achieving self-sufficiency (CPD 2009).

Second, the level of the public food stock is also an important issue of food policy discourse in Bangladesh. Public food stock is important for several reasons: (a) price stabilization by ensuring a floor price for producers and a ceiling price for consumers. Floor prices for foodgrain producers are ensured through the public procurement system; (b) it provides emergency relief; (c) it provides targeted food distribution. Considering the importance of public foodgrain stocks, the scale of national stock was designed by the World Bank (1979) report, *Food Policy Issues,* which cited optimal national stocks as equal to 1.5 MMT as of 1 July of every year and 1.2 MMT as of 15 November of every year. Security stocks equal to 600,000 MT were considered 'appropriate'. In view of this policy recommendation, the government has calculated that maintaining year-round grain stocks between 0.7 and 1.5 million tonnes is adequate for national food security (Shahabuddin et al. 2009: 4-5). But in practice, food stocks were reduced from about 1.5 MMT in the 1980s to about 0.6 MMT in recent years (Hossain 2010: 178). Recently, the question of the size of food stocks has been raised as the government failed to make an impact during the food crisis of 2007-8 (ibid.; Shahabuddin et al. 2009). In an interview with the daily *Prothom-alo* (5 December 2010), Hossain, a leading food policy expert in Bangladesh, suggests that in order to exert a significant influence in the market the government should have 2.5 to 3.0 MMT of food stock.

The role of the government in public food distribution is another controversial issue in the food security discourse in Bangladesh, considering the societal pressure for promoting food security as political parties promised to provide free food to the destitute, the poor and the vulnerable (see Islam 2012: 114). However, because of leakages and targeting errors, a number of studies (World Bank 1977, 1979, 1992, 2004, 2006 Ahmed et al. 2004, 2007) recommended abolishing many programmes of the PFDS, through which the public supply of foodgrains are handled. As a result, the government has significantly downsized the PFD, making poverty reduction a priority basis for grain allocation (Chowdhury, Farid & Roy 2006). For instance, between the mid-1980s and the mid-2000s, the share of public distribution in market supply shrank from 13 per cent to 5.2 per cent (ibid. 2010: 3). Thus, the role of the PFDS in creating state-led entitlement has declined significantly. Many suggest that by reducing food subsidy bills, Bangladesh has created notable gains (ibid. 2010; Ali et al. 2008). In contrast, many believe that reducing public distribution is not the solution. For them, a well-targeted entitlement generation programme is essential for reducing hunger but the problem is with its implementation. For example, a noted Bangladeshi economist rightly stated that 'one of the challenges in attaining food security is to ensure smooth transferring of resources to the rural sector either in the form of subsidies or through transfer payments' (Sobhan 2009: 116).

Fourth, the question of input prices, subsidies and farmers' incentives is a vital issue of the food security discourse. I will illustrate in Chapter 5 that it is not easy to formulate a simple food policy to ensure food security in Bangladesh, where food-insecure people are both 'peasants' and the 'rural and urban poor'. On the one hand, a large majority of the poor people in Bangladesh depend on markets for access to food. Adverse movements in terms of trade between purchased food and the goods or services they produce and sell (including wage labour) can cause entitlements failure (Barrett 2002: 17). On the other hand, many net food sellers in Bangladesh are poor themselves, and declining relative food prices hurt them. This is the question of the 'food price dilemma' (Timmer, Falcon & Pearson 1983)—higher food prices are necessary to induce increased local food production and to increase the incomes of poor, net seller food producers, yet high food prices threaten the food security of low-income countries like Bangladesh. Hence, the question of input prices, subsidies and farmers' incentives gains currency in the food security debate in Bangladesh. Over the years Bangladesh's agriculture sector has been liberalized and has deregulated input markets. A number of studies suggest that liberalization and privatization of input markets began gradually but has substantially influenced the growth of rice production (for example, see Ahmed 1995; Ahmed, Haggblade & Chowdhury 2000; Ahmed 2001). In contrast, in view of poor governance, Azmat (2009; also Azmat & Coghill 2005) demonstrates that despite notable achievements, the reforms have not achieved their expected outcomes, and more importantly, in cases in which they have been achieved, their sustainability is in question. Some suggest that the government will need to play a more proactive role in ensuring sufficient supply of quality inputs (Rahman & Deb 2005). A study of Asaduzzaman et al. 2009) suggests that the government can seek to influence farmer incentives by subsidizing agricultural inputs or by procurement of foodgrains and open market sales.

The Food Security Discourse within NGOs: Is There any Consensus?

There are few local NGOs which directly or indirectly work to promote food security in Bangladesh. A survey of NGOs in Bangladesh calculated their sector specific activities as follows—credit (90 per cent of small NGOs and 96 per cent of big NGOs), health care (60 per cent and 48 per cent), sanitation (56 per cent and 43 per cent), employment, child education, safe drinking water, agricultural training, adult education, other, roads, land rights/tenure, transportation, electricity, and communications (see Gauri & Julia 2005: 2050). Nevertheless, in the wake of the 2007-8 food crisis, a FAO/WFP mission estimated that 'as many as 8.1 million people, representing just over 12 per cent of the estimated 65.3 million food insecure population, could be receiving assistance from non-Government channels' (FAO 2009: 16). International NGOs like CARE and Save the Children-US were providing assistance to approximately 4.8 million people, and the Bangladesh Rural Advancement Committee (BRAC), the country's largest NGO was providing food rations and monetary assistance to around 1.4 million people (FAO 2009: 15). And the World Food Programme disbursed food to approximately 4.7 million people in the same period (FAO 2009: 15).

In addition to this assistance, many NGOs concerned with awareness-raising programmes do give importance to nutrition. This activity was ranked third out of nine major focus areas (Gauri & Julia 2005). And apart from these direct activities, it is to be noted that a number of NGOs such as UBINIG, Proshika and CARE Bangladesh have launched initiatives in different parts of the country to promote alternative agriculture—they emphasize reduced use of external inputs, including agro-chemicals and increased use of local and on-farm resources in order to make the system both environmentally and economically sustainable (Akter 1997). One of the main drawbacks of such initiatives is that they are confined to certain pockets of the country. However, they are gaining importance gradually, as there is increasing awareness of the adverse health and environmental impact of conventional agriculture (Rasul &

Thapa 2004). Not surprisingly, despite the growing importance of the role of NGOs in promoting food security in Bangladesh, the voice of NGOs in respect to food policymaking is still unheeded. The central role played by the state and donors in food policymaking in Bangladesh is illustrated by the manner in which the National Food Plan was developed.

Following the 1999 Development Forum held in Paris which emphasized the need to adopt a comprehensive food security policy, the Government of Bangladesh established a task force of nine ministries. Based on the recommendations of this task force, an initial draft of the NFP was produced in 2001. After consultations with a parliamentary sub-committee on food, and with support from FAO, the draft went through a series of revisions between 2002 and 2004. The National Food Policy was finally approved by the Cabinet on 14 August 2006 (see NFPCSP 2012).

NGOs in Bangladesh can be categorized in two main groups which work for food security. In a personal interview, a Bangladeshi political analyst, activist and noted economist states that: 'Bangladeshi non-governmental organizations (NGOs) can be categorized into two main groups: (a) corporate NGOs with huge amounts of capital who are mainly involved in business, which includes agribusiness; and (b) other types of NGOs who are mainly dealing with environmental issues. But I have not seen the types of NGOs who work on food issues with rights-based perspectives. Very few NGOs work on seeds and agriculture' (IvCSPol10).

In order to examine the food security discourse among NGOs, here I make a brief comparison between two NGOs in Bangladesh, the Bangladesh Rural Advancement Committee (BRAC), one of the leading NGOs in Bangladesh; and UBINIG, a policy and action research organization which is well-known for its Nayakrishi Andolon or New Agricultural Movement. One interesting comparison of these two NGOs is that while UBINIG suggests to 'keep seeds in farmer's hand; in situ and ex situ conservation of seed and genetic resources' (UBINIG 2012), BRAC is the pioneer in hybrid rice variety development, seed production and marketing in Bangladesh (BRAC 2012).

In the field of Bangladesh's agriculture and food security, BRAC works on several issues, which include research on biotechnology and soil testing, work with hybrid rice and maize varieties, mitigating *monga*, combating climate change threats on food security and crop intensification (ibid.). It also has multi-dimensional programmes which are designed to reach the poor including the most vulnerable segments, with a particular focus on women. Shahabuddin (2010: 122) points out that the major BRAC interventions directly linked to food production include development of poultry, livestock, fisheries, agricultural crops, and fruit and vegetable production programmes. In addition, BRAC has a number of income generation programmes. One of these is Income Generation for the Vulnerable Group Development (IGVGD). A study of Matin and Hulme (2003) notes that BRAC's IGVGD programme has deepened the outreach of its poverty reduction activity and differed markedly from other programme plans. On the other hand, the Nayakrishi Andolon of UBINIG is now a major ecological movement in Bangladesh involving over 300,000 farming families (as of October 2009). It is worthy to note that:

> The strategic focus of agriculture at present is biodiversity and genetic resources. The *Nayakrishi* distinguishes its practice from commonly familiar 'organic' agriculture for various reasons. Emphasis is on the biodiversity based life activities, developing an operational notion of 'ecosystem', ensuring various natural cycles of water, elements, nutrition, energy, evolution and demonstrating the validity and authenticity of experiential knowledge. These are some key features that distinguish *Nayakrishi* practice from the commonly known 'organic' agriculture. *Nayakrishi Andolon* is not simply about production of 'food', but regeneration of communities with conservation and enhancement of their wealth for a healthy, happy and enriched life. (UBINIG 2012)

UBINIG is concerned with international trade, intellectual property rights, and biotechnology and genetic engineering from the perspective of food-producing communities. The fact is that UBINIG advocates the concept of food sovereignty instead of food security. In other words, the major difference between BRAC and UBINIG is that while BRAC practises neoliberal strategies of promoting food security, UBINIG challenges the concept of food security, although their aim is also to promote sustainable food and agriculture for society. In the context of the present study, it is difficult to quantify the significance of UBINIG in promoting food sovereignty or the role of BRAC in promoting food security.

Based on this discussion, we can draw two important conclusions. First, local NGOs in Bangladesh are not actively involved in promoting food security. Second, considering the role and activities of two major NGOs in Bangladesh whose focus is on food security issues, it is clear that there is no consensus among NGOs in Bangladesh with regard to which strategies and policies are most important in addressing food security.

A study of FAO (2009b) shows that non-government sources of food security have also played a critical part in providing assistance to a large number of poor households in Bangladesh. NGOs such as CARE and Save the Children-USA (USAID's PL 480 Title II NGOs) are reported to be providing food assistance to about 4.8 million people. The WFP is currently assisting approximately 4.7 million people (3.8 million of which are also beneficiaries of the Government programmes). BRAC, Bangladesh's largest NGO, is reported to be assisting 1.4 million people with food rations and cash assistance. There are also various other NGOs operating similar programmes and the FAO/WFP mission estimated that as many as 8.1 million people, representing just over 12 per cent of the estimated 65.3 million food insecure population, could be receiving assistance from non-government channels (FAO, 2009b: 15-16).

CHALLENGES OF FOOD AVAILABILITY IN BANGLADESH

Food consumption patterns: Before analysing the problem of food production and availability, it is important to discuss the nature of the main foods consumed in Bangladesh. Cereals amount for a high percentage of calories in Bangladesh, which is about 78 per cent of total consumption (FAOSTAT 2012). Rice is the staple food and it dominates cereal calorie consumption as well as total calorie consumption. It accounts for about 70 per cent of the total cropped area and 93 per cent of total cereal production (BBS

1996). Agriculture, the main occupation of the people, sustained the livelihood of about 44.41 per cent of the active labour force in 2011, compared to 58.79 per cent in 1996 (FAOSTAT 2012). As the largest private enterprise, agriculture (crops, livestock, fisheries and forestry) contributes about 21 per cent to the GDP, most of which come from crop production (NAP 2010: 1). Thus, as a source of both calories and rural employment, rice (production) is a very important factor to understand the challenges of food security in Bangladesh. In addition to rice, some main items of food consumed in Bangladesh are wheat, pulses, potato, vegetables and fish. More than 14 per cent of per capita calorie consumption is derived from vegetable products, which is the second largest calorie source. Table 4.1 shows that the normal diet of Bangladeshi people is seriously unbalanced due to the prevailing deficit in total calorie intake and an inadequate consumption of fat, oil, protein and other non-cereal foods. However, the overall calorie intake per capita per day increased by 3.6 per cent to 2,318.3 Kcal in 2010 from 2,238.5 Kcal in 2005. Per capita per day intake of food items has also increased by 5.5 per cent to 999.9 grams in 2010 from 947.8 grams in 2005 at the national level (BBS 2011).

TABLE 4.1: TREND IN PER CAPITA FOOD INTAKE IN BANGLADESH (GRAM PER CAPITA PER DAY)

Food intake (gram per capita per day)	HIES 2010			HIES 2005		
	National	Rural	Urban	National	Rural	Urban
Rice	416.01	441.61	344.20	439.64	459.71	378.53
Wheat	26.09	23.38	33.69	12.08	7.99	24.52
Pulses	14.30	13.23	17.30	14.2	12.7	18.6
Vegetables	166.08	170.04	154.95	157.0	156.5	158.7
Fish	49.41	45.67	59.91	42.1	39.7	49.6
Meat	19.07	14.32	31.41	8.4	7.0	12.6
Eggs	7.25	5.80	11.32	5.2	4.4	7.4
Milk & Milk products	33.72	31.78	39.16	32.4	31.0	36.6
Fruit	44.80	42.73	50.59	32.5	32.4	32.9
Protein	66.26	65.24	69.11	62.52	61.74	64.88
Calories (Kcal/capita/day)	2,318.3	2,344.6	2,244.5	2,238.5	2,253.2	2,193.8

Source: BBS 2011.

Table 4.1 indicates the growing diversification of food intake that has taken place from 2005 to 2010. Most noticeably there has been a decline in the consumption of cereals. The average quantity of rice intake decreased to 416.01 grams in 2010 from 439.64 grams in 2005 at the national level. On the other hand, consumption of both wheat and potato increased to 26.09 and 70.52 grams in 2010 from 12.08 and 63.30 grams in 2005, respectively (BBS 2011). Similarly, the consumption of vegetables, fruits, meat, onion and other items also increased in 2010, relative to 2005.

The impact of the prevailing deficit in total calorie intake and the nature of an imbalanced diet are huge. For example, as noted in Chapter 1, over 75 per cent of households with children under the age of five were food insecure in the period of February-May 2011 (FSNSP 2011). A study of FAO (2001) shows that between 2006 and 2008, out of total 157.7 million people, 41.4 million were undernourished in Bangladesh—26 per cent of the total population.

Foodgrain Production and Food Availability

Historically, Bangladesh is a country with a food gap, as the imbalance of demand and supply of foodgrains is a prevalent fact of the nation's history (see Table 4.2). Over the years, however, Bangladesh's food production has increased manifold. A significant breakthrough in production can be seen in the period of 1975-6–1983-4 when the production of cereals was able to keep ahead of population growth (Osmani 1991: 313). Ahmed et al. (2000) argue that improvements in agricultural science in the 1970s roughly doubled farm yields, while in the 1980s the liberalization of irrigation restrictions, the lifting of import barriers to irrigation technology and the privatization of fertilizer distribution rapidly increased rice cultivation. They further assert that these increases in production, coupled with improvements in infrastructure and a more slowly growing and increasingly urban population, have substantially changed the structure of foodgrain markets, leading to increased marketing volumes, lower prices and significantly larger private grain stocks. More precisely, the respectable growth in rice

TABLE 4.2: CEREAL PRODUCTION, IMPORTS AND FOOD AID IN BANGLADESH, 1981-2010

	Average quantity (1,000 tonnes)			Trend growth (per cent)*		
	1981-90	1991-2000	2001-10	1981-90	1991-2000	2001-10
Total Production	16,103	20,172	28,336	2.07	2.34	2.48
Rice	15,021	18,772	27,228	2.31	1.96	2.97
Wheat	1,092	1,400	1,108	-1.41	7.58	-8.97
Net imports	1,838	2,115	2,697	4.83	8.90	5.78
Food aid	1,233	794	166	2.92	-6.97	-9.22
Net supply	16,194	20,189	29,617	2.38	3.05	3.44
Net supply/person	163	168	211.49	0.23	1.39	2.22
Imports/net supply	11.25%	10.17%	9.19%	2.44	5.85	2.33

* Trend growth rate has been calculated by using semilog model (for details see, Gujarati 2003).

Source: Author's calculation from Directorate of Food.

production was propelled by adoption of high-yielding modern varieties of rice, facilitated by an expansion of irrigation infrastructure (Hossain, Naher & Shahabuddin 2005: 105). The adoption of modern rice varieties has reached 70 per cent of rice cropped area. Almost 90 per cent of the growth in rice production came from the increase in yields made possible by the technological advances in rice cultivation (ibid. 2005: 105).

Similarly, Chowdhury, Farid and Roy (2006) suggest that three factors—the advent of new technology (High Yielding Varieties, hereafter HYV), the development of infrastructure and market liberalization and working in tandem—have delivered favourable food security outcomes for Bangladesh. The HYV gains were most notable for the *boro* season (planting: December-February and harvesting: April-May) harvests, which converted the customary hungry season into a welcome harvest season. They further argue that, based on values corresponding to the lower limit, overall effects on food security are actually quite small. However, despite the success of production, in order to feed an increasing population, a former top state official for the food ministry suggests that 'our [food] productivity is not yet at the maximum level, not even at the optimal level. Therefore, we must increase our production [in order to ensure food security]' (IvGoB4).

My discussion in Chapter 5 will clarify that several factors such as poor governance, weak state capacity, rent-seeking and so on can be seen as major challenges for future agricultural production. Yet, here a brief discussion is called for in order to clarify this section. Some studies (Azmat & Coghill 2005; Azmat 2009) show the negative impacts of market reforms in agricultural development. They assert that lack of good governance affects the success and sustainability of the market-based reforms undertaken in the agricultural sector of Bangladesh. As governance is a basic factor explaining the poor economic performance of many developing countries (Hayami & Ruttan 1985) a country of better governance can end up with more agricultural outputs, given the same amounts of agricultural inputs, the same education levels and the same climate conditions (Lio & Liu 2008). Throughout the 1980s, when market reforms in the agricultural sector took place in Bangladesh, the country was under extremely poor governance of military regimes. Hence, it is difficult to claim that market-based reforms were the leading factor in the growth of agricultural production. Rather, it was the advent of new technology (HYV), an expansion of irrigation infrastructure and the development of other forms of infrastructure that caused the boom of increased agricultural production. Not surprisingly, Bangladesh could not even maintain its production rate compared to the global trends of rice production. Recently, because of the lack of large developments of new technology, the growth of production stalled for the first time since the early 1990s. As a result, dependency on food grain imports has considerably increased in the last four years (see Table 4.3), and many people have joined the ranks of the hungry because of high food prices. The food-insecure population has become the largest in the history of Bangladesh. In the following section, I will discuss the challenges of food availability in Bangladesh.

Fluctuations of production and the challenges of food availability. Table 4.2 illustrates that domestic food production is the major source of food supply of Bangladesh, and thereby fluctuations in

TABLE 4.3: VALUE OF IMPORTS BY MAJOR AGRICULTURE COMMODITIES

(*in million US dollar*)

Commodity	1999-00	2000-1	2001-2	2002-3	2003-4	2004-5	2005-6	2006-7	2007-8	2008-9	2009-10
Rice	115	172	15	211	144	262	117	180	874	239	75
Wheat	266	177	171	198	287	312	301	401	537	643	761
Oilseeds	90	64	72	64	73	86	90	106	136	159	130
Edible oil	256	218	251	364	471	440	473	583	1,006	865	1,050
Fertilizer	140	129	107	109	150	332	342	357	632	955	717

Source: *Bangladesh Economic Review*, 2010 and 2011.

production are a major cause of instability in food availability. The Table further indicates that foodgrain production significantly increased during the 1980s and 1990s. However, in the last decade, the growth trend of production has failed to keep pace with that registered in the previous two decades. Again, foodgrain imports still play a significant role in the stability of food availability as the country is not yet self-sufficient in food production. There has always been a food gap between foodgrain production and demand. In contrast with India, stability in food supplies in Bangladesh was provided mainly through food aid from the mid-1970s up to the early 1990s, and since the early 1990s via private sector imports (del Ninno et al. 2007: 420).

Despite success in food production, fluctuations in production are still a major threat to food security in Bangladesh. The major causes of fluctuations are—poor harvest, flood, drought and artificial food crises caused by traders. Bangladesh is extremely vulnerable to floods and cyclones because of its geographical location. The country is located within the world's largest delta, formed by the Padma (Ganges), Jamuna (Brahmaputra) and Meghna rivers and their tributaries, all of which empty into the Bay of Bengal. Therefore, while its alluvial soil is highly fertile, natural disasters such as floods and drought are also very common phenomena, particularly floods, adversely affecting the agriculture sector. Since the mid-1950s, the frequency of floods and the extent of flood damage have increased manifold. Severe (measured in terms of loss of life and property) floods occurred in 1954, 1955, 1956, 1962, 1963, 1968, and 1969 (Alamgir 1980: 110). After the War of Independence in 1971, major floods occurred in 1974, 1984, 1987, 1988 and 1998. Small scale floods occurred almost every year. All of these floods caused severe crop damage and brought misery for poor people in many ways. For example, in explaining the Bangladesh famine of 1974, Sen (1981) shows how the impact of flood created entitlement failure and caused famine. Moreover, Bangladesh has been affected by many tropical cyclones, which are usually formed in the Bay of Bengal and mainly hit the coastal districts of Khulna, Patuakhali, Barishal, Noakhali and offshore islands like Bhola, Hatiya, Sandwip, Ramgati and Kutubdia.

Several studies (Montgomery 1985; Brammer 1990) have examined the extent of crop damage caused by flooding, but they have virtually ignored the temporal dimension of flood damage. Paul and Rashid (1993: 150) suggest that the extent of damage caused by both 'normal' and 'extreme' floods varies not only spatially but also from year to year. They show the spatial patterns of damage to rice crops resulting from flooding during a specific period, 1962 to 1988.

In addition to the loss, of life, according to Paul and Rashid (1993: 151), the most costly consequence of floods in Bangladesh is rice-crop damage. Rice production is the main victim of both normal and abnormal flooding, even though floods damage other crops such as jute, sugarcane and summer vegetables. The loss of rice production attributable to floods accounts for nearly three-quarters of the total annual loss of agricultural output. During the 27-year (1962-88) study period, floods damaged rice crops every year, with only one exception. The average annual loss of rice production resulting from flooding in Bangladesh was approximately four per cent of the total countrywide rice production figure (see ibid.). However, this figure is manageable in the context of food availability despite the huge loss it represents, as it is a normal trend of production. In contrast, abnormal floods create a severe threat to food availability. In addition to the damage and fluctuation in availability of foodgrains, it also creates challenges for the policymakers to mitigate unexpected crises through food import. For example, in recent history, Bangladesh experienced severe floods in 1974, 1984, 1987, 1988 and 1998. Among these, the 1974 floods caused famine in that year, whereas others created famine-like situations, although actual famine was averted.

To cope with the regular crop damages caused by natural disasters, cereal production has become more resilient to natural disasters because of the dramatic change in the seasonal composition of production (for example, see Hossain, Naher & Shahbuddin 2005: 106). In addition to the seasonal varieties of rice production, attempts are also taken to develop flood-tolerating rice varieties that would help farmers prevent millions of tonnes of annual crop lost during flash floods. However, floods and other natural calamities are still unavoidable and are unbridled threats to stable domestic foodgrain production.

Drought is another cause of fluctuation of food grain production in Bangladesh. Although drought is not as regular as floods it is still one of the causes of poor harvest of foodgrains and fluctuations of food availability. For example, a severe drought in 1979 caused rice prices to fluctuate heavily—upto more than four times that of the previous year. The drought of 1982 also caused similar troubles in foodgrain availability and price hikes.

Challenges of production and availability: Is the road ahead blocked? There is a complex relationship between agriculture and food production and the impact of environmental changes. The outcome of this complex linkage can, in turn, impact food systems which lead to further environmental changes and so on. There are various ways how environmental changes can jeopardize food production, which include impacts on land and soil; water use and water quality; habitat and biodiversity loss; energy use; and climate change (McDonald 2010: 98-9). Sadly, because of the geographical location, environmental changes will adversely affect the food security of Bangladesh.

On the one hand, to ensure food availability via domestic production, it is imperative to keep pace with population growth since it is assumed that the food demand will significantly increase in the near future in Bangladesh due to its high population growth rate. For example, the population is still growing by about 2 million per year in Bangladesh, which means an increase in rice production by 0.5 million metric tonnes is required every year (Hossain 2010: 172). On the other hand, the impact of global climate change is widely considered as a big threat to future foodgrain production in the world in general and Bangladesh in particular. Climate change may affect food systems in several ways, ranging from direct effects on crop production (e.g. changes in rainfall leading to drought or flooding, or warmer or cooler temperatures leading to changes in the length of growing season), to changes in markets, food prices and supply chain infrastructure (Gregory, Ingram & Brklacic 2005).

All current quantitative assessments show that climate change will adversely affect global food security (WSFS 2009). The most direct implications of climate change for food security are through its impacts on food production worldwide (Devereux & Edwards 2004). It is projected that countries in sub-Saharan Africa and South Asia in particular are most vulnerable and may suffer the greatest share of damage in the form of declining yields and a greater frequency of extreme weather events (WSFS 2009). In southern Asia, Bangladesh may suffer the greatest share of damage in the form of agricultural production. Its 'low ability to cope with shocks and to mitigate long-term stresses means that coping strategies that might be available in other regions are unavailable or inappropriate' (Gregory, Ingram & Brklacic 2005).

Again, other drivers, such as labour issues and the availability and quality of groundwater for irrigation, rank higher than the direct effects of climate change, as factors influencing food security (ibid.). While natural disasters are very common in Bangladesh, in future, the country is likely to be suffering more natural disasters due to the impact of climate change. According to a projection, out of many devastating impacts, most strikingly Bangladesh will lose about eight per cent of its rice and 32 per cent of its wheat production by the year 2050 (see Islam 2012). Bala & Hossain (2010) show that Bangladesh, which will be the most affected by a rise of its total population, lives close to the coast. Elsewhere, I have shown (Islam 2012) that already about 830,000 hectares of arable land have been affected by varying degrees of soil erosion and this will increase in coming years. More than 60 per cent of Bangladesh's land lies six metres below sea level (Mirza 2002) with 25 per cent of it is experiencing regular floods. This is projected to increase to 40 per cent (see Islam 2012). Hence, as Herrmann and Svarin (2009) rightly suggest, the effects of climate change, including frequent natural calamities, will have serious implications for food security in Bangladesh.

In addition to the threat of deforestation, coastal erosion and flooding due to the impact of climate change, some other challenges are also evident for Bangladesh in relation to foodgrain production and availability. For example, Bangladeshi farmers have already adopted high-yielding varieties (HYVs) in most of the areas suitable for foodgrains, and have used groundwater for increased food production. However, Bangladesh is still a food deficit country and the future challenge is huge in relation to the future demand of foodgrains. 'To overcome the challenges to meet the future challenge of foodgrains production', according to a former agriculture minister of Bangladesh, 'further increase in yield of foodgrains at the farm-level will depend on making breakthrough in development and diffusion of new varieties and hybrids that have higher yield frontier. To this end, research on hybrids and biotechnology needs to get adequate importance from the government side' (Anwar 2009: 110). It is also important to note that developing varieties for unfavourable ecologies (flood, drought, salinity) is also required to overcome the challenges of food production in a hostile environment. In response, a downward trend of Research and Development (R&D) investments have been observed in Bangladesh; and a lesser priority for agricultural research is evident.

In order to catch up the future growth of food demand, the expansion of arable land could be an easy solution for food deficit nations. In this regard, Bangladesh stands out as a stark example where arable land is under challenge for two chief reasons.

Firstly, Bangladesh is the most densely populated country in the world and, therefore, it has one of the lowest land/person ratios in terms of arable land and land under permanent crops availability; in 2009, this was only 0.06 ha compared to 0.08 ha in 1994 (FAOSTAT 2012). The high population growth (around 2 per cent annually) further reduces the availability of land for agriculture by creating increased demand for land for settlements, roads, industry and other non-agricultural uses (Ali 1995; Rahman & Thapa 1999; FAO 2000; Rasul & Thapa 2004), particularly rapid urbanization, reducing arable land dramatically. For example, in 2009, the total area of arable land in Bangladesh was 7.57 million ha, compared to 8.41 million ha in 1994. Between 2004 and 2009, in terms of the annual growth rate, the arable land of Bangladesh was significantly decreasing (-1.63 per cent) (FAOSTAT 2012). Moreover, Rahman (2003: 487) notes that Bangladesh agriculture, dominated by rice production, is already operating at its land maximum and has very little or no scope to increase the supply of land to meet the growing demand for food required by its ever-increasing population.

Secondly, the expansion in crop areas, which was a major source of production growth until the 1980s, has been exhausted and the land under the rice started to decline thereafter (Husain, Hossain & Janaiah 2001; cited in Rahman 2003: 487). As a result, the area under pulses, oilseeds, fodder and natural inland fisheries is also declining rapidly (FFYP 1998; quoted in Rahman & Thapa 1999). For example, the rapid expansion in the area of *boro* rice and wheat was achieved partly through the reduction in the area and production of pulses and oilseeds. These two crops were important sources of protein and micronutrients, particularly for the poor (Hossain Naher & Shahabuddin 2005: 106). Therefore, the expansion of one particular crop results in the reduction of other kinds of crops as the arable land is not expanding. The impact of this trend can be seen in Table 4.3 which shows that the value of imports of major agriculture commodities such as edible oil, oil seeds and wheat, has dramatically increased in recent years.

While the impact of climate change and the gradual decline of arable land are only two aspects of the future challenges of foodgrain production in Bangladesh, there are also some other impediments which demand attention as a threat to the sustainability of conventional agriculture. Rasul & Thapa (2004) suggest two factors as potential threats—the continuous degradation of land and water resources; and declining yields due to indiscriminate use of agro-chemicals. Several studies (Osmani & Quasem 1990; Rahman & Thapa 1999; Rasul & Thapa 2004: 328) identified that the use of chemical fertilizers increased sixfold between 1970 and 1990, and the use of pesticides increased about threefold in just one decade, from 1982 to 1992. The mono-cropping trend of agriculture, as well as an unbalanced use of chemical fertilizers, pesticides, and intensive use of land without application of organic fertilizers, has led to the deterioration of both soil quality and fertility (Task Force Report 1991; Hossain & Kashem 1997; Rahman & Thapa 1999; Rasul & Thapa 2004). Consequently, crop yields are decreasing steadily, despite an increased use of agricultural inputs (Ali 1995; Pagiola 1995; Hossain & Kashem 1997; Ahmad & Hasanuzzaman 1998; Rahman & Thapa 1999; Rasul & Thapa 2004). Coelli, Rahman and Thirtle (2002: 608) explain two bleak scenarios of the current levels of production—(1) there has been an apparent decline in the average yields of modern rice varieties; and (2) the level of adoption of new methods has stagnated. Thus, Rasul and Thapa (2004: 329) claim that given the present state of declining soil fertility, decreasing yields, and the increased and imbalanced use of chemical fertilizers and pesticides, producing food and fibre on a sustainable basis for the growing population has become a serious challenge for Bangladesh.

Beyond Domestic Production: International Trade and the Availability of Food

Like many other food deficit countries, domestic food production is only one source of food availability in Bangladesh. Despite an upward trend in domestic production since the 1980s, Bangladesh still remains a food deficit country where foodgrain availability depends on imports. Particularly during the time of natural disasters and poor harvest, the food security of Bangladesh, with respect to food availability, is highly dependent on imports. It is often stated that one of the reasons for the Bangladeshi famine of 1974 was the failure of the government to import foodgrains. In the recent food crisis of 2007-8, Bangladesh again failed to import foodgrains to ensure its food availability from international markets, mainly because of rice export bans by main rice exporters such as India and Thailand. My discussion in Chapter 5 exclusively focusses on the challenges of timely imports in Bangladesh. However, in order to develop the framework of the challenges of food availability in Bangladesh, here it is imperative to discuss it briefly.

We know that floods and droughts are common in Bangladesh and are the main causes of fluctuations in food availability, which adversely affect employment and food prices. As a consequence, international trade is an important means to ensure food availability in Bangladesh (see Islam 2012: 131). Over the last four decades, it has been observed that rice production was adversely affected by the frequency of natural disasters. As a result, a significant number of years yielded poor harvests. In other words, food availability through domestic food production is heavily dependent on the nature and frequency of natural disasters. Hence, foodgrain imports play a very vital role in promoting food availability in Bangladesh.

In the 1970s and 1980s, the Government of Bangladesh was responsible for all necessary imports of foodgrains. In contrast, in 1997, a year of poor harvest and in 1998, a year of massive flooding, private sector traders in Bangladesh imported several million metric tonnes of rice from India. Drawing on the case of Bangladesh-India rice trade, Dorosh (2001) finds a positive contribution of trade liberalization to short term food security in Bangladesh. However, despite the possible contribution of trade liberalization to short-run food security in Bangladesh in recent years, widespread concerns remain regarding possible adverse affects on long term food security. This concern was particularly revisited among food policy experts in Bangladesh after the recent food crisis of 2007-8 (for examples, see CPD 2009). Due to the poor regulation of the state, it is difficult to trust and/or rely on the private sector. International markets, particularly the rice market, are also extremely volatile and, therefore, not a reliable source of foodgrains. However, as Dorosh (2001: 674) suggests, the implications of trade liberalization for public sector price stabilization and food distribution is also complicated. The recent global food crises in 2007-8, which hit Bangladesh severely, validated these concerns. To explain the recent global food crises, Timmer (2010: 5) argues that panicked hoarding caused the rice price spike. He states that: 'Price panics usually have their origins in the fundamentals of supply and demand. But the sudden surge in rice prices in 2007-8 demonstrated that something was happening beyond these fundamentals. Exporting countries were clearly willing to sharply restrict exports of rice to protect their own consumers. In responding, nearly all importing countries realized they were too dependent on foreign supplies for food security (this was also a lesson from the 1972-3).

Timmer (2010: 5) adds that 'lessons from the world food crises in 1972-3 and in 2007-8, especially lessons from how the world rice market functioned, point the way toward improved food policy management at national and international levels in the future'. Though there has been little implication, it is evident in Bangladesh that the policymakers are concerned about the improved food policy management.

In both global food crises in 1973-4 and 2007-8, Bangladesh failed to arrange the timely import of foodgrains to manage its foodgrain shortage. In the 1973-4 crisis, Bangladesh faced two import-related difficulties: it experienced high inflation and a balance-of-payments crisis; and it had political tensions with the USA, one of the major food suppliers in the world, which resulted in food suspension. However, in recent crises, Bangladesh has not faced problems importing foodgrains, mainly, as there was no coinciding crop shortfall in India. Despite several high-level diplomatic attempts on the part of Bangladesh, India eventually restricted exports of rice to protect their own consumers. In addition to the negative attitude of international markets, the liberalization policies of the government, particularly of relatively small government interventions on market, and its total dependency on the private sector, were seriously criticized as the reason of the failure of crisis management policy. At this point, it is important to note that until 2005, policymakers in Bangladesh believed that rice demands could be met by international trade, which was proved wrong during the 2007-8 crisis. Today, after the shocking downturn of global markets, many analysts suggest that 'the most important thing to attain sustainable food security is achieving self-sufficiency' (for example, see CPD 2009: 106-7).

It is imperative to note that rapid urbanization, as well as economic growth in Bangladesh, will bring other major changes in lifestyle and consumption patterns of food in the future. Changing food habits have already increased the demands of vegetable, fruits, edible oil, meat, dairy and fish (see Table 4.1). As a consequence, according to Hossain, Naher and Shahabuddin (2005), imports of other food items such as fruits, edible oil, meat, dairy pulses, sugar and milk have been growing very quickly (see Table 4.3 also). While the demand has been increasing, the area for producing pulses, oilseeds, fodder and natural inland fisheries has been declining rapidly. As a result of the hasty expansion in the area of *boro* rice and wheat, the area for producing other items has reduced over the years, while the gradually decreasing trend of arable land is further widening the crisis. Thus, the rapidly rising import of food items (both grain and non-grain items) has become a major drain on the limited foreign exchange earnings of the country, while the high food prices of imported items affects poor people in different ways—and for many of them it is simply unbearable.

PROBLEMS OF FOOD ACCESSIBILITY IN BANGLADESH

Food availability and food self-sufficiency are necessary but are not sufficient conditions for food security. Some nations with food production deficits, like Japan, enjoy considerable national food security as they can import to satisfy their population's food consumption needs. On the other hand, some countries, for example Brazil, have national food self-sufficiency but export so much food that many of their own citizens go hungry (Hollist & Tullis 1987: 1). Bangladesh neither has the ability to import enough foodgrains to satisfy its population's food consumption needs, nor does it have its own food self-sufficiency. For Bangladesh, food self-sufficiency means employment opportunities for thousands of poor people to generate entitlements through agricultural development. It is imperative to note that food availability and self-sufficiency does not denote and/or guarantee food accessibility at the national level.

In food security literature, Sen (1981) is credited with shifting the discourse towards 'entitlement' and 'access' (Maxwell & Slater 2003: 532). Accessibility is now considered as the major pillar of food security. To establish his entitlement theory, Sen (1981) argued that the 1974 famine in Bangladesh could not have been predicted on the basis of food supply per capita, because this measure was high then. To him, even in the severe Bengal famine of 1943, food was available. In 1974, it was the floods and their destructive impact on rice production that left workers without the means to secure food. In both 1943 and 1974, many people did not have access to food because—the government failed to regulate and monitor the market which caused excessive food prices; people lacked buying power; and people did not have access to transfers. In the words of Sen (1982: 451) 'in a private ownership market economy, how much food a person can command will depend on (1) what he owns, and (2) what he can get in exchange for what he owns either through trade, or through production, or some combination of two'. If a person cannot do either of these, they will go hungry. Sen (1981) suggests that the root causes of hunger are poverty and inequality—inequality in access to land and other production resources, inequality in wealth and inequality in power.

Poverty, Inequality and the Challenge of Food Accessibility

If we analyse the problems of food accessibility based on the entitlement approach and in the context of the poverty and inequality of the society, it is clear that Bangladesh is still far away from achieving food security for all of its citizens. As can be seen in Table 4.4, various dimensions of poverty are the main reasons for the food crisis in Bangladesh. Table 4.5 also indicates that, although

TABLE 4.4: MAIN REASONS FOR FOOD CRISIS (MULTIPLE ANSWERS)

Main reasons for food crisis	Per cent
Low income	59.6
Lack of agricultural land	44.8
Incapable of buying agricultural equipment	6.6
Business is slow	8.1
No employment	9.6
Sickness/death of income earner	9.5
Loss by flood/drought/ natural calamity	17.9
Loss in river erosion	2.4
Other	26.2

Source: BBS 2010.

TABLE 4.5: INCIDENCES OF POVERTY IN BANGLADESH

Year	Head Count Ratio			Number of Poor (million)		
	Rural	Urban	Total	Rural	Urban	Total
1983-4	59.6	50.2	58.5	50.3	5.6	55.9
1988-9	59.2	43.9	57.1	54.1	6.2	60.3
1991-2	61.2	44.9	58.8	57.6	6.3	63.9
1995-6	55.2	29.4	51.0	53.6	5.8	59.4
2000	53.0	36.6	49.8	53.4	9.3	62.7
2005	43.8	28.4	40.0	45.8	9.7	62.7
2010	35.2	21.3	31.5	–	–	–

Notes: The head count ratio refers to the percentage of the population living below the upper poverty line as measured by the Cost of Basic Needs (CBN) Method. The number of poor has been derived using estimated population and its rural-urban distribution implicit in respective surveys.

Source: Mujeri 2000, BBS 2011.

the incidence of poverty, as measured by the head-count ratio, declined from about 59 per cent in 1983-4, it still remained at 40 per cent in 2005. In other words, the proportion of the national population living below the poverty line is still 40 per cent. The per capita expenditure was still very low in Bangladesh in 2000, at US $189 for rural households, and US $329 for urban households (Hossain, Naher & Shahabuddin 2005: 113-14). Again, Sen, Mujeri & Shahabuddin (2007: 86) suggest that, although growth accelerated in the 1990s, leading to greater poverty reduction than in the 1980s, the pattern of growth became increasingly inequitable. Both consumption expenditure and income data point to this trend. Moreover, analysis of current income distribution further confirms the increasing trend in relative inequality. Thus, we see the impact of this inequality in access to real income and, hence, food. Based on the time series data on real wages, Shahabuddin (2010: 102) shows that the index of real wages is observed to be lower in agriculture, which employs most of the labour force, as compared to those in manufacturing and construction. Available data also suggests that the rate of underemployment was still 28.7 per cent in 2009, and it is somewhat worrying to note that the rate of decline has slowed down considerably over the last decade compared to the preceding one.

The trends of poverty, wages, income and non-income indicators of poverty and the increasing trends of inequality provide sharp evidence that a large number of the population cannot maintain food security, mainly, because of entitlement failure. While the poverty dimensions explain the failure of trade-based entitlement, labour-based entitlement and transfer-based entitlement, incidences of poverty and land ownership can be helpful in explaining the failure of production-based entitlement. In Bangladesh, about 63 per cent of the labour force is employed in agriculture, forestry and fisheries. As much as 50 per cent of rural households involved in agricultural production are landless, defined as those having less than 0.05 ha of land. Out of a total number of agricultural households, 11 million are landless. This huge number of landless people needs to purchase food from the market to cover deficits from household-based production. For landless people, income opportunities are extremely limited. They depend heavily on selling labour in both agricultural and non-agricultural labour markets for their livelihoods. The seasonal nature of agricultural employment and limited opportunities for non-farm employment cause millions to suffer from chronic and transitory food insecurity (Hossain, Naher & Shahabuddin 2005: 116). Thus, the failure of producing food because of lack of land as well as the failure to buy food as a result of poverty and inequality, has led to a huge number of the population to suffer from food insecurity. These people further lose their minimal access to food for several basic reasons—sudden price hikes, lean season traps and during natural disasters. Particularly, the lean season reduces people's access to income, which is a shock on their food security. In the north-western part of Bangladesh, this seasonal food insecurity caused by unemployment and income deficit, is generally known as *monga* (famine-like situation). Every year, *monga* appears from September to November or in the Bangla months of Aswin and Kartic. In these two months, rural people of the northern part of Bangladesh experience seasonal hunger because of extreme shrinkage of job opportunities. In this situation, people can access food neither by producing it themselves nor by buying it in the market due to a lack of money. When they fail to do either of these, they go hungry.

Urban Poverty and the Challenge of Food Security

To understand the problems of food accessibility we also need to explain the magnitude of urban poverty in Bangladesh, which is generally ignored by both policymakers and policy analysts in relation to food security.[3] Rapid urbanization will bring drastic changes to every aspect of life including food habits, food distribution, consumption patterns, structures of market chains and so forth. In Bangladesh, where urbanization is a rapidly growing phenomenon, the increase in urban poverty will add further difficulty to food security systems.

Table 4.5 indicates that over the period of 1984-2005, while the absolute number of poor in the country remained almost the same, the number of urban poor registered an increase (by about four million, almost double) during the same period. There are two main reasons for this trend of increasing urban poverty. The first reason is the rapid migration from rural to urban areas. A study by S. Hossain (2010) reveals that poverty in the slums of Dhaka was most strongly influenced by recent migration from rural areas, household organisation, participation in the 'informal' sector of the economy and access to housing and land. And the second reason is the unequal distribution of growth. As a result, S. Hossain (ibid.) notes that almost half of the poor households in Dhaka were identified as 'hardcore poor' that is having insufficient income for their physical needs. The remainder were found to be 'absolute poor', those who experienced poverty and vulnerability but varied in their levels of income and consumption. Data drawn from a 2009 Multiple Indicator Cluster Study (MICS) clearly show that living conditions in urban slums are often appalling and, in fact, much worse than those in most rural areas (UNICEF 2010). Despite the widespread poverty, poor living conditions, and fast growing migration from rural to urban areas, the country has no comprehensive policy on urbanization or urban poverty reduction (UNICEF 2010). Rather, historically, most development programmes in Bangladesh have focussed on rural areas (ibid.).

In a similar vein to urban poverty, the country also has no comprehensive policy on the problems of urban food insecurity. Benson (2007) states that 'the limited number and ambiguity of available studies in the country on urban poverty and food insecurity contributes to inadequate policy development and public sector response to address the needs of the hungry and undernourished urban poor'. In an interview with a leading Bengali newspaper, Rahman, a former advisor of the caretaker Government of Bangladesh (2010), argued that 'in dealing with urban poverty, our success is negligible compared to rural poverty. There are almost no creative schemes/initiatives for promoting food security among the urban poor. It is imperative to explore appropriate schemes that can ensure food security in a metropolitan area (Dhaka) as well as in other small cities' (*Prothom-alo*, 10 October 2010). In this regard, it is worthwhile to explain the strategies of the National Food Policy (2006) of Bangladesh. Under the objectives of increased purchasing power and people's access to food, it has three sub-strategies—first, Transitory Shock Management; second, effective implementation of Targeted Food Assistance Programmes (e.g. VGF, FFW, VGD, etc.) to improve food security; and third, employment generating (e.g. TR, 100-Day Employment Generation Programme) income growth (NFP 2006). Interestingly, both targeted food assistance programmes and Employment Generating Programmes are focussed on rural areas. In other words, urban poverty is simply missing from the government policy to promote food security. Although there is a nationwide Open Market Sales (OMS) programme, its effectiveness is in question due to poor governance. The fact that as Rahman stated that 'many people who are most adversely affected because of food price hikes do not get benefits from Open Market Sale (OMS) because of its faulty design and poor implementation mechanism. Moreover, OMS has many other limitations and, therefore, fails to reach the urban hardcore poor or absolute poor' (*Prothom-alo*, 10 October 2010).

Over the years food policy has changed dramatically: while old food policy gives emphasis on 'peasants' as the main target group, new food policy focusses on both the urban and rural poor (Maxwell & Slater 2003). In a very old-fashioned style, the National Food Policy (NFP) of Bangladesh exclusively focusses on 'peasants' and the 'rural poor' as the target group of food-insecure people.[4] This policy failed to include the growing number of food-insecure urban poor. In the present context, Bangladesh desperately needs a food policy that will address both the rural and urban poor as the urban population is increasing significantly. The increasing trend of urban poverty definitely needs special attention/concern.

High Food Prices and the Problem of Food Access

As noted earlier, a provisional study of FAO/WFP (2008: 7) indicates that in 2007, 7.5 million more people were added to the total number of undernourished since 2003-5. While several factors are responsible, high food prices are driving millions of people into food insecurity, worsening conditions for many who were already food-insecure, and threatening long-term global food insecurity (FAO 2008). This study shows that the vast majority of poor urban and rural households are hit hardest by higher prices. Among the poor, it is the landless and matriarchal households that are most vulnerable to sharp rises in basic food prices.

Bangladesh is one of the most vulnerable countries in the world in respect to the adverse affect of price hikes in food commodities. Recent global food crises in 2007-8 along with the impact of natural disasters in January 2008, led to domestic rice prices soaring to 53 per cent above January 2007 prices (in real terms), and, as late as July 2008, rice prices were still 45 per cent above those of a year earlier (Figure 4.1; and FAO 2009: 33). Hossain (2010: 177) shows that during the financial year 2007-8, the rate of increase in the rice price was 62 per cent. The impact is largely negative across income groups, and it is particularly high for the poorest and landless households (FAO 2008). In this section, I examine the magnitude of poverty and landlessness in Bangladesh. Most of the poor households are net food buyers and seldom produce enough food to feed themselves because of the lack of land entitlements. In the short term, high food prices usually hurt net food buyers, rich or poor; but the impact can be devastating for the poorest of the poor (FAO 2008). A huge proportion of rural households' budgets in Bangladesh is spent on basic food items, produced mostly in the farm

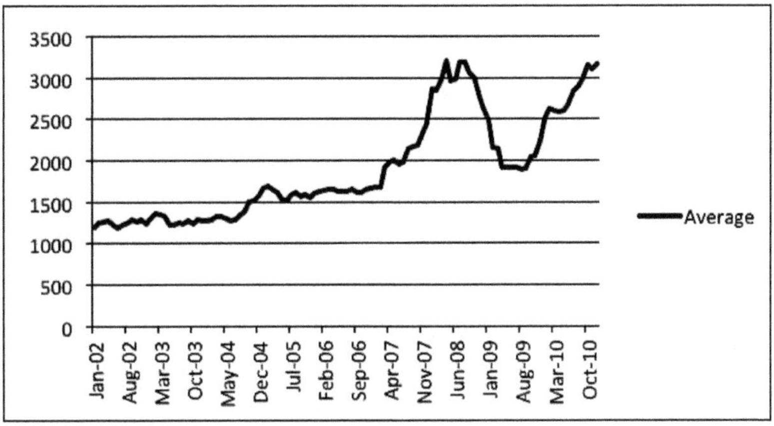

Source: Directorate of Food and author's calculation.

Figure 4.1: Prices of Coarse Rice in Bangladesh (monthly average Taka/QTL), 2002-10

sector, leaving very little room for non-farm products. For instance, on average at the end of 2008, households were spending 62 per cent of their income on food, up from 52 per cent in 2005 (ibid. 2009: 33). Some argue that low income groups, such as transport operators and petty traders in the informal market and agricultural laborers were initially adversely affected but later they were able to adjust their earnings somewhat through increases in wages and margins. Thus, Bangladesh was able to avoid serious food insecurity and famine that many influential elites predicted. It is argued that it was possible as the agricultural wage rate was increased from Taka 100 to 130 per day from June 2007 to April 2008 (Hossain 2010: 178). However, this explanation has at least two major weaknesses. First, famine and serious food insecurity do not denote similar meanings. It is true that a famine was averted despite serious food inflation but the magnitude of hunger was not prevented but rather increased significantly in spite of increases in wages. Second, while the agricultural wage rate was increased 30 per cent, the rice price was increased 62 per cent in the financial year 2007-8. In fact, low income groups were seriously affected by the surge in rice prices in 2007-8, which caused serious food insecurity. According to a Welfare Monitoring Survey of 2009 (BBS 2010), the households who reported food insecurity mentioned that they managed such crises by starving (54.3 per cent), borrowing money (49.2 per cent), reducing consumption of their favorite foods (49.3 per cent) and eating less food (39.3 per cent). It may be noted that households used more than one measures to cope with the situation. Moreover, data from successive rounds of Household Income and Expenditure Surveys indicate that per capita intake of calories increased steadily in Bangladesh from about 1,990 kcal in 1973-4 to 2,266 kcal in 1991-2, but has since been falling slowly, standing at 2,239 kcal in 2005 (Osmani 2010: 46). Despite increasing food availability, it is perhaps the high food price that is the reason for the gradually declining calorie intake. It may be noted that rice prices in Bangladesh have been highly volatile since 2003, although in 2003 and early 2004 prices increased slowly and from then on it increased dramatically which caused the low calorie intake. Thus, in this age of media hype, the ruling elites avert famine in Bangladesh for political reasons, particularly for their self-interests. However, food insecurity or 'silent hunger' is still unavoidable as it does not pose a challenge to the state elites as famine can do.

The adverse effects of the high price of food commodities is not new in Bangladesh. In the beginning of its journey as a nation state, Bangladesh experienced devastating famine in 1974. The main stream analysis of the causes of the Bangladesh famine of 1974 focussed on a few key words such as 'panic', 'hoarding', 'speculation' and 'price hike of rice'. However, there is no doubt that it was mainly because of a dramatic increase of rice prices which caused the 'panic', 'hoarding', 'speculation' and eventually the famine. Sen (1981: 131) suggests that 'the price of rice rocketed during and immediately after the floods. . . . In some of the most affected districts, the rice price doubled in the three months between July and October'. In addition to the Bangladesh famine of 1974, in subsequent years several natural disasters caused extraordinary surges in rice prices which, I contend, is one of the main reasons of persistent hunger in Bangladesh.

In Chapter 6, my discussion will exclusively focus on how the government has responded to the food inflation that hit millions of urban and rural poor in Bangladesh in recent food crises. However, here it is imperative to note that the debate between government intervention and the role of markets in providing food security is part of a broader and long-standing debate over the 'role of the state' in sectoral and overall growth (Timmer 1991). After the liberalization of foodgrain markets in the 1980s and early 1990s, the role of the Bangladesh state in stabilizing markets through intervention and economic management weakened in such a manner that many Bangladeshi policy experts, analysts and members of civil society explicitly criticize the state and many also saw it as a key cause of the failure of the government in 2007-8 food crises (for examples, see CPD 2009). Previously, the government influenced prices through its 'foodgrain stock maintenance policy' that involved public procurement, public distribution, and imports. In response to the crises of 2007-8, available evidence indicates the failure of the government in all of these three sectors—it failed to influence the market because of its relatively small stocks (e.g. food stocks were reduced from about 1.5 million MT in the 1980s to about 0.6 million MT in recent years (Hossain 2010: 178); the PFDS was virtually ineffective as the government downsized it in the previous years; the government failed to arrange timely imports as the responsibility of commercial imports of foodgrains was transferred to the private sector; and the government key import agency, TCB, was inactive.

Moreover, in the last couple of years, it has widely been discussed in Bangladesh that because of the failure of market regulation, a business syndicate is controlling the market. Politicians point the finger to the so-called syndication for the surge of price hikes of daily essentials. Therefore, successive governments are persistently dealing with the business community to decrease the price of essentials. To control the unbridled price hikes of daily essentials in recent years, the government recently fixed the wholesale prices of essentials. For instance, in August 2009, the government fixed the wholesale price of potatoes, onions, garlic and ginger to ensure stability in the essential commodity market during Ramadan (*The Daily Star*, 21 August 2009). However, the following day the prices of essentials witnessed a sharp rise in both wholesale and retail markets, a day after the Commerce Minister had fixed the wholesale prices of some daily necessities. Many shoppers and small traders alleged that taking advantage of weak market monitoring, traders in kitchen markets were charging higher prices (*The Daily Star*, 22 August 2009). In Chapter 6 my study exclusively focusses on the issue of market regulation and the role of the Bangladesh state, where I argue that instead of taking reliable actions to rectify market prices, successive governments often act to create media hype to show that they are proactive in controlling the market. This does not eventuate in any positive outcomes.

Intra-Household Disparity and the Challenges of Food Security

Bangladesh is a patriarchal society where gender discrimination is evident in almost every aspect of life, including intra-household disparity of food distribution. It has been observed that in most patriarchal societies, one salient aspect of the distribution of food in low income settings is the disparity in nutrients received by women compared to men, particularly in south and west Asian societies (For details see Behrman 1990; Pitt, Rosenzweig & Hasan 1990). Disparities by gender in food consumption in a low-income society like Bangladesh are clearly observed in quite a few studies.

As a result of the biased intra-household distribution of food, food insecurity poses a serious threat to vulnerable people (poor women, children and the disabled). A survey conducted by the Institute of Nutrition and Food Science (INFS) in 1981 indicated that the extent of malnutrition within households varied substantially according to individual characteristics such as age and sex (Chowdhury 1993, cited in Shahabuddin 2010: 105). The INFS Survey (1981) further suggests that acute mal distribution of food was observed within households, with mothers and young children being particularly vulnerable (Shahabuddin 2010: 105). The follow-up survey carried out in 1998 shows that the shortfall of calorie intake from a norm of requirement was much higher for women than men in 1990s. The highest shortfall was noted for lactating and pregnant mothers whose calorie intake was deficient by as much as 30 per cent of their daily requirement, as against an average of 13 per cent deficit for a household as a whole (INFS 1998; cited in Osmani 2010: 47). The nutrition survey conducted by BIDS in 1990-1 also reveals similar findings of mal distribution of food within the household, which indicates that none of the boys and girls under the age of 20 years met the calorie requirement. Girls were in a more disadvantageous situation than the boys (Shahabuddin 2010: 105).

Islam (2012: 145) shows the intra-household distribution of nutrient intake between males and females in Bangladesh. It indicates that male intake of all nutrients is considerably higher than that of their female counterparts for all age groups.

CONCLUSION

This chapter examines the challenges of food security in Bangladesh by focussing on three major issues. It first illustrates the discourse of food security in Bangladesh. My discussion demonstrates that—(a) the state itself generates discourse that providing food to all people at all times shall be a fundamental responsibility of the state; (b) the issue of food gained importance as a political agenda in Bangladesh, which particularly can be seen in the major political parties' election manifestos during national elections; and (c) although political parties are very interested in the issue of food, the fact that it is neither an issue of parliamentary debate, nor a matter of street agitation, and not even of intra-party policy debate, shows that the issue of food security is merely political rhetoric in Bangladesh. One important feature of the food policy discourse in Bangladesh is that there is a lack of consensus with regard to policy. This chapter shows four different key issues of policy in order to mitigate the challenges of food security where there is no consensus. First, whether the country should come out of the strategy of self-reliance to self-sufficiency in promoting food availability? Second, what would be the appropriate level of public foodgrain stock? Third, to what extent should the state intervene in PFDS? and fourth, the unsettled issue of the role of the state in input prices, subsidies and farmers' incentives. Finally, this section suggests that NGOs do not play a significant role in promoting food security as a development partner of the state and there is also a lack of consensus among the NGOs as to who plays a role in promoting food security.

This chapter demonstrates that both food availability and accessibility in Bangladesh is under serious threat. The supply side or the availability of food includes some factors which are involved with agri-governance, environmental degradation, stagnation of new technological development and an uncertainty of trade to mitigate the shortfall of production. The key question that it raises is—can future production meet increasing future demands? It argues that the present nature of the state does not have the ability to overcome the existing challenge nor can it attempt to deal with future challenges. Then this chapter examined the problems of food accessibility in Bangladesh, focussing on the vulnerable section of the population. With particular focus on entitlement theory, it demonstrated several major challenges of food accessibility in Bangladesh, which include poverty, increasing numbers of the urban poor, intra-household disparities of food and the impact of sudden price hikes. With the existing crisis of ensuring food accessibility, this chapter shows the only way to promote food accessibility to the chronic poor is state-generated entitlement. However, the finding of this chapter is that, with regard to entitlement generation, the Bangladesh state is gradually shrinking its role.

NOTES

1. Importing food from the world market when prices are cheaper than growing it at home, so as to release land for other uses for which Bangladesh has a comparative advantage (Deb, Hossain, & Jones 2009).
2. Growing within the country all the food the country needs (Deb, Hossain, & Jones 2009).
3. According to Benson (2007), 'The existing knowledge base on the welfare and food security of the urban poor is slim and partial, with no studies that are representative of the broad population of the urban poor. The limited

number and ambiguity of available studies in the country on urban poverty and food insecurity contributes to inadequate policy development and public sector response to address the needs of the hungry and undernourished urban poor.'

4. Bangladesh has set its target at reducing the number of poor people to a half by the year 2015. In order to achieve this target the National Food Policy (NFP) 2006 highlighted three key objectives: (1) To ensure adequate and stable supply of safe and nutritious food; (2) To enhance the purchasing power of the people for increased food accessibility; (3) To ensure adequate nutrition and food for all (especially women and children). The plan envisaged achieving these objectives through key market-based strategies. These included (i) strengthening the liberal credit delivery system through advisory and monitoring services; and (ii) supporting the expansion of banking facilities to rural and outreach areas (NFP 2006: 6). The NFP was approved by the government on 14 August 2006. In 2010, in order to provide programmatic guidance in implementing the National Food Policy, the government formulated the National Food Policy Plan of Action (PoA). The Plan identifies 26 strategic areas of intervention and priority actions that cover all dimensions of food security. The Plan, which is in line with the Millennium Development Goals, stretches over the period 2008-15 (see NFPCSP 2012).

CHAPTER 5

Governance, Food Availability and Food Security in Bangladesh

INTRODUCTION

In order to investigate the role of the Bangladesh state in promoting food availability, this chapter examines all three components necessary for food availability—domestic production, international trade and food aid.[1] The central question that I attempt to examine here is—how has the state approached the task of ensuring food availability in Bangladesh in the period from 1975 to 2010? This question then fosters several different new questions to explain three different aspects of food availability which I have developed in the light of the central framework of this thesis. For instance, with regard to domestic production, I raise two questions. Firstly, how do rent-seeking, corruption and partial reform impede agricultural production in Bangladesh? Secondly, how do other problems of the state relating to state weakness and poor governance impede agricultural production? Similar questions will be employed to investigate the role of the state in two other components of food availability: trade and food aid. Throughout this chapter, I seek to examine the role of the Bangladesh state in promoting food availability, with the central intention of investigating the process of policymaking and its implementation mechanisms. In particular, I am interested in the interactions between the actors. In doing so, I frequently raise a series of questions in order to understand the origin of state policy with regard to agriculture, timely import and/or receipt of food aid, the market regulation mechanism, and economic management.

This chapter continues with four further sections. In the next part, the chapter deals with agricultural governance in Bangladesh. I begin with the policy changes that have taken place in Bangladeshi agriculture in order to identify the role of the state: this is followed by an examination of the relationship between agricultural production and governance. I then consider the state's (in)ability in the agriculture sector based on a number of cases. After assessing the role of the state in agricultural development in Bangladesh, in part two of this chapter, I analyse the role of the state in mitigating the food availability crisis via trade during a time of relative vulnerability as a result of temporary production shortfalls. Discussing the case for international trade as a source of food availability, this section also examines the underlying causes of trade liberalization and the state's ability to deal with trade as well as its capacity to respond in a timely manner. The third part of this chapter critically examines the importance of food aid as a means of food availability. The final section of this chapter presents the conclusion.

THE STATE, DOMESTIC PRODUCTION AND FOOD AVAILABILITY

The agriculture sector of Bangladesh is not only the single largest contributor to the nation's Gross Domestic Product (GDP) but is also the primary source of income for the majority of the population of Bangladesh, as they live in rural areas and earn their living from agriculture.[2] In addition to its important role in the overall economic development of Bangladesh, agriculture plays a vital role in relation to food security, income generation, and poverty reduction. In Chapter 4, I have shown that as Bangladesh is a food-deficit country, domestic food production is the major source of food availability and, therefore, promoting the agriculture sector is important for ensuring food availability. Most of the farmers who are the basic producers are near-subsistence peasants. As a result, any radical policy changes affecting Bangladesh's agriculture have important implications for people's livelihoods, including their food security (Rahman & Deb 2005: 86).

In this section, my aim is to explicate the role of the Bangladesh state in agricultural development to ensure food availability in order to promote food security. Here, I am particularly interested in investigating how the state is dealing with the agriculture sector. In doing so, I discuss the underlying changes that have taken place in Bangladesh's agriculture in the past few decades and the resulting market-based reforms which began in the 1980s. Before examining the linkages between the state, domestic production, and food availability, I begin by discussing the macroeconomic policy shift in Bangladesh that has led to low budgetary allocations to the agriculture sector and the market reforms in agricultural inputs, as both provide evidence of the state's absence from agricultural governance. I then draw the nexus between agricultural growth and governance using six case studies in Bangladesh.

The Political Economy of Pro-market Reforms in Bangladesh Agriculture

In 1976, there was a massive reduction of the public sector which took place by the new government after the assassination of Sheikh Mujibur Rahman. Although symbolically the 'reforms programme [had] begun in May 1975, with the devaluation of the Taka and the agreement with the IMF', the process of privatization actually began and accelerated under the new military government of General Ziaur Rahaman, which proved to be an early version of what is now called 'crony capitalism'. The new military regime 'confirmed that it intended to introduce such further economic reforms as subsidy reduction, agricultural taxation, and import liberalization' (World Bank 1976: 3). The process of reforms continued, and consequently, in the mid-1980s, the market oriented liberalizing policy reforms were initiated with the support of the IMF and the World Bank, and have been followed through since then in various phases (Mahmud 2008: 9). In the late 1980s and early 1990s, Bangladesh negotiated the Structural Adjustment Facility (SAF) and Enhanced Structural Adjustment Facility (ESAF) with the IMF, and implemented Structural Adjustment Programmes (SAP) with assistance from the World Bank and Asian Development Bank (ADB) (for details, see Muhammad 2006; Mahmud 2001; Mahmud, Ahmed & Mahajan 2008). Because of these reforms, as Sobhan (2002) argued a decade ago which is still the fact that Bangladesh has today attained a largely liberalized import regime, a largely reduced public sector, very limited input subsidies for the agricultural sector and in the area of manufacturing, a significantly reduced public sector where virtually no new investment has taken place in the last decade.

Nuruzzaman (2006) suggests that market based reforms have not taken place in Bangladesh without any challenge. Political protest movements and demonstrations against pro-market reforms in Bangladesh were widespread throughout the 1980s and 1990s. However, the two dominant political parties—the Bangladesh Nationalist Party (BNP) and the Awami League (AL)—favour the reform agenda wholeheartedly. Among political parties, only the leftist political parties strongly oppose the pro-market reforms. It may be noted that these parties have insignificant numbers of supporters in Bangladesh. Basically, the urban industrial workers and rural peasants were at the forefront of political resistance to economic reforms. In spite of protests, successive regimes in the 1980s and 1990s have undertaken wide-ranging reforms to create market-friendly governance structures in Bangladesh. Their policies have focussed primarily on restructuring the public sector, constructing a strong private sector, liberalizing trade and exchange rate regimes, and establishing an enabling environment for private enterprise (Quadir 2000: 198). Examining the politico-economic factors that have led the successive regimes (both military and democratically elected) in Bangladesh to implement economic liberalization programmes, Quadir (ibid.) argues that pro-market reforms were implemented in Bangladesh neither to stabilize the economy nor to meet broader development challenges. Instead, Quadir (ibid.) argues that economic reforms were used primarily to consolidate the power of the ruling elites.

As part of the pro-market economic reforms, Bangladesh undertook a series of policy reforms in agriculture in the 1980s. These included the liberalization of investment in minor irrigation, the privatization of trade in fertilizer, the import of agricultural machinery, seed delivery systems, food distribution systems, the management of agricultural research and extension systems and so forth. It may be noted that during the 1960s and early 1970s, the agriculture sector in Bangladesh, particularly the rice sector, had been receiving a significant amount of domestic support in the form of fertilizer subsidies, output price support, provision of seeds and irrigation equipment at subsidised prices and the provision of soft credits from public financial institutions. During this period, the Bangladesh Agricultural Development Corporation (BADC) was a public monopoly controlling the promotion and distribution of new agricultural inputs and services. In the process of economic reforms, BADC was crippled. In other words, there had been an ideological shift from the state to the market in the agricultural sector of Bangladesh.

The driving force behind the economic reforms was that 'the reforms would increase the efficiency of the delivery system, increase easy access by farmers to inputs at a reasonable price and decrease the budgetary burden of subsidy' (Azmat & Coghill 2005: 629). It was also aimed at creating a competitive market environment so that the market itself can rectify its crises automatically, if any arise. Now it is the matter of inquiry as to what happened as a consequence of these economic reforms. In order to understand the outcome of the state policy that aimed to promote agricultural growth throughout this section of this chapter, I will show the way in which rent-seeking, public corruption and/or partial reform syndrome impacted on policymaking as well as implementation.

It is imperative to examine the nexus between agricultural production and governance. In Chapter 4, I have discussed the relationship between agricultural production and good governance. In order to clarify my position in the following discussion, here I cite again the study of Hayami and Rettan (1985), which asserts that the basic factor constraining agricultural performance is neither the meagre endowment of natural resources nor the lack of technological potential to increase output from the available resources, but rather, poor institutions and policies that impede both the adoption of appropriate technology and the outcome of organizational innovation (as cited in Lio & Liu 2008). Using the six indicators of governance Lio and Liu (ibid.) also suggest a crude framework for exploring the effects of governance in the context of agricultural development. In the subsequent discussion, we will see how poor institutions and faulty policies affect the agricultural production in Bangladesh.

Budgetary Policies for Agricultural Development in Bangladesh: State Inertia?

Because of the importance of agriculture in the Bangladesh economy, this sector is regarded as the 'lifeline' or 'life blood' of Bangladesh. Given the fact that agriculture is an important sector for not only promoting food security, but also for overall development and well-being of the society this section examines the role of the state in agricultural development. To understand the intentions of the state in promoting agricultural development, public expenditure through the budget can provide a clear explanation. Therefore, it can be useful to understand the role of state in dealing with agriculture. Although budgetary allocation is an important aspect to understand the state's role with regard to promoting agricultural growth, similarly the budget making process itself (i.e. politics of budget making) can explain how well the state is doing in agricultural development.

A measure of prioritising concern for agricultural development can be understood by the amount of budgetary allocation for the agriculture sector in Bangladesh. In other words, government spending through the budget is an important way to understand the government's intention in developing agriculture to promote food security. The National Agricultural Policy 2010 of Bangladesh itself admits that one of the major threats to the Bangladesh agriculture sector is that budgetary allocation for agriculture, especially for research is inadequate (NAP 2010).

Table 5.1 shows that actual expenditure for agriculture under the Annual Development Plan (ADP) has been declining gradually. During the period from 1991-2 to 2004-5, the percentage share of total actual expenditure has decreased from 7 per cent to 3.1 per cent, which is almost half of the annual expenditure in agriculture. In other words, although the budgetary expenditure on agriculture has increased in absolute terms, the relative share of the

TABLE 5.1: ADP ACTUAL EXPENDITURE FOR AGRICULTURE, 1991-2 TO 2009-10

Year	Total Actual Expenditure (Million Taka)	Actual Expenditure in Agriculture (Million Taka)	Percentage Share of Total Actual Expenditure
1991-2	60,240	4,217	7.0
1992-3	65,500	3,734	5.7
1993-4	89,830	5,210	5.8
1994-5	103,030	5,358	5.2
1995-6	100,160	4,507	4.5
1996-7	110,410	5,521	5.0
1997-8	110,370	5,408	4.9
1998-9	125,090	5,379	4.3
1999-2000	154,710	7,581	4.9
2000-1	161,510	7,308	4.5
2001-2	140,902	6,229	4.4
2002-3	154,343	6,398	4.1
2003-4	168,174	6,788	4.0
2004-5	187,703	5,870	3.1
2005-6	194,729	10,117	5.2
2006-7	172,063	10,500	6.1
2007-8	184,190	12,272	6.7
2008-9	197,008	12,352	6.3
2009-10	259,174	16,277	6.3

Source: Author's calculation from *Bangladesh Economic Review* (Various Issues), Ministry of Finance, Government of The People's Republic of Bangladesh.

agriculture sector in relation to Total Public Expenditure (TPE) showed a declining trend with fluctuations in various years. Sobhan (2010: 225) shows that government spending in the agriculture sector remained abysmally low, amounting to 1.7 per cent of value added in agriculture in Bangladesh and 2.4 per cent of ODA despite the fact that Bangladesh's farmers have tripled food grain output between 1971 and 2008.

As can be seen in Table 5.1 there has been an upward trend in budgetary allocation since 2005-6 although it is still low compared to the early 1990s. It is important to bear in mind that since 2005-6, two factors caused this increasing trend in budgetary allocation, which suggest that this is not a permanent trend—

firstly, it was the policy outcome as a result of the global food crisis which caused a sudden price hike; secondly, 2005-6 coincided with an election budget and after that budget was prepared by a military backed caretaker government.

The budgetary allocation for agriculture has continually been decreasing again since 2007-8. For instance, in 2010, compared to other sectors, agriculture was again relegated to low priority, where it was allocated Tk 7,492 crore, only 5.4 per cent of the budget (Farida 2010a). The chasm between the rhetoric and reality of the government's intention in promoting agriculture is clear in the budget speech of the Finance Minister (FM). On one hand, he declared that 'in the next year's budget, we plan to keep fertilizer prices within the reach of the farmers' (Muhit 2010: 22). On the other hand, the subsidy on agricultural inputs including fertilizer had actually been slashed by about 24 per cent (down from Tk 4,950 in the FY 2009-10 to Tk 4,000 in the FY 2010-11) (ibid.).

Again, how the government sees a particular sector can be used as a measurable tool to assess the government intention to develop that sector. For instance, despite the agriculture sector's 21 per cent contribution to the GDP, it is not a separate/independent budget segment. Rather, this sector is under the segment of 'agriculture and rural development'. In his budget speech in 2010, Muhit, the Finance Minister of Bangladesh, stated that 'we do not perceive agriculture as a separate sector. Rather, we treat the rural non-farm sector and rural development including rural infrastructure, rural electrification, rural housing, using land and water resources, and development of rural small and medium enterprises as an integral part of agriculture'. Moreover, he added, it is 'our belief that food security along with accelerated economic growth can be achieved by developing the rural economy' (ibid.: 21-2). Some suggests that this argument is indeed an over simplification of two different aspects of development, which principally overlook the agricultural development. For instance, Farida (2010a), an activist in agriculture, environment and health issues notes that 'agriculture is integral to rural development, but that does not mean any rural development is necessarily promoting agriculture . . .

Making agriculture less important leads to denial of importance of cultivation of food and other crops, ensuring self-sufficiency in food and livelihood of people engaged in farming, fishing and livestock rearing'.

There are, of course, strong linkages between agriculture, rural development and food security. However, there is a question of importance—the budget speech of the FM implies that the government is keen to promote food security and agriculture development through rural development. When the developmental policy is the outcome of politics, it is difficult to separate political choice, development strategy and the interest of ruling elites. In other words, the question can be raised as to why the government does not perceive agriculture as a separate sector of the national budget. Why is rural development placed above agriculture and/or food security with regard to priority? Sobhan (2010: 199) suggests that, in the budget making-process, most FMs in South Asia remain relatively unconstrained in preparing their annual budget beyond their own perception of a need to consult constituencies which they deem politically important. As a consequence, FMs tend to prioritise particular political constituencies such as regional governments, parliaments, key business constituencies, professional bodies and occasionally some civil society groups (ibid.).

In Bangladesh, historically, the FM pays special attention to the demands of the ruling party lawmakers in the budget making process. In 2005, at a pre-budget discussion, the then Finance Minister argued that 'the budget will certainly be election-oriented. We're a democratic government. If we renege on our commitments, we will betray the cause of the people'. He also assured his audience that he would try to minimize pressures from the ruling party lawmakers while undertaking politically motivated projects (see Haque 2005). Although this is an example from a particular year (which was the pre-election year), politically motivated projects are common phenomena in the Bangladesh budget, like in many other developing countries. In rural areas, all politically motivated projects are linked to rural development—ruling lawmakers always make promises to build a bridge, road, school, health centre and so forth that will help them to be re-elected. Although agriculture and food security are important national issues, these are not considered determinant factors in the context of voting politics. It may be mentioned that the target group for the politically motivated budget is always middle class or lower middle class people, who play a vital role in voting politics/election mechanisms. On the other hand, because of inadequate organization and ineffective associations, the demands of farmers hardly reach the ears of the government. Similarly, hungry people are also neglected by the policymakers as their voice is even fainter than the farmers'. As rural development clearly provides better opportunities for political gains when compared to agriculture or rural development, and the government is not officially required to disclose its actual budget allocation within the 'Agriculture and Rural Development' budget section to the agriculture sector, the government opts not to view agriculture as an independent budget sector. In other words, it is easy to show that the budgetary expenditure on agriculture has increased in absolute terms, while the relative share of the agriculture sector in relation to total public expenditure under 'Agriculture and Rural Development' has, in fact, declined over the years.

Reforms, Agricultural Input Market, and its Impact: Exploring State Capacity

The major changes that took place in the Bangladesh agriculture sector in the past three decades constituted the policy outcome of market-based reforms, whether directly or indirectly. Therefore, the underlying policy of market-based reforms and their impact is necessarily synonymous with addressing the agricultural policy of the Government of Bangladesh. A critical analysis of the reforms in the Bangladesh agriculture input sectors can provide a clear understanding with regard to the role of the state in agricultural development. A key aspect of the reform programme was the withdrawal of agricultural input subsidies. In addition, reform measures were related to the privatization of fertilizer, privatization of irrigation equipment, privatization of production, processing and distribution of seeds, management of agricultural research, extension systems and so forth.

In the following section, I will analyze whether or not the above-mentioned changes helped to improve agricultural productivity and thus promote food security. In doing so, I first discuss the underlying changes that took place in the agricultural sector and then discuss how effective these changes were for agricultural development in Bangladesh in relation to food security. Here, however, I will particularly look at the role of the state in the agriculture sector of Bangladesh.

(a) *Political Economy of the Privatization of Fertilizer*

The privatization of the fertilizer market in Bangladesh was completed in 1994 and all fertilizer imports were handled by the private sector.[3] In other words, BADC or the Ministry of Agriculture lost its monopoly of retail and wholesale markets of fertilizer. Although the World Bank claimed unprecedented success of the Fertilizer Distribution Improvement Project II (FDI II), the fact is that in the year following the project's completion, 1995, the government issued the Revised Fertilizer Control Ordinance in consultation with the private sector and the International Fertilizer Development Corporation (IFDC) for quality control and the regulation of fertilizer prices. According to some accounts, 18 farmers were killed following disturbances in the supply of urea (Ali 2005). As a result, the government was compelled to make change in fertilizer distribution. Begum and Manos (2005: 6) suggest that 'in the last quarter of 1994, the privatization programme was subjected to widespread concern and criticism due to rapid and exorbitant increases in retail prices of urea. . . . The crisis of 1995 was seen by many as a demonstration of the failure of the liberalization policies so far followed in fertilizer distribution'. In relation to the liberalization policy, AMM Shawakat Ali, the Former Secretary of Agriculture for the GOB, observes that during the process of fertilizer privatization which was formed as part of the aid policies of the World Bank, USAID, and ADB:

> The government argued about the need for (a) buffer stock and (b) appointments of dealers in different districts. Both these proposals were rejected by

the aid-giving agencies. There was no monitoring of fertilizer availability. . . . The government decided to implement the system of both buffer stock and appointment of dealers. All donors led by the World Bank reacted by sending a letter. This letter was signed not only by the heads of major donors' agencies but also some foreign ambassadors. A reply was sent by the Minister for Agriculture affirming strongly that it was not a reversal of trade liberalization policy but rather a means to assist farmers. The matter ended there (Ali 2005).

There are at least three reasons which suggest that this crisis was a result of poor governance as well as weak state capacity. First, due to the lack of regulation, after the liberalization of the market, the government did not have any effective control over the fertilizer traders. Second, there was a lack of actual statistics of real demands of fertilizer. And third, despite the possibilities of upcoming fertilizer shortages and ignoring the internal demand, in 1995, about 400,000 MT of urea were exported by the Bangladesh Chemical Industries Corporation (BCIC). In dealing with this crisis, the government initially used/employed force (military and police) in every stage of fertilizer distribution including transportation and sale. After the crisis of 1995, the government introduced a new distribution system of fertilizer under a new dealership system.

However, the crisis of fertilizer management in Bangladesh has not yet been resolved. Since the beginning of privatization, there have always been seasonal crises of fertilizer in Bangladesh. This is known as the existence of 'artificial fertilizer crisis' by successive governments. As a result of the crises, on the one hand, farmers do not get fertilizer when they need it, which severely hampers agricultural production. On the other hand, under these circumstances and following from the lack of rules and regulations, instances of fertilizer contamination and/or adulteration have taken place. Based on newspaper reports, Azmat & Coghill (2005: 630) shows various forms of contamination and/or adulteration: (1) there have been cases of fertilizer contaminated with cement; (2) there have also been reports of the sale of adulterated fertilizers, i.e. Tri Super Phosphate (TSP) mixed with Single Super Phosphate (SSP) granules; (3) there are also reports of banned and unregistered pesticides being sold to illiterate farmers. Admitting the widespread incidents of fertilizer adulteration, in 2005, the then Agriculture Minister, M.K. Anwar candidly called upon the district commissioners to be more active in stopping production and sale of adulterated fertilizer and marketing of substandard seeds (*The Daily Star*, 12 April 2005). In fact, in the last two decades, as a by-product of market liberalization, the incidence of fertilizer adulteration has become an open secret in Bangladesh. Furthermore, as the content of any particular input is not visible, it has become easy for extra profit-seeking businesses to cheat the farmers and sell poor quality inputs at prices at par with high quality input prices (Zohir 2001: 38, as cited in Azmat & Coghill 2005: 630). According to a study by SAPRI (as cited in ibid.), these poor quality inputs not only decrease yields but also affect the micro-nutrient component of the soil, diminishing soil fertility and productivity. For example, as demonstrated by the case of the soyabean farmers' experiences, an editorial of the most circulated Bengali daily newspaper *Prothomalo* (5 December 2009) stated that it is sad to learn that farmers are the victims of adulterated fertilizer—soyabean farmers bought and used fertilizer they did not know that was adulterated and only realized this when their soyabean did not grow well and crops eventually failed.

Kafil Uddin Ahmed, Chairman of the Bangladesh Fertilizer Association (BFA), suggests that, in the last four decades, there has been huge experimentation taking place in Bangladesh with relation to the Fertilizer Distribution System. He criticizes the new system which monopolized fertilizer trade to only one dealer in a defined area. He argues that, because of the new system, farmers have to spend a huge number of working hours buying fertilizer, as there is only one dealer and there are no other small traders (as cited in Rahman 2009: 84). Islam 2012: 162, has shown effects of the mismanagement of the Fertilizer Distribution System in Bangladesh. I argue that this mismanagement is the result of the neo-patrimonial nature of the state which promotes public corruption, and is unable to provide basic services due to weak state capacity. As a result, over the years, an acute crisis of fertilizer has been affecting the cultivation of crops in Bangladesh.

In Chapter 4, I have shown the consequences of the excessive use of fertilizer in Bangladesh. Here, further elaboration is also necessary in accordance with the context of the present discussion. In fact, it is a matter of concern in relation to soil productivity or soil quality that fertilizer inputs are unbalanced, which can lead to nutrient mining, particularly for potassium (World Bank, 2006). In Bangladesh, the use of chemical fertilizers increased sixfold between 1970 and 1990, and the use of pesticides increased about threefold in just one decade, from 1982 to 1992 (Osmani & Quasem, 1990; Rahman & Thapa, 1999; Rasul & Thapa 2004). Since 1992, this trend of excessive fertilizer use has continued to increase (Hossain & Bayes 2009: 391). Over the years, the intensity of fertilizer use more than doubled from 87 kg per ha in 1988 to 209 kg in 2004, and to 213 kg in 2007 (see ibid.). The number of farmers using fertilizers in paddies has increased, particularly in traditional paddies. Various studies show that mono-cropping, along with imbalanced use of chemical fertilizers and pesticides and intensive use of land without application of organic fertilizers have led to the deterioration of both soil quality and fertility (Task Force Report 1991; Hossain & Kashem 1997; Rahman & Thapa 1999; Rasul & Thapa 2004). Consequently, more than 65 per cent of the total agricultural area is suffering from declining soil fertility, and about 85 per cent of the net cultivable area has less organic matter than the minimum requirement for maintaining soil productivity (Hossain 1990; Task Force Report 1999; Rasul & Thapa 2004).

This excessive fertilizer use is the result of poor agricultural governance.[4] There is no given that lack of awareness among farmers is the key reason of this threat to sustainability of land resources and conventional agriculture of Bangladesh. A lack of awareness surely also indicates the weak extension service and thus the state's inability to protect its land and water resources from continuous degradation and also from declining yields due to indiscriminate use of agro-chemicals. Poor agricultural governance can also be understood in relation to fertilizer subsidies. While other forms of subsidies are difficult to manage because of corruption, fertilizers are subsidised in order to encourage farmers to try new technology. Among the main fertilizers used, urea is relatively more subsidized and every government tries to keep the price at a level at which it can remain affordable to farmers. For example, generally, the price of non-urea fertilizer is four times higher than urea. As a consequence, there is a trend of disproportionate use of urea which has been substantiated by various studies (Asaduzzaman et al. 2009). The existing tenancy system is another important reason why farmers use excessive fertilizer. As Ahmed (2009) observes, 'the reasons for using chemical fertilizers are, therefore, not only related to market availability and the scarcity of the indigenous fertilizers; they are also related to the notion of greater short term gains, given that farmers may not have access to the land next year'. While market-based reforms only encourage the use of more fertilizer to produce more rice, the absence of the state in relation to its proper management is the real threat to the sustainability of ecological and conventional agriculture which is, in turn, a threat to food security.

(b) *Privatization of Irrigation, the State and its Consequences*

As a result of the privatization of irrigation, on the one hand, the role of the government in irrigation reduced completely, as BADC ceased the procurement and distribution of all kinds of irrigation equipment; on the other hand, the government started to promote irrigation through the private sector.[5] In promoting irrigation, the government took a number of actions including: (1) the removal in 1986-7 of restrictions on the import of diesel-operated minor irrigation equipment such as STWs; (2) duty-free imports of such equipment were allowed from 1988-9; (3) the subsidy on DTW was removed in 1992 to discourage it; (4) the government encouraged importing agricultural machinery by the private sector (Rahman & Deb 2005: 89). Consequently, the policy of the government indeed encouraged small scale irrigation and, therefore, STWs became a major source of irrigation. As of now, as a result of the privatization of irrigation, 1.2 million shallow machines are operating and all of them are under private owners (Hossain & Bayes 2009: 270).

It is true that since the 1980s, access to irrigation has increased all over the country. Currently, about 90 per cent of the irrigated area is provided by the private sector, mainly from groundwater with minimal public sector financing (ADB, 2009: 1). As a result, in 2008, the total harvested irrigated cropped area was estimated at 5.98 million hectares (ha), of which the most important crops were rice accounting for 4.34 million ha (73 per cent), wheat at 0.31 million ha (5 per cent), potatoes at 0.26 million ha (4 per cent) and vegetables at 0.24 million ha (4 per cent) (see FAO irrigation survey, 2010). This dramatic expansion of irrigation infrastructure played a significant role in increasing cereal grain production along with some other factors such as the increased use of modern variety, seeds and fertilizer and so forth. Hossain (2009) argues that the policy shift of the government (i.e. privatization) improved farmers' access to minor irrigation equipment and opened the door to the rapid expansion of groundwater irrigation, which increased production and decreased prices. He further points out that the gross effect of market liberalization for minor irrigation equipment is an additional 5.9 million metric tonnes of rice production per year, enough to feed an additional 22 million people. Conversely, one practitioner as well as Bangladeshi agriculture and food security expert suggests that 'trade liberalization policies, market reform and privatization have their strengths. These have also weaknesses that need to be addressed without going in for blind to be a dogmatic approach to development' (Ali 2005). Thus, it is imperative to investigate the weaknesses of the privatization of irrigation.

Given the political culture, the dilemma of development in Bangladesh is that the state can neither promote agricultural development by its policy of direct involvement in the input market, which was inefficient and unsustainable, nor can it monitor and regulate the privatization process of irrigation, unlike many other inputs. In other words, due to poor governance, BADC, a state parastatal, could not increase the irrigated area. On the other hand, under the auspices of the free market, although irrigated area has expanded, it has not helped to eliminate hunger significantly, which I attempt to discuss here.

It is imperative to take into consideration that privatization of irrigation, without control or regulation of the market or lack of governmental monitoring, produced a very costly irrigation system in Bangladesh. The cost of irrigation in Bangladesh is high relative to India, Thailand and Vietnam, although the per capita income of all of these three countries is very high compared to Bangladesh. A study of Deb, Hossain & Jones (2009: 6) suggests that diesel pump-based irrigation in Bangladesh is more expensive than subsidised canal irrigation in Vietnam or electric pump sets in India. Thus, they recommend that 'the country must provide electricity for irrigation if it is to attain a cost-efficient irrigation system and reduce unit costs of rice production. Promotion of electricity-operated irrigation systems will also help the Bangladeshi farmer achieve comparative advantage in rice production and may open up export opportunities'. Field-level data suggest that, because of high costs, farmers are not willing to use diesel pumps. However, farmers need to go for diesel pumps as the government cannot provide uninterrupted and enough electricity for irrigation. In a personal interview, an agricultural extension officer notes that 'in *boro* season farmers mostly complain about electricity as they cannot run irrigation pumps. This crisis has been affecting *boro* production . . . currently, the government is very keen to provide uninterrupted electricity for irrigation and decided to provide electricity from 11 p.m. to 7 a.m. uninterrupted, only for irrigation purposes. It seems, however, despite the good intentions of the government, they are unable to do it' (IvGoB1).

Hossain & Bayes (2009) hypothesize that because of the widespread expansion of pumps, the 'water market' is more competitive now than ever before. They argue that it is quite likely that the dominance of the 'water lords' would dissipate with the presence of thousands of water sellers entering the market with small irrigation equipment. However, Hossain (2009: 74) reminds us that 'ownership is skewed toward larger landholders, with 2007 data showing shallow tubewells in the hands of almost 90 per cent of farmers operating farms of more than 2 ha of land, compared to only 6 per cent of farmers operating up to 0.4 ha'. It may be noted that the latter group constitutes 52 per cent of farm households in Bangladesh. Thus, it can be concluded that the advent of shallow tubewells failed to dissipate the dominance of the 'water lords'. However, my field-level data shows that, in the absence of agricultural governance, the dominance of the powerful owners of pumps notably means the interruption of irrigation and the charging extra fees to small farmers. A farmer states that

> . . . we are paying Taka (Tk) 1,500 to Tk 2,000 for (the purpose of) irrigation to our land. What is the actual cost of this irrigation? It is about Tk 500 to Tk 700. We are paying this amount of extra money because there is no agency to regulate it. If we could have a cooperative system, if that could be established with the help of the government, then farmers could benefit, but the government is not taking any initiatives to do so. As a result, the manager of the irrigation scheme is making thousands of Taka. But farmers are not getting any benefits. Rather, if a farmer cannot pay his water bill (irrigation), the powerful manager of the scheme may take the entire paddy from the farmer's field (IvFmr13).

Therefore, on the one hand, the failure by the government to provide electricity for the promotion of electricity-operated irrigation systems, which is cheap compared to diesel-operated pumps, caused the irrigation to become costly. On the other hand, the lack of agricultural governance created a dominant group in the 'water market', and what resulted was the exploitation of small farmers. It would not be wrong to claim that despite the trend of increasing irrigated area, due to poor governance, the success of the privatization of irrigation failed to eliminate hunger as the small farmers were deprived from the benefit.

(c) *Production, Processing and Distribution of Seeds*

As part of market liberalization of agricultural inputs, in early 1990s, the GOB initiated a number of reform measures to liberalize the seed market (Rahman & Deb 2005: 89-90).[6] As a consequence, significant changes have occurred in Bangladesh's seed sector. Needless to say that one of the central aims of the National Seed Policy 1993 is to strengthen seed certification, quality control and testing facilities to ensure the availability of quality seeds to farmers (NSP 1993). However, about two decades later, M.K. Anwar, the Former Minister of Agriculture, lamented the fact that certified and quality seeds had not yet reached the 50 per cent mark (CPD 2009: 108-9). Like other agricultural inputs, the privatized and market-oriented seed sector of Bangladesh is also witnessing a serious lack of monitoring. For example, regular monitoring of seed quality is vital. Without monitoring, farmers can be cheated in several ways—low quality seed can affect agricultural production, lack of proper distribution can be the reason for the high cost of seed, profiteers can be encouraged to take illegal advantage, and so forth. Sadly, Bangladesh has not established any standard seed certification process yet, whereas neighbouring Nepal has a Seed Production Council (Faruk 2009: 109). As a result, as an agriculture extension officer candidly argued that 'there is no quality seed in the market without the supply of BADC as other sources (private) mostly provide adulterated seeds' (IvGoB1). A seed trader in Dhamrai Bazar of Dhaka district personally confessed that 'despite knowing that the expiry date is over, we often sell seeds' (IvSeedtrd14). He also points out that 'except BADC, no other company provides exact dates of production and expiry on the packet of seeds . . . look [showing me a packet], an expiry date has been mentioned in this packet but there is no manufacturing date'. 'This date of production and/or expiry appears on some packets of some brands of seeds at the whim of a company' (IvSeedtrd14) as it helps to gain farmers' trust. Farmers are sometimes helpless as they don't know about the quality of particular seed brands. He further states:

> Many farmers are not aware of which particular seed brand is good and which is not. As they don't have any idea about the quality of a particular brand, [they depend on us]. We recommend to them based on our own interests . . . basically businessmen recommend to them some new brand that can make their profit margins high . . . Farmers are completely dependent upon traders (ibid.).

The privatization of the seed sector can be meaningful in relation to food security only if it can ensure that the public-private partnership is able to provide quality seeds to the farmers at affordable prices. While almost everybody is unanimously in agreement that 'the Seed Certification Agency (SCA) is a rather weak organization' (Faruk 2009: 109), the challenge of ensuring quality seed, of course, remains high. Moreover, some suggest that it is important to reform the Department of Agricultural Extension (DAE) so that it can play an effective role in the distribution of seeds to rural areas. It was also observed that in the *boro* season, adequate seed supply of BRRI Dhan-28, BRRI Dhan-29, BRRI Dhan-25, BRRI Dhan-36, and BRRI Dhan-47 is necessary (Aktaruzzaman 2009: 109). In other words, in making quality seeds available to farmers, 'technologies developed locally for ensuring the quality of seeds should be made readily available to farmers' (Karim 2011).

Again, policymakers in Bangladesh are sharply divided on the issue of using hybrid seeds. Some suggest that Bangladesh should end the debate on hybrids, i.e. debates as to whether these new products will create evil effects and hamper the fertility of the soil (CPD 2009: 111). On the other hand, some argue that HYV is not required in Bangladesh to increase agricultural production. It is argued that the government permits hybrids in Bangladesh without any feasibility study. For example, in 1998-9, the GoB permitted four private seed companies to import seeds of rice hybrids. A study of Hossain, Janaiah and Husain (2003) suggests that 'hybrids were introduced in Bangladesh without a clear deployment strategy and without scientific evaluation of new rice hybrids under farmers' conditions before importing seeds'. UBINIG (Policy Research for Development Alternative), a platform that promotes the 'Naya Krishi Andolon' (New Agricultural Movement) among other development activates, is a leading movement in Bangladesh against hybrid seeds. For instance, Farida (2010b), Executive Director of UBINIG and Founding Member of Nayakrishi Andolon, points out that:

> Agriculture is a national security issue, but we are giving access to the germplasm of our major staple food crop, rice, to the foreign organisations without even disclosing the facts to the general public. . . . It goes without saying that Bangladesh being a major rice producing country and rice production being the source of livelihood, employment, economic activities and [also] for various cultural and social reasons, any attempt to 'engineer' rice without full and authentic research about safety, impact on local varieties and farmers' livelihood, etc., would be disastrous.

Similarly, Mazhar, the managing director of UBINIG, argues '. . . we are allowing them [the corporate giants of seed trade] to plunder our seeds and genetic resources, allowing them to destroy the environment and putting the age-old bio-diverse farming practices at stake for profiteers. A community cannot survive with this kind of strategy' (*Star Magazine*, 26 March 2004). Some fear that we are losing control of our seeds and 'some companies are grabbing control of our seeds' (IvNGO3).

In order to provide uninterrupted supply of quality seeds, a farmer-friendly seed policy needs to be formulated based on expert opinion with full and authentic research about safety, the impact on local varieties and farmers' livelihood, and then it should go through democratic institutions. Nation states also should aim to produce seeds locally so that production can be more environmentally friendly as compared to production under imported seeds, which also can ensure national security in relation to agricultural production and food security. However, it seems that the Bangladesh state neither deals with this complex issue in a scientific manner nor does it see seed as a possible threat to security. For example, while the experiences surrounding hybrid rice varieties are not beyond controversy, according to the Director General of BRRI, Bangladesh is soon going to introduce Genetically Modified (GM) rice. It is not clear whether or not BRRI has done its study on health safety issues as regards GM rice. Farida (2010b) doubts 'whether BRRI research protocol has such provision and whether they have the capacity to carry out research on health and environmental safety aspects of GM crops'. She further suggests that 'it is not apparently stopping BRRI from introducing GM rice in Bangladesh as the International Rice Research Institute and the biotech industry are behind this project and are using BRRI facilities including their scientists to introduce the controversial GM rice crops in Bangladesh'. Bangladesh is introducing GM rice while there is a strong global movement against GM crops, which is testament to its unfavourable impacts.[7] Interestingly, while it is the responsibility of the state to prove whether or not GM food is harmful, in a move towards introducing GM food, Agriculture Minister, Matia Chowdhury ridicules that 'those who are opposing GM crops should come up with proof that this is hazardous. Without proof, if anyone issues a fatwa [pronouncement] claiming that it is harmful, it cannot be accepted' (*The Daily Star*, 30 March 2011). Here my argument is that the Bangladesh state has been approving the planting and consumption of GMF—a crucial agricultural policy—without any consequential scientific study eventhough this is one very controversial issue in the global politics of food. Theoretically, a capable state needs to protect its citizens by an effective regulation system as governments in Europe and many other countries have by developing a different approach to regulating GMFs. While the poor governance of the Bangladesh state sheds light on the underlying failure of the state in protecting farmers from adulterated or poor quality seeds, the weak state capacity of the states suggests the reason of the state inability in making and regulating appropriate policies with regard to GMFs.

(d) *Research and Development in Agriculture: in search of the Contribution of the State*

Since Independence, Bangladesh has made significant progress in increasing the production of foodgrains despite an acute scarcity of land resources. It is widely believed that new technologies have been the major causes of increased agricultural production. However, growth in the agricultural sector has stalled in the last few years. It is argued in Chapter 4 that arable land is declining in Bangladesh and its quality is deteriorating, forming one of the key constraints among many other challenges in agricultural growth. In this context, growth in crop agriculture and productivity depends ultimately on what the technology generation system in the country can deliver. Regrettably, according to a World Bank report (2005), in more recent years, the system (National Agricultural Research System or NARS) is finding it increasingly difficult to generate new and profitable technologies suited to the changing needs of farmers. There are two basic reasons for the state's inability to deliver new and appropriate technologies—poor agricultural governance and 'inadequate and unstable funding'. Poor agricultural governance includes 'weak management of the research system including inefficient allocation and use of available resources, declining quality as well as the relevance of research and limited access to new sciences; ineffective institutional arrangements for coordination of research, including weak governance, poor scientific incentives and an eroding human resource base' (World Bank 2005: XI).

Public investment in agricultural technology (research and extension) is very important as it plays a vital role in the overall economy of a particular country. Investment in agricultural research and extension (a) yields high economic returns; (b) improves the competitiveness of agriculture; (c) provides food security; and (d) reduces poverty (ibid.: 13). Despite its critical importance, investment in agriculture research and its extension is completely neglected by the Government of Bangladesh. In order to understand the state's role in promoting agricultural technology, I will explain the budgetary allocation and agricultural governance in this section.

With regard to food security in Bangladesh, BRRI is one of the main research institutes that play a significant role, relative to other institutes, as it directly researches rice varieties.[8] The major achievements of BRRI have been in the development of High-Yielding Modern Varieties (MVs) of rice. BRRI has so far released 57 MVs (53 inbred and 4 hybrid). Very recently, eight additional varieties have been developed, which are awaiting a final evaluation by the National Seed Board (NSB) for release as new cultivars. Moreover, about 8,000 germplasms, most of which are local, have been collected and preserved in the BRRI gene bank (BRRI 2011). Interestingly, the contribution of the Bangladesh government to these achievements is very low as the research is aided by the International Rice Research Institute (IRRI) and International Center for Wheat and Maize Improvement (CIMMYT). Thus, Farida asserts 'we know that BRRI is nothing but an affiliate institution of the International Rice Research Institution'. Recently BRRI has also received support from organizations like the Bill & Melinda Gates Foundation and the Rockefeller Foundation. As a result, 'although the farmers of Bangladesh do not have access to the rice germplasm collection, it is more readily available to the corporations and to international institutions such as Syngenta, Monsanto, Bill & Melinda Gates and, of course, Rockefeller Foundation' (Farida 2010b).

It is important to note that donors' policies of aid commitment and disbursement are not always determined based on Bangladesh's necessity for technological development. Thus, any major changes to donors' policies can severely affect agricultural research in Bangladesh. For example, because of the considerable budget cut for agriculture by the World Bank and other sources, Sundaram (2010: 36) suggests that agricultural research and development has fallen for all crops in all developing countries. He adds that 'as budgets have been cut, spending on plant-breeding programmes—needed to improve crop productivity—has declined. IRRI's budget, which comes from governments, foundations and development institutions such as the Asian Development Bank, has been halved after adjusting for inflation—since the early 1990s'. As a result, 'several dozen important varieties of rice have been lost from the institute's gene bank through poor storage. Promising work on rice varieties that could withstand high temperatures and saltier water—ideal for coping with global warming and the higher sea levels that may follow—had to be abandoned' (Bradsher & Martin, as cited in Sundaram 2010: 36). Thus, the policy changes of donors' countries are ultimately threatening the agricultural research potentialities in Bangladesh.

To understand the public intention in agricultural research and extension, it is now worth mentioning the budget allocations of the Government of Bangladesh. M.K. Anwar, Former Agriculture Minister, observed that since the mid-1980s, the agriculture sector of Bangladesh has been utterly neglected by both domestic and international leaders (agencies). To explain the probable causes which have acted as factors limiting breakthroughs in technological development in Bangladesh, he argues that from the mid-1980s, international research organizations showed less interest in funding national research institutions, which resulted in a stagnation in this sector (Anwar 2009: 111). A study by the World Bank (2005) clearly indicates that agricultural research has received low priority from policymakers in terms of budgetary resource allocation at the national level. According to the study (World Bank 2005: 22-3):

- The public expenditure (revenue, development and total) on agricultural research has substantially declined over the years.[9]
- The share of total expenditure on agricultural research was only 0.22 per cent of agricultural GDP in 2004-5.[10]
- Over 90 per cent of the revenue expenditure is allocated to finance salaries, allowances, operational costs and some investment costs. Less than five per cent of the revenue budget is actually used to finance activities, materials and chemicals that are needed to undertake agricultural research.
- The share of development expenditure on agricultural research, including human resource development activities, declined significantly.

Inadequate budgetary resource allocation initiates public inertia in agricultural production through research and extension, while poor agricultural governance is another important obstacle to further development. Bureaucratic systems impede the timely release of funds, create difficulties in purchasing research materials and hamper other forms of expenditures as well as obstruct timely and appropriate recruitment (World Bank 2005: 23). It has been observed that some positions always remain vacant from among the total number of sanctioned positions of scientists and other staff.[11] It is alleged that the recruitment of scientists is also problematic—rather than merit, nepotism; political connection and money play a vital role in the recruitment process. Moreover, because of the lack of reward and poor governance, many meritorious scientists are frustrated and, therefore, leave their profession prior to their retirement for better opportunities, while the retirement age itself is only 57 years (the daily *Kaler Kontho*, 14 November 2011).

While increased sustained investment in agricultural research is important for efficient and sustainable increases in food production to ensure food security, it is particularly important for Bangladesh, since challenges of food production here are acute due to natural calamities and the trend of decreasing land arability. However, the above discussion indicates that the role of the Bangladesh state in agricultural research is minor and declining, while the capacity for existing funding to be useful is negated because of poor agricultural governance.

(e) *Agricultural Extension: 'Nothing will be of Benefit to the Poor Farmers'*

Growth in crop agriculture not only depends on technology generation, but is also important to disseminate new technologies to the farmers. Hence, agricultural extension is one of the major driving forces for the growth and development of agricultural productivity, since it can speed up farmers' access to new technology. According to NAP (2010: 8) 'the Government recognizes agricultural extension as a service delivery system which will assist farmers through appropriate technical and farm management advice and information, new technology, improved farming methods and techniques aimed at increasing production efficiency and income'. However, despite the rhetoric of the government, the reality is that the past results of the extension services cannot be regarded as very satisfactory.

Similarly, for agricultural research and development, the nature of public expenditure is also obstructive to the agricultural extension system in Bangladesh. The public sector continues to dominate the agricultural extension in Bangladesh although the private sector and NGOs are gradually increasing their participation for extension work. Available research indicates that unlike agricultural research, the share of total expenditure on agricultural extension has been gradually declining since 2003-4.[12] It is also interesting to observe that almost 95 per cent of the revenue expenditure is used to finance salaries. The remaining 5 per cent is used to finance operational costs. Thus, staff are paid salaries but funds are not used to actually deliver adequate agricultural extension services to farmers (World Bank 2005: 37). One field-level agricultural extension officer suggests that,

> each staff member is responsible for delivering agricultural extension services to 800-1,200 farmers' families in principle, but they need to do it for 1,500-2,000 families in practice. For this service, they receive Tk 100 for operational/field costs which is very inadequate. Moreover, they neither receive any transport support from the government, nor does the government provide a vehicle, such as a motorcycle or bicycle, for the extension service (IvGoB1).

On the one hand, the inadequate and inappropriate funding policy for agricultural extension does not have an impact on agriculture or farmers that is commensurate with the resources used or national needs. On the other hand, the bureaucratic procedure of funding is another obstacle of agricultural extension development—the release of funds for agricultural extension is often timely, while the process of getting funds released is very long and time consuming. It is worthwhile to note that agriculture is a very seasonal activity and, therefore, receiving funds at appropriate times is essential. Otherwise, funding would be completely misused (See World Bank 2005).

Bangladesh has many institutions providing extension services, which could be encouraging for agricultural development. However, because of poor agricultural governance, the proliferation of extension organizations in different sectors of rural development activities resulted in duplication of work, conflict and the underuse of scarce human and capital resources, which were, in turn, manifested in their poor performance. Moreover, it created an imbalance of resource allocation and use, further resulting in regional imbalances in productivity through wrong priority and emphasis (Hossain 1991: 244). Similarly, outside of externally financed projects (e.g. the World Bank), there are few examples of working relationships among various institutions where a set of activities have been planned and implemented through the mutual sharing of resources, knowledge and experience between public and private organizations (World Bank 2005: 46). Not surprisingly, within a government institution, there is a lack of coordination, which is mostly an outcome of patronage politics, corruption. For example, the number of total extension service staff members employed in Dhamrai and Savar, two adjacent Upazila (sub-districts) of Dhaka district, is 46 and 58, respectively (during my fieldwork period). Interestingly, the job responsibility in Savar is less than that in Dhamrai—Savar is an industrial area where arable land is less than that in Dhamrai and much likely, there are fewer numbers of farmers' family members (IvGoB1). The reason is crystal clear. Savar is a lucrative work station for any government officer as it is very much in vicinity of Dhaka city. Thus, the additional posting in Savar only serves interest groups, and not the extension service.

Available fieldwork data suggests that farmers hardly get any extension service from government institutions. For instance, according to a farmer, 'sometimes government officials (extension staff) come to see the field. They come, meet the rich farmers, take some snacks, and if there is any opportunity to offer help (from the government), they offer those to them. In this way, poor farmers never get anything—no benefits are given to them' (IvFmr13).[13] The fact is that:

> The coverage, as measured by direct contact between Department of Agricultural Extension (DAE) field staff and farmers, has remained at around 10 per cent of farmer population. The number of clients entitled to service is large, some in geographically difficult-to-reach dispersed communities and with differing needs. In practice, therefore, extension staff can only establish direct contact with a few farmers (World Bank 2005: 50).

In addition, in the past few decades, fewer qualified people were employed with little or no logistic support, and many of them were not properly trained for effective extension work. As a consequence, it is argued that the extension agents are poorly educated to advise adult, experienced clients (Hossain 1991: 245). A seed trader suggests that the 'know-how of the extension field staffs is utterly poor' (IvSeedtrd14).

(f) *Landownership, Land Reforms and Land Tenancy in Bangladesh*

Hartmann and James K. Boyce (1982: 17) suggest that the pattern of landownership in Bangladesh profoundly affects both the production and distribution of food. In 2008, about 4.5 million households (15.63 per cent) were landless, a majority of whom (73 per cent) lived in rural areas (BBS 2008). According to an estimate, 86.70 per cent of households owned only 0.02 to 1.0 ha (landless, sub marginal and marginal) of land in 2005, which implies that the distribution of agricultural land is highly inequitable (see Table 5.2). Over time, the number of small farmers have been increasing substantially, which is mainly because of land fragmentation whereas the number of medium and large farmers have been declining. Table 5.2 also indicates that approximately 52.60 per cent of rural households in Bangladesh are either landless or functionally landless, which implies that many of them make their living principally from land they do not own. According to a study of BBS (2010), 60.0 per cent households were reported (multiple answers) to be landlessness or having inherited nothing as the reasons for being poor or extreme poor.

While landless people depend mainly on selling labour or completely rely on rented-in land for their livelihoods, historically, small and marginal farmers of Bangladesh have been cultivating owned as well as rented-in land—either in sharecropping (*Barga Chash*) arrangements or in exchange for rent to a landlord. As a consequence, landlessness stands as the root cause of social injustice, deprivation of political rights and basic human needs in Bangladesh. It particularly affects the agricultural production, income generation, and eventual food security. To explain how the landownership and land tenancy system can be threatening to agricultural production and food security, an agricultural extension officer (IvGoB1) suggests one example: 'there is no guarantee whether or not next year a farmer can cultivate a land which someone is cultivating this year. Thus, they are always careless about the fertility of the land'.

TABLE 5.2: DISTRIBUTION OF AGRICULTURAL HOLDINGS IN 2005 (IN PERCENTAGE)

Holdings Size	Percentage of Holdings	Percentage of Area
Landless Holdings and Sub Marginal Holdings (below 0.2 ha)	52.60	6.94
Marginal Holdings (below 0.2 ha-1.0 ha)	34.10	35.76
Landless, Sub Marginal, and Marginal Holdings (1+2)	86.70	42.70
Small Holdings (1.0 ha-below 4 ha)	11.70	40.43
Medium Holdings (10 ha and above)[14]	1.70	16.87
Large Holdings (10 ha and above)	–	–
Total	100	100

Source: BBS 2005; Adapted from Sobhan 2010.

As Jannuzi & Peach (1990) suggest, 'within the framework of this system, with ownership and control of land traditionally separated from labour and investment, neither the owner nor the tiller of the soil has a strong incentive to increase productivity'. In the absence of a formal tenancy agreement system in Bangladesh (almost all are verbal agreements), tenants have always been subject to extreme insecurity. In other words, there is no right of tenants in their rented-in land which is an important source of earning as well as food security. This situation is worsened, because this landlessness or functional landlessness combined with 'the seasonal nature of agricultural employment and limited opportunities for non-farm employment cause millions to suffer from chronic and transitory food insecurity. The access to food for these people depends on trade-based entitlement relationships, i.e. on the wage rate and food prices and their fluctuations in the market' (Hossain, Naher & Shahabuddin 2005: 116).

In addition to the fact that tenancy arrangements are inherently inefficient compared to owner cultivation, stories of plight resulting in severe exploitation by the landlord of the tenant are very common phenomena in the history of Bangladesh. With respect to the 'power' relations that can be threatening to somebody's right to food, Osmani (2010: 48) suggests two possibilities that may be relevant in the context of Bangladesh. Firstly, the village elite may unlawfully usurp the land of the poor. In that context, according to Osmani, obligation would require the state to ensure proper land registration and enforcement of land rights. Secondly, there is the possibility of unlawful eviction of tenants or cases of tenants being forced to accept exploitative contract terms. Therefore, in the following discussion, I will examine the role of the state in the context of land reforms where I will address the following questions (borrowed from FAO 2006): Have necessary (contextually relevant) land and tenure reforms (land consolidation, titles to tillers, redistribution, etc.) been undertaken to support an improvement in domestic capacity for agricultural production? Do property, inheritance and other regulatory laws support an improvement in capacity for agriculture production?

Griffin, Khan, and Ickowitz (2002) argue that redistributive land reform is necessary to accelerate agrarian growth in developing countries. Similarly, some suggest that it is possible in Bangladesh to reduce rural poverty through land redistribution, particularly by distributing publicly owned *khas* land to landless people. However, because of widespread corruption as well as an inefficient land administration system in Bangladesh; on the one hand, most of the public *khas* lands are under the control of powerful elites. On the other hand, it is a common phenomenon in Bangladeshi society that village elites almost regularly unlawfully take the land of poor persons. In other words, the state has not sufficiently challenged the inequalities in land ownership and capture due to poor governance, partial reform and weak state capacity. A complicated land administration system in Bangladesh, according to Osmani (2010: 48-9) leads to 'a perennial source of litigation and harassment for resource-poor households, especially in the rural areas', and also 'leads to the problem of falsification of records, which is perhaps the major factor behind the endemic nature of land disputes in Bangladesh'. The extent of complicatedness of land administration of Bangladesh can be understood by the report, *National Household Survey 2007 on Corruption in Bangladesh*, conducted by the Transparency International Bangladesh. This study indicates that in terms of specific sectors, a staggering 52.7 per cent of households who interacted with land administration agencies experienced corruption, while 53.03 per cent experienced bribery. The rate of bribery was reportedly highest for the allotment of *Khas* land, followed by land registration and mutation respectively. Moreover, 70.0 per cent of households experienced bribery for obtaining documents, followed by *Khas* land allotment (65.6 per cent), land survey (64.7 per cent), mutation (63.4 per cent) and payment of land tax (26.0 per cent) (TIB 2008: VIII and XII). Under these circumstances, it is almost impossible for poor people to control their own land or to receive allotment of *Khas* land since they are unable to bribe.

Before Independence in 1971, a series of initiatives for land reforms were taken in the 1950s and 1960s, which included tenancy reforms, ceilings imposed on landholdings, and efforts at distribution of public land to the landless (Uddin & Haque 2009; as cited in USAID 2010). However, these initiatives proved not very fruitful. After liberation, an attempt was made under the Land Reforms Ordinance of 1984. The aim of this ordinance was to reform the law relating to land tenure, landholding and land transfer, with two major goals—to ensure increases in agricultural production and to establish the basis for better relationships between land owners and *bargadars* (sharecroppers or tenants). However, given the existing distribution of power (*de jure* and *de facto*) in rural Bangladesh, it proved almost impossible to enforce provisions of the ordinance (Osmani 2010: 49). It is also argued that the ordinance of 1984 is an ineffective means of establishing a land system that would be conducive to sustained economic growth (Jannuzi & Peach 1990). In fact, various reform initiatives suggest that 'the agrarian reform . . . would not be likely to be implanted within the existing political economy of Bangladesh' (Jannuzi & James 1990: 98).

The empirical application of the five analytical frameworks of rent-seeking, public corruption, partial reform, poor governance and weak state capacity provides clear understanding of the reason why there have been limited outcome of the state initiatives in agricultural production. As a result, the domestic production cannot guarantee uninterrupted supply of foodgrains to ensure food availability in Bangladesh.

THE STATE, TRADE AND FOOD AVAILABILITY: THE BANGLADESH CONUNDRUM

In the previous discussion, I have shown the state's failure in developing effective policy necessary for agricultural production, and the state's inability in policy implementation, resulting in poor agricultural production which is directly opposite to the aim of promoting food availability. In this section, I will discuss trade as a means of food availability in the context of Bangladesh. While the previous section shows that because of the poor administrative capacity of the state, over the years, the Bangladesh state has failed to achieve self-sufficiency in foodgrain production, this section aims to investigate the state's failure to facilitate a steady supply of food through trade. Using the central analytical framework of this study,

I will endeavour to examine how poor governance, rent-seeking behavior, and public corruption impede effective imports of foodgrains. Furthermore, I will also aim to examine how two other factors, relating to state weakness and poor governance, impede effective imports.

Before undertaking the main discussion, I will first attempt to shed light on the importance of trade in maintaining food availability in Bangladesh. I will then seek to understand the underlying reasons and politics of the Bangladesh state behind its turning to the world market instead of achieving self-sufficiency in foodgrain production. My discussion then suggests that it is important to import foodgrains to ensure food availability, but that early warning and timely imports are more crucial than merely importing foodgrains. Considering that timely imports are crucial, I raise the following question—Has the Bangladesh state the potential capacity to import foodgrains when needed? In order to examine the administrative ability of the decision making system, I will explicate the political economy of statistics—the most important factor for scientific decision making. I will then discuss the potential and pitfalls of the state as well as the private sector in making timely imports of foodgrains.

Bangladesh is heavily dependent on imports of almost all items of food in considerable amounts. This includes rice, wheat, maize, sugar, pulses, soya bean oil, palm oil, animal fat, milk, etc. However, in this discussion, I will mainly focus on cereal grains since cereals amount to a high percentage of calories consumed in Bangladesh and, therefore, are the main source of food (see Chapter 4 for details about the food consumption pattern). Table 5.3 shows that Bangladesh is still not self-sufficient in cereal grains, so the import of cereal grains continues to be an important factor for food availability. Between 2000-1 and 2010-11, the total imports of cereal grains as a percentage of total availability remains at 10 per cent (see Table 5.3). It is argued in Chapter 4 that the imports of rice substantially increased in Bangladesh in the years following poor harvests, mainly because of floods and droughts. For example, after the massive floods in 1998, Bangladesh imported over 22.3 per cent of the total available foodgrains in the fiscal year of 1998-9,

TABLE 5.3: BANGLADESH FOODGRAIN IMPORTS, 1980-1 TO 2010-11 (000 TONNES)

Year	Public Imports			Private Imports			Total Imports			Total Imports availability of foodgrains	Total imports as per cent of total availability
	Rice	Wheat	Total	Rice	Wheat	Total	Rice	Wheat	Total		
1980-1 to 1989-90	266	1,571	1,838	0	0	0	266	1,571	1,838	16,194	11.2
1990-1 to 1999-2000	120	1,135	1,255	540	320	860	661	1,454	2,115	20,189	10.2
2000-1 to 2010-11	198	325	524	708	1,713	2,422	936	2,042	2,949	30,221	10

Source: Author's calculation from Directorate of Food, Government of Bangladesh (GoB).

compared to only 5 per cent of the total imports of foodgrains in 1996-7 which was a good harvest year. On average, imports remained stagnant at around 0.5 million tonnes per year, whilst actual imports increased in years of bad harvest such as the 3.45 million metric tonnes in 2009-10 (Food Planning and Monitoring Unit (FPMU) 2010).

Towards The Invisible Hands: Food Availability and the State Under Trade Liberalization

Until the 1980s, the Government of Bangladesh was solely responsible for all necessary foodgrain imports; at that time, the private sector was not allowed to import. In contrast, since the early 1990s, private sector imports have been playing an important role, while the role of government has reduced significantly. As a consequence of trade liberalization, for the first time, in 1992-3, the private sector was allowed to import wheat. Then, in 1997-8 and 1998-9, when poor *aman* harvests threatened national food security in Bangladesh, the government response was completely different. The government almost handed the responsibility for rice imports over to the private sector—imports of the private sector were about 6.77 times higher than government imports in 1998-9 (compared to 393,000 tonnes of public imports, the private imports accounted for 2,663,000 tonnes of rice). In this section, I will firstly outline the government policy changes (i.e. towards trade liberalization) and its mechanisms, and I will then examine the underlying factors behind the policy changes.

It is argued that after the massive floods in 1998, the government policymakers were faced with the prospect of large production shortfalls, a sharp increase in rice prices, inadequate foodgrain stocks to stabilize prices, and major difficulties in government foodgrain procurement. Several issues that further complicated the policy issues and decision making were the uncertainty surrounding projected production, the market's behaviour, an atmosphere of humanitarian and political urgency, etc. (Dorosh et al. 2004: 155). In this regard, it was hoped that the privatized foodgrain trade, with minimal government interference, would function more efficiently, and thus the domestic market would behave appropriately. As a consequence, the government took steps to encourage private-sector imports to boost market supplies. A study by Dorosh et al. (ibid.: 159) suggested that several steps were taken to provide incentives for private-sector imports—firstly, the Government of Bangladesh removed a 2.5 per cent rice import surcharge making rice imports completely duty-free in January 1998; secondly, the government raised the Open Market Sales (OMS) price, bringing it closer to import parity; thirdly, ministry of food officials met with major rice traders, explaining policies and encouraging traders to import grain; and fourthly, despite pressure from some high-level officials, the Government of Bangladesh did not reinstate anti-hoarding laws which would have seriously disrupted incentives for both domestic and international rice traders. As a result, private sector traders in Bangladesh imported several million metric tonnes (mmt) of rice from India which was indeed prior to the offer of the government's incentives. Dorosh (2001) found that trade liberalization made a positive contribution to short-term food security in Bangladesh, based on the case of the Bangladesh-India rice trade following a poor harvest in late 1997 and the massive floods in 1998. However, as I have argued in Chapter 4, in the following section, I will further illustrate the uncertainty of the global rice market.

It is imperative to analyze the necessity of providing incentives for private-sector imports instead of direct government procurement from the international market. Before discussing the importance of the incentives, it is important to examine the nature of the business community in Bangladesh. Historically, the business community in Bangladesh, until the early 1990s if not at present, was not considered trustworthy enough for the government to rely on (for details, see Kochanek 1993 and also Chapter 3 of this thesis).[15] In other words, historical experience suggested that, because of poor market regulation, it was difficult for the government to completely rely on traders. Secondly, the experience of traders was also in question as, prior to the 1997-9 crises, traders had little experience in the large-scale import of foodgrains and thus there was huge uncertainty about private sector import. Along with some other reasons, according to Dorosh et al. (2004: 159), 'private trader uncertainty over possible changes in Government of Bangladesh rice policy could also inhibit private sector imports'.

Here it is noteworthy to examine why the government took initiatives to encourage private-sector imports. The political-military-bureaucratic elites' interest played a vital role in prompting the policy changes—it comprised both rent-seeking as well as political gain for the regime through speeding up trade liberalization. In other words, as Quadir (2000: 197) suggests that 'these reforms [trade liberalization] were used primarily to consolidate the power of the ruling elites . . . [it was] an instrument to build and maintain political coalitions in particular with traders and industrialists'. However, the following points could be considered as the main reasons which explain the underlying factors behind private-sector imports of foodgrains.

Firstly, the regime was patronizing the new business class, particularly those people who were associated with the ruling party. Kochanek (1996) shows the rise of interest politics in Bangladesh, and particularly how business was attempting to become the kingmaker of Bangladeshi politics during the 25-month-long political crisis which ended in 1996. In addition to patronizing the business community which supported Sheikh Hasina in the movement against the previous government, Hasina also had the patronage of a new group of businessmen who became members of parliament in the 1996 election. The notion of rent-seeking may thus provide an insightful explanation into the provision of incentives for private-sector imports (for further discussion on the business-politics nexus in Bangladesh, see Chapter 3).

Secondly, encouraging private-sector imports of foodgrains was an attempt by the government to accelerate the pace of trade liberalization. This was an opportunity for the ruling government to consolidate its power by implementing economic reforms, mimicking the footsteps of the previous regimes of Zia, Ershad, and Khaleda Zia. It is imperative to mention here that while the military regimes of Zia and Ershad largely used economic reform programmes as a tool to both legitimize and consolidate their unconstitutional power base, reform programmes were also used to consolidate power under the democratically-elected regime of

Khaleda Zia (Quadir 2000). Later, the Awami League (AL) also joined the reformers' club. It is argued that Hasina's Awami League was no less ready than the Bangladesh Nationalist Party (BNP) to undertake the economic restructuring measures to engineer rapid economic growth (Nuruzzaman 2006: 175). Quoting a senior trade union leader, Nuruzzaman (ibid.) suggests that:

> In 1994 Sheikh Hasina sent a confident note to the IMF, the World Bank, and other bilateral donors, promising quick implementation of the privatization process in Bangladesh. That note dispelled the suspicion of the donors about the AL's socialist overtones, and the party had the blessings of the donor community to win the 1996 elections to the national parliament.

Therefore, after forming the government in 1996, the Awami League wholeheartedly favoured the reform agenda which testified its support in the massive private-sector imports in the instances of both the 1997-8 and 1998-9 crises.

Moreover, the context of the global policy shift in relation to trade and food security in developing countries can provide us with the basis of the policy changes in Bangladesh. It is now widely believed that before the looming food crisis in 2007-8, policy-makers in Bangladesh believed that the demand for rice could be met by international trade.

Challenging the Imports of Foodgrains: What to do? When to do it? How to do it?

Considered as the landmark event because of its importance in the history of hunger and food insecurity in Bangladesh, I will refer to the example of the Bangladesh famine of 1974, throughout this study. To understand to what extent Bangladesh can rely on the international market, it is again worthwhile to recall the 1974 food crisis in Bangladesh. As I have argued, Bangladesh was the most affected nation in both the recent global food crises in 1973-4 and 2007-8. Sadly, in both of these crises, Bangladesh failed to arrange the timely import of foodgrains to manage its food availability. While many argued that Bangladesh failed to import foodgrains in the first crisis mainly because of the balance-of-payment crisis as well as its political tension with the USA, in the more recent crisis, Bangladesh had neither of these problems. However, over the years while the policymakers ignored the lesson of the 1974 crisis, the most recent global food crisis emerged as a wake-up call for the Bangladesh policy of self-sufficiency. As Bangladesh still needs foodgrain imports as its domestic production continues to fall short of its foodgrain requirements, the questions which I will deal with in this section are—What are the problems regarding foodgrain imports in relation to the capacity of the Bangladesh state? To what extent can the Bangladesh state rely on imports? What are the best alternatives? Here, I begin by examing the historical experience and then I will discuss the issue of statistics. As mentioned in Chapter 1, in dealing with any crisis, this study analyses government performance based on three questions—What to do? When to do it? How to do it?

It is important to import foodgrains to ensure food availability, but early warning and timely imports are more crucial than merely importing foodgrains. It is argued that output and per capita availability of domestic foodgrains fell sharply from 1970 to 1973 in war-torn Bangladesh which was then followed in 1974 by catastrophic floods. During these years of foodgrain crisis, the Government of Bangladesh frustratingly failed to ensure food availability and, in particular, the regime failed to import foodgrains in a timely manner. As a consequence, Bangladesh experienced famine in 1974. On the other hand, in subsequent years, Bangladesh experienced several floods and droughts such as the drought in 1979 and floods in 1984, 1988 and 1998. With multidimensional damage including damage to infrastructure and a drastic reduction in employment for the rural landless, these floods and droughts were no less devastating than the 1974 floods. However, famine did not recur despite a couple of close calls. Clay (1985; Curtis, Hubbard & Shepherd 1988) first draws attention to why there was no repetition in 1984 of the famine of 1974. According to Clay (1985: 202-3), several important institutional changes in the agricultural system, in the food system as managed through governmental intervention, and in the political system more generally, appear to have contributed to famine being averted.

Clay (1985) indicates several features of institutional building which included the development of an early warning system.[16] In the context of the present discussion, I find this very useful. A better warning system can provide an appropriate signal to the policymakers: What to do? When to do it? In 1984, Clay (ibid.) indicates that the Government of Bangladesh immediately imported rice on a large scale from Thailand amounting to over 400,000 tonnes to ensure food availability. These imports prevented a sudden price hike that would have been unbearable to the poor, thus also preventing hoarding and speculation. Similarly, during the crises of the 1988 and 1998 floods, the government successfully imported or encouraged private importers to import. Therefore, it was possible to avert the recurrence of famine.

However, it is not always easy to import in a timely manner. One of the main obstacles to timely imports is the government decision-making mechanism. According to a former Food Secretary of the Government of Bangladesh (GoB), 'it is very complicated as well as challenging to import foodgrain in a timely manner. It is complicated mainly because of two reasons: (a) procurement policy of the government, and (b) international market situation' (IvGOB8). He candidly adds, 'Unfortunately, here [in Bangladesh] the decision-making process is very slow'. With regard to the international market, he argues that:

> Despite the contract, suppliers often fail to supply in a timely manner due to some unavoidable reasons . . . and they seek extensions of time. The problem is that if we cancel the contract for delayed supply, it will take another three months for the process of a new tender. Otherwise, we have to import foodgrain late. By this time, import may be not necessary anymore (ibid.).

Recent experience also shed some light on some uncertainties in relation to foodgrain import from the international market. These are: First, the experience associated with the sudden surge of rice prices in the recent global food crisis of 2007-8 demonstrated that the government should learn from this lesson and that high priority should be given to domestic production instead of relying on the international market. It appeared that the major rice-exporting countries were sharply restricting exports to protect their own markets. For example, soon after the price increase in the international market, India introduced export restrictions followed by an export ban. India continued its export ban for three consecutive years although the public stocks in the country reached a new record (FPMU 2010). During the crisis of 2007-8, major exporting countries such as Thailand, Vietnam, Cambodia, and Egypt banned rice exports altogether. As a consequence, Bangladesh found it difficult to import foodgrains which caused a serious shortage of availability (Deb, Hossain & Jones 2009). It is important to keep in mind that there is a huge risk of coincident crop shortfalls between Bangladesh and India due to their geographical locations.

Second, for over a decade, India has been the major source for rice imports for two reasons: (a) Bangladesh mainly imports milled rice for which India is the major source; and (b) as India is the neighbouring country, imports face lower transport costs, and shipments are also comparatively easy and timely and, therefore, reliable in mitigating an emergency crisis. In addition to India, Bangladesh imports rice from Thailand, Myanmar, Pakistan, and Vietnam. However, a study by Deb, Hossain and Jones (ibid.) shows that: (a) Myanmar does not have the capacity to provide the relatively large quantities of rice required to meet Bangladesh's needs; (b) although Thailand has the ability to meet Bangladesh's needs, the prices are generally higher than those of India and transport costs are often higher; and (c) India could be the best source but uncertainty remains high in relying on it. So, the options for an emergency market are very limited indeed.

Thirdly, the global rice market is very small although almost half of the world's population consumes rice as a staple food. Rice is mostly consumed where it is produced. Of the global production of nearly 440 million metric tonnes (mmt), less than 30 mmt rice are accounted for in international trade or about 7-8 percent of global production (Timmer 2010: 4). Some of the underlying characteristics of the global rice market can be the cause of the volatility of rice prices. Timmer (ibid.) suggests that 'the world rice market operates with highly incomplete and very imperfect information about short-run supply and demand factors. Because of this disorganized industrial structure and lack of information about the behaviour of its participants, rice is a very different commodity from the other basic food staples, wheat and corn'. By analysing the nature of the rice market, Timmer (2010: 4) further shows how it can drive 'destabilizing speculative behaviour' among millions, even billions, of market participants. Thus, the rice market and its global trade are seen as a politically sensitive issue by the governments of both importing and exporting countries. Consequently, the rice market is subject to a variety of trade distortions even in normal times (Headey 2011). While it is argued that trade shocks are still one of the 'great uncertainties' in world food markets (ibid.), available evidence suggests that the rice trade is more uncertain than the trade of any other foodgrain (e.g. see Timmer 2010).

The Political Economy of Statistics: Statistical Mess, Weak State Capacity and Foodgrain Imports

Scientific study is important for the effective import of foodgrains in order to ensure food availability at the national level. It is particularly important in a country like Bangladesh where higher food prices are necessary to induce increased local food production and to support poor farmers. Again, it is imperative to import foodgrains to mitigate crises in order to tackle any adverse impacts of a sudden price hike. As I noted earlier, natural disasters such as floods and droughts are very common in Bangladesh and are the main reasons for the fluctuation of food availability. Thus, understanding the challenges of foodgrain imports is critical: policy issues in relation to both timeliness and quantity must be designed in a scientific manner. I have noted that foodgrain imports in Bangladesh vary significantly from year to year—while in 1996-7 total imports as a percentage of total availability were only five percent, they were 22.3 per cent in 1998-9. In this regard, statistics play a very important role as in any particular year food shortage is only for certain periods of time—delay or miscalculation can be not only meaningless but disastrous for the market. In other words, the crucial political decision regarding foodgrain imports is completely dependent on scientific analysis based on statistical data analysis. It is the state's responsibility to carry out scientific research to secure the interests of its citizens. In not doing so, the state's failure can jeopardize the interests of its citizens. Here, any form of dependency on any other organization, local or international, can be seen as the state's inability since the supremacy of other institutions over the state can jeopardize its authority.

Controversy over the recent population census (BBS 2011) indicates that the statistical service of Bangladesh has completely broken down; now, very basic national accounts data are increasingly of suspect quality. Echoing the thousands of people who claim to have been left out of the enumeration process of the recent census, the Agriculture Minister of Bangladesh, Matia Chowdhury, terms this census as 'unrealistic', and argues that '[h]ad the population been 142.3 million, we should have been sitting on sacks full of food grains now, and there would have been no requirement [for] food import' (*The Daily Star*, 19 July 2011). Controversy over three important sources of statistical data such as the size of the population, the grain production volume and the per capita rice consumption level is indeed an old problem which can be seen as a main obstacle to appropriate decision making. For example, according to Hossain and Deb (2009: 81):

> The rapid increase in imports of rice in recent years raises question[s] about the accuracy of the official statistics on rice production, on the basis of which the food balance sheet data indicates surplus rice production in the country. The report of the National Level Sample Survey conducted in 2005 shows the area under Aman rice is one million ha less than reported in the Statistical Yearbook (BBS 2006). If the survey data is correct, total rice production in Bangladesh would be three million tonnes less than reported in official statistics. Such inconsistency of data from the same source needs to be resolved for effective policymaking.

Conventional wisdom suggests that without an accurate statistical service, sound decision making is virtually impossible. Now, the following questions arise: Why is there this statistical mess? How are decisions being made about whether or not Bangladesh needs to import foodgrains? Who are the decisionmakers?

The Food Planning and Monitoring Unit (FPMU) of the Ministry of Food and Disaster Management is the government unit responsible for monitoring the food security situation in Bangladesh and for the implementation of related policies. Major activities of this organization comprise collecting, storing and disseminating information for food security analysis and policy formulation, and delivering evidence-based policy advice to the government on issues relevant to food security—on its own initiative or on demand by the government (see NFPCSP 2011). However, the Bangladesh Bureau of Statistics (BBS) is one of the key actors for statistical data not only for the FPMU, but also for other research agencies including major international organizations such as the World Bank, FAO, etc. In addition to the BBS, other sources also provide statistical data such as the individual ministries (e.g. Ministry of Agriculture), Space Research and Remote Sensing Organization (SPARSO), the data wing of FPMU, etc. Over the years, the strength of the BBS in relation to data collection has improved significantly. However, the capacity of the institution is still not beyond question; in particular, the field level data of food production and availability are still disputed. However, it is important to note that data of some other agencies such the Ministry of Agriculture is less acceptable than the data provided by BBS. For example, recently, the World Bank's country director in Bangladesh argued that he preferred the data provided by the BBS instead of that from the Ministry of Agriculture as it provided wrong data. In response, the Agriculture Minister, Matia Chowdhury, alleged that the multilateral development agency was promoting incompetence in the government. She stated that 'you are promoting incompetence. Why are you encouraging incompetence? Whose interest [are] you looking after? You have not been sent to secure anyone's interest' (Chowdhury 2010). This conflict between the minister and the World Bank is an important point in understanding the state's weakness in ensuring a basic statistical service. A closer investigation further reveals that the total statistical service is in a mess particularly with regard to food policy, which I am going to evaluate in the next section.

Based on his personal experience while he was in office in 2003, a former food secretary of the Ministry of Food and Disaster Management argues that Bangladesh did not even have any benchmark study reports to indicate the exact amount of food required per head. Explaining every detail of the imperatives of scientific study, he further claims that there is the lack of a proper study to find out the actual food gap, that is, total production and total requirements (IvGoB4). In developing a better food policy and responding to crises, the issue of 'statistical error' is further clarified by another former food secretary of the government. He suggests that data from various sources (mainly three sources: field level data from FPMU, BBS and SPARSO) are always contradictory, which complicates the policymaking process. As a result, it is not clear to the policymakers as to what amount of foodgrains is needed to tackle any particular food crisis. In other words, there is always a debate on the total requirement of foodgrains in Bangladesh (IvGOB8). Similarly, in an interview, one rice trader points out that policy fails mainly because of statistical errors. He argues that:

> When the government claims bumper production of rice in any particular year we often understand that there is a fallacy of policy analysis of the government due to the error of field level data. For example, sometimes we see production of the paddy is very good but the quality is poor (e.g. *Chita* or paddy grains containing no substance) which means that the crisis of rice is going to be inevitable and, therefore, the price hike of rice would be inevitable. Here you need a sincere and better analysis in order to understand the problem (IvRTrd12).

This failure of the state to provide a better statistical service in order to design better policy is seen as a sign of a state's low capacity as Van De Walle (2001: 129-37) shows in the context of postcolonial Africa. Thus, due to the weak state capacity in Bangladesh with regard to statistical services, the state is unable to design the policies that are necessary for effective imports to ensure food availability.

'The Government is simply unable to do Business': Institutional Incapability of the Trading Corporation of Bangladesh (TCB) and Foodgrain Imports

In this section, my purpose is not to claim that public sector food imports are better than private sector food imports or vice versa, rather, I argue that economic management and market regulation are vital—while sound monitoring and market regulation are crucial for private sector food imports, administrative efficiency is required for public sector imports. After the recent global food crisis in 2007-8 which badly affected Bangladesh, the question of the importance of state regulation and state control over international trade gained currency, particularly in the media and popular discussion. In the quest for a scapegoat, many blamed 'syndication' as the major reason for food price hikes in Bangladesh. While it is the responsibility of the state to crack down on syndication (if there is any), many influential ministers also suggested that a form of syndication was the driving force behind the dramatic price hike of essentials. For example, the Finance Minister of Bangladesh stated that 'a monopolistic force is controlling the market . . . there is no logical reason for the current price level' (bdnews 24, 2011). Considering 'syndication' as the failure of governance, in a personal interview, a Bangladeshi economist and political analyst suggests that 'market syndication has always been patronized by the government. It is always only politically-connected businessmen doing business under every regime: mostly, a small clique of the party followers'. He adds, 'Why doesn't the government allow more people to do business? To provide a licence to a handful of importers is the government policy, in order to promote a few people to get rich. If the government wishes, it is not impossible to crack down on the syndication. It is simply a matter of political will' (IvEcn11). Market syndication is a situation where a single buyer or seller or a small group of buyers or sellers may be able to control market prices. This ability to control and influence market prices is known as market power which is the key factor of market failure. In order to rectify market failures under these circumstances, governments need to intervene to prevent the formation of monopolies; to control acquisitions, mergers, and foreign ownership; to guarantee market share for new operators; to break up existing monopolies; etc. In doing so, governments need institutional and infrastructural strength as well as political will.

In order to break up the sorts of monopolies known as 'market syndication' in Bangladesh, some emphasize the necessity of mobilizing the Trading Corporation of Bangladesh (TCB), the government wing for facilitating the steady supply of essential commodities, which has failed to create any impact in the market with its recent sporadic activities. The necessity of an active TCB came to the forefront in 2007 when a study by the Centre for Policy Dialogue (CPD) revealed that a small group of traders was controlling the daily essentials' market. Since then, the general opinion of society, which is particularly reflected in the media, is that the TCB needs a total renovation as the present format of the organization is of no use. The core argument in favour of strengthening the TCB is that 'the government would struggle to keep essentials' prices stable unless state-run Trading Corporation of Bangladesh succeeds in improving the supply chain' (*The Daily Star*, 16 August 2009). Here, it can be recalled that the TCB was established in 1972 with the objective of ensuring a steady supply of essential consumer goods and industrial raw materials and of making them easily available to consumers at reasonable prices. But then the TCB was crippled in the 1990s in the process of market-based reforms. In relation to the institutional capability of the TCB, in an interview with the daily *Prothom-alo* (10 October 2010), Rahman stated that 'some believe that TCB needs to be strengthened. While I was the commerce advisor [of the government], we had several meetings to improve its institutional capacity. This organization became so weak that there is no way to strengthen it'. In a personal interview, another policy expert suggests that 'the government is simply unable to do business. We have seen the state's performance in doing business. State-owned corporations and industries cannot work, only a few people involved in these businesses are making fortunes but the institutions are unable to run' (IvEcn11).

The concepts of institutional inefficiency, public corruption and rent-seeking can all shed light on understanding the capability of the TCB. It is not unlikely that businessmen may take the initiative to keep the TCB inactive while the institutional set-up of the organization itself has already been crippled. Its institutional inefficiency can be traced by the following news in a daily Bengali newspaper:

TCB opened its first LCs [Letter (s) of Credit] for importing 10,000 tonnes sugar on 17 April. It was unknown to the authority of the TCB that 12,000 tonnes is the minimum requirement for a shipment. So, TCB was obliged to cancel the LCs. On 3 June, it reopened LCs for 12,000 tonnes after correcting the previous inaccuracy . . . till now [14 August] TCB could not provide the delivery order to the lowest bidder. It has no stock of sugar at all, and there is still uncertainty whether or not it would be able to import any (*The Daily Prothom-alo*, 14 August 2009).

The above-mentioned initiatives were taken to keep the market stable during the Ramadan month when prices usually go up. The above news shows that despite a five-month long struggle, a week before Ramadan, the TCB neither had any stock to support the market supply chain nor was it able to show its ability to import foodgrains. On the eve of Ramadan, renewing his pledge to ensure the availability of essentials including sugar, the Commerce Minister, Faruk Khan, admitted that 'local businessmen have a common mistrust in the performance of TCB that has caused some difficulties for activating the agency. . . . The organisation is still not very efficient in its functions, as it is yet to ease and accelerate its procedure to import and distribute' (*The Daily Star,* 17 August 2009). So, the fact is that the TCB is an 'inefficient institution' that cannot be strengthened. In the context of the patronage politics in Bangladesh, the public agency would not be strengthened due to at least two interest groups—strengthening a public business agency is the antithesis of a free market so it is against the neoliberal reforms agenda, and it is against the emerging business community. On the one hand, like the Bangladesh Agricultural Development Corporation (BADC), the TCB was crippled by the pressure of the international agencies (IvCSPol10); on the other hand, business community members are not willing to see it as an active institution (IvGoB4) as they will lose their monopoly over the market.

The government failure to maintain the effective institution necessary for market rectification is mainly the outcome of patronage politics, in particular, public corruption and rent-seeking behaviour (for details, see Chapter 3). These failures must be seen in the context of large-scale and visible corruption, weak state capacity, and the elite's beliefs. For example, on 12 April 2011, one of the most influential daily Bengali newspapers, the daily *Prothom-alo,* reported that the government was importing rice at $580 and $575 per tonne from Thailand and Vietnam respectively, when at the same time private importers were importing it from Vietnam at between $420 and $430 per tonnes. A report of the daily *Bangkok Post* (29 March 2011) 'questioned' the deal between Bangladesh and Thailand. The report went on to suggest that under this deal some requirements were designed so that only certain major exporters can get the opportunity to export to Bangladesh. By citing Pranee Siriphand, Deputy Director-General of the Foreign Trade Department of the Thai government, the *Bangkok Post* added that these conditions were set to meet the demands of the Bangladeshi government.

This section illustrated four major challenges faced in the effective import of foodgrains in Bangladesh in order to promote food availability by means of international trade. Firstly, uncertainties with regard to foodgrain imports which are focussed on the global rice market. Secondly, weak state capacity and the inefficient decision-making mechanism of the government. Thirdly, lack of effective state regulation and monitoring of private sector traders. Fourthly, because of rent-seeking, public corruption, and administrative inefficiency, the TCB (the government institution) is not capable of carrying out effective imports.

THE POLITICS OF FOOD AID, FOOD AVAILABILITY AND ITS SIGNIFICANCE IN CONTEMPORARY BANGLADESH

In the previous two sections of this chapter, my discussion has reflected on the two most important components of food availability in Bangladesh—domestic production and international trade. Here, I endeavour to examine food aid as a component of food availability, which is generally considered as an important means of promoting food availability, particularly in a least developed, low income, food deficit country. Food aid is particularly applicable as 'poorer countries often lack the foreign exchange necessary to purchase commercially all the food needed to meet their population's nutritional requirements' (Barrett 2001: 335) which was the case for Bangladesh in the 1970s. However, in this section, I am keen to investigate whether food aid is an important means of promoting food availability in contemporary Bangladesh. This issue is worth investigating as the conditions of food availability mean that there is a steady supply of foodgrains at all times, while the fact is that there is no guarantee that Bangladesh can receive food aid in a crisis. Moreover, by employing the central framework of this thesis, here I attempt to explicate the way in which rent-seeking, corruption and partial reform impede the receipt and allocation of food aid along with two other factors relating to weak state capacity and poor governance.

I begin this part of the chapter with a critical review of the food aid literature and then examine the historical background of food aid in Bangladesh which suggests that food aid played a significant role in meeting food availability in Bangladesh in the 1970s and then gradually became insignificant. It then examines the reliability of food aid as a source of food availability focussing on two major food crises in Bangladesh. The chapter then deals with the justification for food aid in the context of contemporary Bangladesh. I then discuss factors that impede the allocations of food aid programmes.

A Brief Review of Food aid Literature

Highlighting the positive contributions of food aid in disaster relief and in assisting several European and East Asian countries to improve their economies after periods of major political and economic crises, some suggest that food aid has been effective in achieving its objectives (for details, see Awokuse 2011). In contrast, a plethora of food aid literature attempts to address a moot question: whether or not food aid stabilizes food availability. So far, most of the researchers tend to be skeptical. For example, Barrett (2001) suggests 'unlikely'. Critics of food aid suggest that it not only fails to adequately benefit the recipient country to compensate for these costs but it actually puts farmers out of business, leads their children to adopt exotic tastes that can be satisfied only by imports, and enables their governments to neglect agricultural reform (Stevens 1979: 13). In other words, it has the potential to create disincentive effects in recipient countries (see Schultz 1960; Isenman & Singer 1977; Maxwell & Singer 1979; Cathie 1981).

The Political Economy of Food Aid in Bangladesh

The economy of Bangladesh suffered a serious setback during the war of liberation in 1971. As a result, there was an absolute fall in gross domestic production in the post-liberation period. Per capita income in 1971-2 was about 22 per cent lower than in 1969-70 in constant prices of 1972-3 (Islam 1978: 4). As with many other sectors of the economy, agricultural production was seriously affected by the war of liberation. Consequently, the new nation went through a famine-like situation although it was able to avoid a large-scale famine until 1973 in spite of war-related disruptions in food production, infrastructure, and marketing. Maniruzzaman (1975: 117) noted that in the first two years after Independence, war-ravaged Bangladesh was able to avoid a major economic crisis and large-scale famine mainly because of the massive relief operation carried out by the United Nations Relief Organization in Bangladesh (UNROB) and other international organizations.[17] In this period, humanitarian concerns became the overwhelming motivator of food aid shipments to Bangladesh. In the first few months, India was the chief food aid supplier (Sobhan 1982), followed by a number of countries which responded with shipments and the new government which began significant commercial imports (Atwood et al. 2000: 151). However, with the winding up of UNROB operations on 31 December 1973, the Bangladesh economy began to show increasing signs of crisis (Maniruzzaman 1975: 117) which was followed by the catastrophic famine of 1974.

Lessons of the Bangladesh famine of 1974 made it imperative for the successive governments in power to organize swift relief, import foodgrains to stabilize the rice price, and work hard to prevent famine. As a result, it has been observed that while famine became a recurrent feature in some parts of Africa in the 1970s,

1980s and 1990s, Bangladesh has successfully avoided a recurrence of famine since 1974. After the famine of 1974, Bangladesh experienced several floods in 1984, 1988, and 1998 and droughts in 1979. The cost of these floods and droughts was more devastating, in terms of crop and property damage, than the 1974 floods. Why then did famine not occur in 1984, 1988, or 1998, years of severe floods, or in 1979, a year of drought? Drawing on the 1984 floods' case, Clay (1985: 202-3) suggests that several important institutional changes in the agricultural system, in the food system as managed through governmental intervention, and in the political system more generally, appear to have contributed to famine being averted.

The fact, as Clay (ibid.) points out, is that the better relationship between the government and donors helped the government to avert famine, particularly in the period of 1975-90. In November 1975, General Ziaur Rahman (Zia) emerged as the 'strong man' after a series of coups and counter-coups. Unlike the Mujib regime, Zia formed a closer relationship with the United States and its Western allies. Zia also moved to harmonize ties with Muslim countries, particularly Saudi Arabia and the People's Republic of China, which had opposed Bangladesh's creation and had not recognized it until August 1975. As a result, Zia's regime received unprecedented international support to rebuild the war-torn nation;[18] particularly food aid which helped his government to secure food availability to avert famine.

Under the new political setting, the mounting flow of international aid helped to prevent any famine-like situation during the era of Zia and his successors. The Bangladesh government imported 11.56 lakh tonnes of foodgrains from different sources to meet the food deficit that developed after the drought of 1979. Of the total amount of imported food in 1979, only a negligible amount (0.6 lakh tonnes) was imported in cash (Molla 1990: 40). In this period, US food aid played a major role in stabilizing the foodgrain market in Bangladesh. In contrast to 1974, when political differences between governments and donors, particularly the United States, intensified problems, no such problems exacerbated the crises either in 1979 or in 1984 or more recently. In

1978, the first PL 480 Title III agreement was signed between the Government of Bangladesh and the Government of the United States of America. This agreement was extended with a second agreement in 1982, which was programmed through to 1985. According to the agreement between the two governments, this programme aimed 'to assist the Bangladesh government in accelerating increases in agricultural production by maintaining incentives prices for farmers, improving food security by holding reserves, reducing the food subsidy through the phase down of the ration system, moderating price increases with the Open Market Sales Programme, and providing resources to support specific Bangladesh Government Agricultural and Rural Development Programmes' (as cited in ibid.: 42). In addition to US support for improving the food security of Bangladesh, other donors and international agencies also significantly took part in this mission. For example, a cash programme was funded by international donors (led by the Japanese) to provide additional storage for about 200,000 tonnes of grain by the summer of 1981 (Franda 1982: 207). As a result, storage was widely spread throughout the country. These changes added up to considerably improved capacity within the Public Distribution System to move and store large quantities of food.

While in 1974, government officials including the Prime Minister were persistently appealing to donors particularly to the US government but failed to arrange any foodgrain for the famine victims, Bangladesh received wholehearted support from the international community without any difficulties in 1979, 1984, and 1987-8. In 1979, according to Osmani (1991: 331), not only were the donors generous and prompt in their response, even the IMF was very understanding. The country was under a standby agreement with the IMF in that year and there was, inevitably, an agreed ceiling on government borrowing. That ceiling was breached as the government borrowed heavily from the Central Bank in order to finance its commercial imports, but the IMF did not create any fuss (ibid.). The donors were somewhat less forthcoming in 1984, but nowhere near as niggardly as in 1974 (ibid.). It would not be a generalization to claim that the popular understanding about the government's ability to import foodgrains, either as a form of food aid or by purchasing, was premised on the belief of whether or not the government would be able to implement a suitable stabilizing response to the reported damage to the future crop. In the crises of 1979, 1984, 1987 and 1998, the government lined up imports on both aid and/or commercial bases. As a consequence, it orchestrated a positive belief that the government would be able to maintain the stability of the food market.

Food Aid as a Source of Food Availability: Bangladesh's Experience

Both historical evidence as well as the theoretical discussion of food aid suggest that there is no guarantee that Bangladesh will receive food aid during a crisis. Using historical data, many disparage food aid as they find it inherently politically motivated. A number of studies show that many bilateral food aid programmes and food aid projects were motivated by both political and economic interests of the donors (see Awokuse 2011; Eggleston 1987; Shapouri & Missiaen 1990; Ball & Johnson 1996; Clay, Pillai & Benson 1998; Neumayer 2005). During the 1973-4 food crisis, the CIA believed that increasing grain shortages could give 'Washington . . . virtual life and death power over the fate of the multitudes of the needy' (as cited in George 1991: 16).

Using the case of the Bangladesh famine of 1974 for illustration, I will firstly aim to provide an example where Bangladesh failed to manage food aid in a crisis because of political reasons. In 1974, during a time of severe food crisis, the bilateral relationship between Bangladesh and the USA seriously collapsed over the issue of Bangladeshi-Cuban jute trade. On 29 May 1974, the US ambassador in Bangladesh, David Boster, informed Kamal Hossain, the Foreign Minister of Bangladesh, that Bangladesh's export of four million jute bags to Cuba legally barred it from receiving any American food assistance. According to Boster, US Congressional laws expressly forbade such commitments to any country trading with Cuba or North Vietnam. However, Boster stated that only the President could waive the ban with a certificate that such aid was in the US national interest (Islam 2005; Sobhan 1979). This message was conveyed at a time when the price of rice was on a steadily upward trend. Islam (2005), Deputy Chairman of the first Planning Commission of Bangladesh, suggests that owing to the severe food crisis, in July 1974, the Government of Bangladesh took necessary initiatives to clarify with written assurances that the deal with Cuba, made by the Jute Corporation of Bangladesh, which was not aware of the provisions of US law, would not be repeated. Moreover, the Government of Bangladesh cancelled further exports of jute to Cuba (McHenry & Bird 1977: 82). And the Government of Bangladesh continuously pleaded to Washington for food aid. Despite the initiatives of the Government of Bangladesh, in the words of McHenry and Bird (ibid.), 'the U.S. government employed its food aid leverage in Bangladesh for the most trifling of political purposes' and held back aid to Bangladesh. To seek emergency support from the US, the Prime Minister of Bangladesh visited the US in November 1974 but the trip was frustrating and he was treated quite casually. It is to be noted that despite well-published information about Egyptian-Cuban trade, on 7 June 1974, the United States signed a credit to Egypt under PL 480 Title 1 (Sobhan 1979).[19]

In addition to the 1974 food crisis, in the most recent food crisis of 2007-8, Bangladesh also failed to receive food aid to ensure food availability at the national level. Bangladesh received the lowest food aid since its Independence in the period of 2006-7 and subsequently (see Islam 2012: 205). Hence, considering these two historical experiences of Bangladesh, food aid does not guarantee an uninterrupted supply of food which is the most important feature of food availability at the national level.

The Winds of Change: Food Aid as a Means of Food availability in the Context of Today's Bangladesh

As noted earlier, during the food crisis of 1974, Bangladesh had two major difficulties in importing foodgrains to ensure food availability and thereby averting famine—it had a shortage of the foreign exchange necessary to purchase commercially and it had a troubled relationship with the USA, the main source of food aid.

Soon after its birth as a nation state, resource-poor Bangladesh was dubbed as a 'test case' for development while Henry Kissinger called it 'an international basket case'. After 40 years of Independence, Banerjee and Duflo (2011: 267) state that 'basket cases, such as Bangladesh or Cambodia, turn into small miracles'. Bangladesh has achieved considerable growth in food production, a good record of disaster management, and famines have become a phenomenon of the past (Chowdhury & Mahmud 2008: 95). In addition to increasing the scale of domestic production and the country's ability to import foodgrains, various indicators such as life expectancy, population growth, child mortality rates and literacy rate all show the country's remarkable progress. The per capita GDP of Bangladesh has also more than doubled since 1975.

As a result of the slow but steady progress of the country, in the context of food availability, the role of food aid has decreased dramatically Islam (2012: 206) shows that food aid is insignificant in contemporary Bangladesh compared to the total national food availability. At present, a very negligible percentage of food aid contributes to the national food availability of Bangladesh. In their influential paper entitled 'Food Aid in Bangladesh: From Relief to Development', Atwood et al. (2000: 161) conclude that:

> Three separate developments have combined to build uncertainty, undermine the standard operating procedures for managing monetized food aid through the PFDS, [Public Food Distribution System] and create the need for both donors and government to forge a new food-aid strategy for the 1990s and beyond—macroeconomic stabilization, increased domestic foodgrain production in Bangladesh, and growing need for emergency food worldwide. These developments have worked together in various ways to reduce food aid levels to Bangladesh . . . it is clear that Bangladesh now has the capacity to produce additional foodgrain if effective demand (primarily dependent on incomes of the poor) were to grow. At the same time, the success of [the] government's macroeconomic stabilization programme has led to an unprecedented increase in public revenue and foreign exchange reserves.

The paper further emphasised that 'while success in promoting investment and economic growth would reduce or eliminate these surpluses, and possibly take up the existing foodgrain productive capacity as well, the three basic rationales for food aid have been seriously eroded in Bangladesh budget support, foreign exchange support, and filling the food gap' (ibid.). Similarly, considering the scenario of the rapid increase in rice and wheat production in Bangladesh, Dorosh et al. (2004: 268) assert that 'if these abundant harvests and low foodgrain prices persist, continued large-scale distribution of food aid through the PFDS could result in disincentive effects'. They further point out that the low flows of food aid will not cause price disincentive effects on Bangladeshi wheat production.[20] In order to avoid producer price disincentives, the study by Dorosh et al. (ibid.) suggested that 'donors could provide the equivalent value of resources in the form of cash, either to permit the Government of Bangladesh to produce foodgrain locally for these programmes or to use direct in re-designed cash for work or other cash programmes'. In other words, food aid is no longer necessary for ensuring food availability, but rather it can jeopardize agricultural growth in Bangladesh.

Despite the fact that Bangladesh has achieved considerable progress in economic growth and food production, a significant proportion of people below the poverty line remain hungry and undernourished. Moreover, as noted in Chapter 4, for a number of reasons, food accessibility is still a major challenge for the hungry poor in Bangladesh. It is argued that 'market-based policies and interventions alone are unlikely to make any noticeable change in the nutritional status of these hard-core poor' (Ahmed et al. 2004: 1). In view of these challenges, Atwood et al. (2000: 162) note that today the question of food aid is not for donors but for government. Most strikingly as a matter of concern is whether or not the government is willing to use some of its own resources to continue targeted food programmes if donors' food aid levels continue to decline (ibid.)? In other words, although food aid is marginally filling the gaps of national level food availability, it is possible to fill these gaps by using alternative means—donors could provide the equivalent value of resources or the state could use its own resources.

It is important to note that although the role of food aid in Bangladesh is relatively insignificant, uncertainty about food aid is huge as there is no guarantee that Bangladesh will receive food aid when it is needed. Ahmed et al. (2004) suggest that the timeliness of food aid arrival is an important determinant in PFDS stock management in Bangladesh. Food aid arrivals frequently coincide with the domestic procurement seasons of the Government of Bangladesh, leading to higher losses due to more movements and higher stock rotation time. Moreover, there is also no guarantee of the timely arrival of food aid.[21] In recent years, the role of food aid in combating global food insecurity has noticeably been declining. For example, according to available data from the WFO, in 2009, total global food aid was only one-third (5,482,296.7 actual tonnes) of what it had been in 1988 (14,048,281.4 actual tonnes). This trend indicates that food aid may further decline in the near future.[22] Hence, while the state has the ability to fill the food gap by using its own resources and the global trend of food aid is declining, there is no doubt that avoiding food aid is the safest way to ensure food availability.

Efficiency of Food Aid in Bangladesh: Corruption, Partial Reform and Poor Governance

Some of the literature doubts the efficiency of food aid throughout the world (e.g. see OECD 2006; Clay, Pillai & Benson 1998; Pillai 2000; Jayne et al. 2001; Subbarao & Smith 2003). Clay, Dhiri and Benson (1996) contend that food aid has been ineffective and has produced dismal results. If food aid is seen as inefficient in general, then it is imperative to examine its efficiency in the context of Bangladesh, particularly with regard to a question relating to this thesis—how does rent-seeking, corruption, partial reform, state weakness and poor governance impede the allocation of food aid in Bangladesh?

Food aid in Bangladesh has been utilized mainly through the channels of the Public Food Distribution System (PFDS) and Social Safety Nets (SSN) programmes. Most of the programmes supported by food aid in Bangladesh are credited with providing poor people with access to food and improving their food security. Findings from the most recent household income and expenditure survey

(BBS 2011) suggest that these programmes are reasonably well-targeted towards the poor. The poverty incidence of the beneficiaries of the SSN programmes is 43.4 per cent overall, compared with 27.5 per cent poverty incidence of the population not included in the SSN programmes. However, the poverty incidence of the population not included in SSN programmes in Rangpur (37.6 per cent) and Barisal (33.5 per cent) is higher than the national average poverty incidence which means that these programmes are reaching the poor but not all the poor everywhere. It is important to note that the Rangpur division consists of eight districts most of which are known for seasonal hunger (*monga*) and that it is one of the 'less included' regions in terms of the beneficiaries of the SSN programmes. Although the recent survey (ibid.) suggests that PFDS and/or SSN programmes are reasonably well-targeted towards the poor, any number of studies conclude that inefficiency, corruption, and political motivation of programmes of the food distribution system are most likely hindering the realization of the full benefits of these programmes (Ahmed et al. 2003, 2004; Murgai & Zaidi 2005). For example, Murgai and Zaidi (2005) doubt that the visible receipts of transfers are significantly pro-poor. Instead, they point out that a large share of the total resources devoted to these programmes disappears before reaching their intended beneficiaries (ibid.). In order to examine the capacity and efficiency of the food distribution system, the study by Ahmed et al. (2004) assesses its three components: (a) food discharge at harbours; (b) the Public Food Distribution System, and (c) food distribution to programme beneficiaries. The study by Ahmed et al. (ibid.) reveals the following points: First, the study shows various types of anomalies in all discharge operations at harbours by the Government of Bangladesh which is inefficient compared to others such as CARE and World Vision. The Government of Bangladesh operations are lacking in systematic record-keeping and in the interagency coordination needed in order to use information for timely actions—the study also unveiled the degree and nature of operational loss and spillage.

Second, the study shows that transit and storage losses in the Public Food Distribution System (PFDS) are still large; the movement of PFDS foodgrains from one Local Supply Depot (LSD) to another LSD within a district is high (17 to 48 per cent of the total PFDS foodgrain off-take); analysis of stock rotation suggests that 35 per cent of the foodgrains distributed to beneficiaries is more than nine months old; the implicit cost of stock deterioration is high; and the timeliness of food aid arrival is an important determinant in PFDS stock management. The study further suggests that food aid arrivals frequently coincide with the Government of Bangladesh's domestic procurement seasons, leading to higher losses due to more movements and higher stock rotation time.

Third, the Union Parishad (UP) chairpersons and members who distribute foodgrains to beneficiaries report lengthy delays or non-receipt of transport and handling commissions: the survey of UP officials indicates that, on average, they received 3.5 per cent less wheat from LSDs than their allotted quantity. In the Vulnerable Group Development (VGD) Programme, one-third of the beneficiaries expressed concern about the quality of the wheat (insect infestation was the most common problem); the overall leakage in the VGD programme is 8.01 per cent of the total wheat allotment: there are also different types of anomalies and leakages in the food distribution.

By examining food assistance programmes in Bangladesh, the above-mentioned study (Ahmed et al. 2004) demonstrates inefficiency, corruption and rent-seeking in all three major components of the study, that is, food discharge at harbours, the Public Food Distribution System and food distribution to programme beneficiaries. It is to be noted that of the many programmes, the study chose two for this food aid leakage study at the beneficiary level—the VGD and the Integrated Food Security (IFS) programmes. The VGD programme in Bangladesh, the world's largest development intervention of its kind that exclusively targets women, is reported to be better targeted to the excluded since it is concentrated in the more deprived areas of the country. On the other hand, the IFS is a new component which began in 2001. In addition to these two programmes, expenditure for similar types of other programmes is also vulnerable to leakage to the non-poor due to the rent-seeking proclivities of the politicians and officials who mediate these payments to the poor (Sobhan 2010). In Chapter 6, my discussion will exclusively deal with the 'target error' and 'leakage error' of the PFDS and SSN programmes in Bangladesh. I will demonstrate that through the channels of PFDS and SSN which are mostly politically motivated programmes, the government food subsidy fails to reach the poor and, thereby, fails to effectively generate entitlement. I will also argue that despite food policy reforms throughout the 1980s and early 1990s, target error or 'pro-better off' programmes still remain in the PFDS of Bangladesh. Thus, I will suggest that food policy reform is, in fact, a classic example of the partial reform syndrome in Bangladesh.

Not surprisingly, the Bangladesh case does not suggest that public corruption, rent-seeking, poor governance, etc., are determinant factors that can impede the receipt of food aid. Islam (2012: 212) that in the 1980s the military regime of General H.M. Ershad received the highest level of food aid in Bangladesh. I also noted in earlier discussion that the largest influx of food aid in Bangladesh was during the first military regime of General Ziaur Rahman. These military regimes were not only corrupt—the toxic political culture they introduced and practised has been the fundamental cause of the abysmally bad governance of contemporary Bangladesh (see Milam 2007). Hence, that rent-seeking, corruption and partial reform impeded the allocation of food aid along with two other factors relating to state weakness and poor governance. However, this chapter does not demonstrate that a regime could receive less food aid because of factors such as rent-seeking, corruption and partial reform.

Based on the discussion in this section, I suggest that further research is needed to understand an important question—to what extent can the Bangladesh state rely on food aid for promoting food availability? The question needs to be considered along with the progress Bangladesh has made, disincentive effects in rice and wheat production, and leakages and errors in food aid-based programmes.

CONCLUSION

This chapter examined the role of the Bangladesh state in promoting food availability in order to ensure food security. In doing so, it examined three aspects of food availability: domestic production, trade, and food aid.

First, this chapter demonstrated a number of key weaknesses of the state in promoting agricultural growth. In addition to the trend of the gradually decreasing budgetary allocation to the agriculture sector, the state has also not been doing 'enough' to take the necessary measures to promote agricultural growth in a manner that can promote food availability in a sustainable manner. Using five key concepts, this chapter shows that poor state performances in economic management as well as agricultural governance that is, rent-seeking, public corruption, partial reform, poor governance, and weak state capacity, either combined or individually, have a clear impact on developing the state's agricultural development policies and/or implementation. As a consequence, the state's initiatives in the development agenda for agriculture, such as the fertilizer subsidy and/or distribution, failed to provide meaningful support to poor farmers. Thus, by demonstrating poor economic management, weak state regulation and monitoring, partial reforms and the state's incapacity to develop appropriate policies and implement them, I suggest that the state has left farmers virtually on their own.

Second, with regard to trade and food availability, this chapter illustrates four major challenges to the effective import of foodgrains in Bangladesh in order to promote food availability by means of international trade. First, there are uncertainties with regard to foodgrain imports which are focussed on the global rice market. Second, the government decision making mechanism in Bangladesh is very slow. There is also a lack of institutional building for a strong early warning system which is particularly critical, as the main reason for the fluctuation of food availability in Bangladesh is natural disasters, such as flood and drought. Third, because of patronage politics and poor governance, there is an 'absence' of effective state regulation and monitoring of private sector traders and, therefore, it often causes harm rather than actuate a steady supply of foodgrains. And fourth, for there to be a steady supply of foodgrains, some emphasize the necessity of mobilizing the TCB—I have argued that the government institution of the TCB is not capable of effective imports due to rent-seeking, public corruption and administrative inefficiency. By addressing these four main failures of the state, I suggest that international trade is not a safe means of ensuring food availability in the neopatrimonial state of Bangladesh.

Thirdly, although historically Bangladesh is one of the largest food aid recipient countries, historical experience also suggests that the country failed to manage food aid during its crises in both 1974 and 2007-8. Moreover, with considerable growth in agricultural production as well as progress in other sectors, the importance of food aid has been seriously eroded. Indeed, questions have been raised about whether food aid could result in disincentive effects on rice and wheat production. However, the truth is that there is still a large segment of poor people who live below the poverty line—state intervention is required to support the nutritional status of these hardcore poor. In the process, my discussion reveals the failure of the Bangladesh state to reach the intended real beneficiaries of the various food aid-based programmes. Expenditure for food aid-based programmes is vulnerable to leakage to the non-poor due to rent-seeking, widespread corruption, poor governance and institutional incapacity.

NOTES

1. The availability of foodgrains can be ensured by domestic food production and/or trade and/or food aid or a combination of these. Many nations enjoy food security from domestic food production as it is considered to be one of the major sources of food availability. On the other hand, trade and/or food aid can also provide important support to ensure food availability in nations experiencing a food deficit, and thereby provide food security. It is believed that improved food production will increase the amount of food available locally; expanded employment will strengthen poor people's purchasing power; countries experiencing food deficits will need to import less food,

thereby reserving foreign exchange for other critical international transactions; and the unit price of food to the local consumer will be reduced, thereby enabling poor people to consume more food (Mellor 1987; Hollist & Tullis, 1987: 3). On the other hand, with today's deeper international markets, lower real prices, and more countries with convertible exchange rates, trade can stabilize food availability and prices for most countries (World Bank 2007: 94-5). However, there is no doubt that foodgrain availability through domestic production is a safe way to promote food security. Domestic foodgrain production, or agriculture, is one of the significant drivers of 'national power', and it is, therefore, the aim of every nation state (except a city state like Singapore) to develop its agriculture sector. Stagnation or decline in domestic production and large fluctuations clearly raise the potential problem of food availability at the national level (ibid.).

2. In pursuance of ensuring food security, agricultural development is vital in Bangladesh as approximately 71.41 per cent of the population live in rural areas, and about 44.41 per cent of the labour force is employed in agriculture (FAOSTAT 2012).
3. Prior to 1987, BADC continued to retain a monopoly on the purchase of fertilizer on the international market and on wholesale distribution by appointing dealers through a complex process. Similarly, all donor-provided fertilizer supplies were also channelled through BADC. In this process, dealers had to sell fertilizer at government fixed prices in a defined area. In March 1987, the World Bank initiated a project or programme entitled 'Fertilizer Distribution Improvement Project II (FDI-II), which was completed in 1994. The aim of this project, according to the Bank, was to increase agricultural production through improved use of fertilizer by focussing initially on technology transfer and on increases in private sector participation.
4. Similarly, using data of a survey of 820 rice, potato, bean, eggplant, cabbage, sugarcane and mango farmers in Bangladesh, Dasgupta, Meisner and Huq (2007) demonstrate the evidence of pesticide overuse. For example, over 47 per cent of farmers were found to be overusing pesticides. With only 4 per cent of farmers formally trained in pesticide use or handling, and over 87 per cent openly admitting to using little or no protective measures while applying pesticides, overuse is potentially a great threat to farmer health as well as the environment. The results of the study highlight the necessity for policymakers to design effective and targeted outreach programmes which deal specifically with pesticide risk and safe handling and averting behaviour.
5. It is important to note that in the 1950s, during the 'Pakistan period', efforts

to increase agricultural productivity by introducing more efficient types of technology commenced with irrigation. It was with water that the Government of Pakistan began its earliest efforts (known as 'Green Revolution') aimed at the technological transformation of agricultural production, as the lack of water control has been considered to be one of the main factors contributing to the decline per capita of agricultural output in Bangladesh (Boyce 1986; also Lewis 1991). After liberation, in the 1970s and in early 1980s, the promotion of irrigation was primarily made through BADC, which retained full ownership of irrigation equipment, which it rented out at a highly subsidized rate to cooperatives and irrigation groups on an annual basis. BADC bought Deep Tube Wells (DTWs)—with the capacity to water 12-15 hectares of land. In addition, Low Lift Pumps (LLPs) were also hired for irrigation via the focussing surface water. At that time, private sector intervention in minor irrigation was banned. Later, however, BADC decided to sell DTWs and LLPs to farmers, and these were primarily bought by rich farmers or land owners (Hossain & Bayes 2009: 270). To avoid a state monopoly over the water and in order to make water accessible to all farmers, a Shallow Tube Well (STW) Project was initiated with the assistance of the World Bank, in which the innovation of private or group ownership (rather than state ownership) was introduced (World Bank 1977). At about the same time, a similar project assisted by the Asian Development Bank also enabled individuals or groups to purchase STWs (Khan 1989: 29).

6. Until the beginning of the 1990s, BADC was responsible for seed production and seed supply. Because of the restrictions on imports of seeds by the private sector, in the late 1980's, the private sector only supplied about 5 per cent of the total requirement for seed (Huda 2001: 258). On the contrary, according to National Agricultural Policy 1999 (p. 5), 'At present, only a small portion of the required quality seeds for different crops is supplied by the Bangladesh Agricultural Development Corporation (BADC). The rest of the seeds are produced, preserved and used under private management, especially at the farmers' level.' To encourage the private sector, a National Seed Policy (NSP) was declared in 1993 whereby the private sector and NGOs were allowed to import, develop and register new varieties of all seeds and distribute them to the farmers. Initially there was a restriction to five notified crops such as rice, wheat, sugarcane, potato and jute. For importing seeds of notified crops, the private sector and NGOs had to observe some procedural formalities. Some private sector companies and NGOs had signed a Memorandum of Understanding (MoU) with the Bangladesh Rice Research Institute (BRRI) to have access to breeders' seed for the purpose of expanding activities in the production of foundation

seed and certified seed (Rahman & Deb 2005: 89). Today, according to the National Agricultural Policy 2010, seed companies and NGOs have started supplying seed primarily the hybrids of rice, maize and vegetables. It further suggests that 'private persons, companies and other agencies will be encouraged to undertake plant breeding programmes and to import breeder/foundation seeds of notified crops for variety development and promotional purposes (NAP 2010)'.

7. As Hans Herren argues, genetically modified crops 'will not feed the hungry, they will make them poorer' (speech to the Overseas Development Institute, London, October 1998; as cited in Madeley 2002: 65). Paarlberg (2010) notes, 'Because of consumer anxieties about GMOs, nearly all of the transgenic crops approved so far by regulators have either been industrial crops (e.g. cotton) or crops used primarily for animal feed (e.g. soybeans and yellow corn).' He further adds, as of 2009, only South Africa approved the production of a GMO variety of white maize in 2002.
8. Here it is important to 'locate' the state's involvement in agricultural research in Bangladesh. Unlike developed countries where the centre of research excellence and knowledge dissemination is universities, universities in Bangladesh, in general, and, in particular, agricultural universities, do not play significant role in research. Under the Ministry of Education, Bangladesh now has three agricultural universities (two of which are quite new and still struggling to be established). The main focus of these universities is largely on teaching in recent years mainly due to declining research funds. In addition, as universities are not involved in the planning or implementation of NARS's research programmes, any impacts of BAU's (Bangladesh Agricultural University, the main university in this type) work is not known (World Bank 2005: 21). Moreover, Bangladesh has in total 11 national agricultural research institutes. Among these, the research of the Bangladesh Rice Research Institute (BRRI) only focusses on rice, the staple food, while the Bangladesh Agricultural Research Institute (BARI) deals with cereals (other than rice). The major responsibilities of the Bangladesh Agricultural Research Council (BARC) are coordination, prioritization and monitoring of agricultural research. Research by the rest of the institutes is primarily centred on jute, sugarcane, application of nuclear techniques, soil, tea, livestock and poultry, fisheries and forestry.
9. For example, expenditure declined from about 14 per cent of total expenditure on agriculture in 1997-8 to about 5 per cent in 2004-5.
10. The share of total expenditure on agricultural research is not only very small but has declined from 0.29 per cent of agricultural GDP in 1997-8 to 0.22 per cent in 2004-5 (the decline is even more dramatic from

0.34 per cent in 1999-2000 to 0.20 per cent in 2002-3). Agricultural research expenditure is about 0.62 per cent of agricultural GDP in developing countries as a group and 2.80 per cent in developed countries as a group (Pardy, Alston and Piggott 2006; cited in WB 2005).

11. For example, out of 304 sanctioned positions for scientists in BRRI, 43 positions remained vacant in 2005, as timely recruitment was not arranged because of the bureaucratic difficulties (see Table 3.1, WB 2005).
12. For example, according to a World Bank study, the share of total expenditure on agricultural extension has increased from 0.83 per cent of agricultural GDP in 1997-8 to 1.05 per cent in 2003-4 and then declined to 1.03 per cent in 2004-5 (WB 2005: 37).
13. A World Bank (2005: 50) study also draw a similar conclusion: 'Field workers have tended to visit mostly the large and more resource-endowed farmers in easily accessible areas. The poor and female farmers, although better served than in the past, still feel neglected. They neither receive regular visits from public extension staff nor benefit from the farmer-to-farmer diffusion of technology from farmers receiving direct service (larger farmers) from DAE, DOF or DLS'.
14. Medium holdings for Bangladesh: 7.5 acres and above.
15. Because of poor economic management as well as patronage politics, historically the business community in Bangladesh was never considered trustworthy enough for the government to rely on. A recent study by the Ministry of Finance (2011) estimated that the total amount of black money in Bangladesh was between 46 per cent (minimum) and 81 per cent (maximum) of total GDP. Generally speaking, black money refers to undeclared money on which income and other taxes have not been paid. Similarly, the World Development Report 2009 indicates that the tax/GDP ratio in Bangladesh is only 10.3 per cent (World Bank 2008). In this regard, it is worthwhile to quote a foreign donor: 'Bangladesh cannot afford a private sector. They (the business community) do not pay taxes; they do not repay their bank loans; and they do not pay their utility bills' (as cited in Kochanek 1993: 199). In his *Patron-Client Politics and Business in Bangladesh*, Kochanek (ibid.) explicitly demonstrates the nature of businessmen in Bangladesh. He argues that: 'rapid growth and government policy have created a large class of 'briefcase' businessmen and indentors who make huge profits by taking advantage of the system without producing anything. They secure huge bank loans which they do not repay, create phantom factories that do not produce, and earn large commissions for doing very little' (1993: 198). Another study also suggests that rich businessmen in Dhaka acquired their wealth through a process of primitive

capital accumulation which included theft, embezzlement, smuggling, hoarding, and black-marketeering, as well as the manipulation of artificial scarcities, and influencing peddling (Siddiqui et al. 1990: 80-1; as cited in Kochanek 1993: 199). Until recently, as I argued in Chapter 2, the business-politics nexus is the predominant characteristic of both politics and business in Bangladesh. The fact is that, over the years, the image as well as the quality of business has improved in Bangladesh. However, public understanding about the major sectors of the business community is still ambivalent and skeptical which is reflected in the popular understanding about 'market syndication'.

16. Other features recommended by Clay are: the development of monitoring of the operation of the foodgrain system; 'there is a hard-to-assess level of government commitment to containing price movements and maintaining distribution of food as well as preventing food-related stress on the poor getting out of hand'; the changing pattern of government behaviour in managing the food system (i.e. in terms of off-take and procurement, the food system is now managed more closely in relation to price movements); improving food security for the rural poor (this includes the 'Food for Work' programme supported by the WFP and USAID); the development of regional and seasonal distribution of allocations for poverty and disaster mapping; and improving storage capacity from something over 1 million tonnes in 1980 to 1.9 million tonnes in 1984. Along with these points, Clay (1985) also includes diversification of the agricultural system and a better relationship between the government and donors.
17. Bangladesh received a total of 1,373 million dollars in grants and credits from friendly countries during the first two years after liberation. See *The Bangladesh Observer*, Dhaka, 26 March 1974.
18. The USA, its Western allies, and Japan provided unprecedented economic support to the regime. Under US auspices, the World Bank, IMF, and other international agencies provided significant support. Over the duration of Zia's regime, US aid to Bangladesh added up to $1,177.15 million (Ali 2010: 151). Zia's regime also secured a total of $808.63 million in aid from Muslim states—of this, $541.84 million came from Saudi Arabia (Halim & Ahmed 1996: 130-6, as cited in Ali 2010: 151).
19. The fact is that the top recipients of food aid are not necessarily the most needy and most food-deficit countries (Barrett & Maxwell 2005: 9). In the words of Barrett (2001: 347), 'food aid has long been intensely political, serving many masters. So long as that remains the case, food aid is unlikely to stabilize per capita food availability effectively'. Similarly, drawing on public and private action in various famines, Cormac Ó Gráda (2009)

suggests that 'foreign aid, even in the form of emergency food aid, is rarely disinterested.' Perhaps no other countries resentfully experienced the bitter taste of food aid and its intensely political use more than Bangladesh, particularly in 1974.

20. Bangladesh mainly receives wheat as food aid. Therefore, the price disincentive effects of food aid will be caused to wheat production.
21. As I have argued in the context of national level food security, the term 'food availability' refers to the availability of sufficient food in a particular country from domestic production and/or international trade and/or food aid or a combination of all, which needs to be always available to the individuals of that country or within their reach in any circumstances without any interruption. As noted earlier, the Bangladesh case suggests that it failed to manage food aid during its crisis in 1974 which turned into famine. In other words, food aid didn't reliably arrive in Bangladesh when it was needed. Considering the recurrence of natural disasters, many suggest that food aid is still essential for emergency relief programmes. While many argue that emergency food aid has a positive contribution to mitigate short-term relief needs, Barrett and Maxwell (2005), OECD (2006) and Shaw (2002) criticize food aid for its lack of timeliness.
22. Harvey and Pilgrim (2011) point out that land as a global resource is likely to become the focus of intensified competition from a variety of uses which include food, energy and climate change. In the words of Tilman et al. (2009), we are living in a world seeking solutions to its energy, environmental, and food challenges. The study by Abbott, Hurt and Tyner (2008) shows how biofuels programmes in the United States and European Union are increasing the prices of these commodities.

CHAPTER 6

Governance, the State and Food Accessibility

INTRODUCTION

While market regulation is important to ensure food availability and protect poor consumers from any abnormal increase in the market price of foodgrains, entitlement generation by the direct initiative of the state is also significant, as many people are still too poor to afford enough food to sustain a healthy and productive life. In order to investigate the role of the state in entitlement generation, I examine the PFDS by offering a historical-political analysis. I examine how the PFDS of Bangladesh has evolved, developed, multiplied and diversified with special reference to its 'target errors' and 'leakage errors'. To understand the political economy of the PFDS in Bangladesh, I raise a series of questions: Is the PFDS designed to promote food security or is its purpose regime survival by using state resources? Do the various initiatives taken by the state to downsize the PFDS imply that the state is avoiding responsibility in creating entitlement to promote food security? Is there any other alternative public funded programme such as Social Safety Nets (SSN), for distribution to improve the accessibility of food? Does SSN promote food security to the vulnerable sections of the population?

On the other hand, considering the impact of the sudden price hike as an important impediment of food accessibility to the poor, this chapter seeks to explore the state mechanisms/initiatives of market regulation necessary for price stabilization. In other words, given the neopatrimonial nature of the state, I endeavour to investigate the challenges of food accessibility in Bangladesh in relation to market, market failure, and market interventions, which in other words can be called market management. In doing so, I am particularly interested to investigate what kinds of measures have been taken by the government to regulate market volatility and how effective that regulation has been.

This chapter proceeds in three further sections. The first section addresses the politics of entitlement generation under the auspices of the state, generally known as the Public Food Distribution System (PFDS) in Bangladesh. The second section deals with the state mechanisms/initiatives of market regulation essential for price stabilization. Finaly it concludes the chapter.

THE POLITICS OF THE PUBLIC FOOD DISTRIBUTION SYSTEM IN BANGLADESH: REGIME SURVIVAL OR FOOD SECURITY?

The food policy of Bangladesh can be described as 'once colonial, now global'[1]—while the origin of food policy in Bangladesh is the colonial legacy of British rule in South Asia; the present food policy of Bangladesh is the outcome of a series of policy reforms that took place throughout the 1980s and 1990s as a consequence of the liberalizing of foodgrain markets. Not surprisingly, donors, particularly USAID and the World Bank, are the key architects of the food policy reforms of Bangladesh (Montgomery 1983; Shahadat Ullah 1988; IFPRI 1993; Adams 1998; Chowdhury & Haggblade 2000). A sequence of studies (World Bank 1977, 1979, 1992; Adam 1998; and more recently World Bank 2004, 2006; Ahmed et al. 2004, 2007) identifies the PFDS of Bangladesh as a system of 'targeting errors' and 'leakage errors'. Since the early 1980s, under serious criticism as well as policy guidance from the donor community, the PFDS has gone through many reforms. As a result, the government has significantly downsized the PFDS, making poverty reduction a priority basis for grain allocation (Chowdhury, Farid & Roy 2006) with particular emphasis on SSN programmes.

The downsizing of the PFDS and attendant market-based reforms of the agricultural sector in Bangladesh in accord with the advice of the World Bank was brought into sharp focus by the 2007-8 global food crisis. As a result of the crisis there has been renewed debate concerning the importance of strategic national food grain reserves in both the academic and policy circles. On one hand, while it has recently been claimed that there is nothing anomalous about recent price rises (Wright 2012) others contend that changes in the agricultural food market has led to 'dramatic increases in price volatility' (Murphy 2012: 3). In this context an interesting debate has arisen concerning the relevance of national grain reserves to food security.[2]

In the context of an assessment of country strategies developed in response to the 2007-8 food crisis, the FAO provided an assessment of PFDS in Bangladesh both as a response to the crisis and its long-term role in providing food security. In terms of the 2007-8 food crisis the FAO provided a positive report and concluded that 'the food crisis in Bangladesh would probably have been worse if there were no public stocks and Public Distribution System in place' (FAO 2009: 16). In relation to the PFDS as a long-term solution to food security the FAO's report suggested a mixed outcome. On one hand, the FAO noted 'the grain reserve has enabled Bangladesh to rapidly respond to humanitarian needs . . .' and it 'appears to have been a rational response to the high and risk of frequent cyclones and floods and very high levels of poverty in the country' (ibid.). On the other hand, the report also claimed that the programme was very costly and inadequate to the needs of the poor. It noted that 'a more concerted effort and additional resources will be required for the food-based safety net programme to effectively cope with high food prices, large numbers of food insecure people and the unprecedented natural disasters that Bangladesh is faced with year in and year out' (ibid.).

Given the volatility of global food prices and the quest for food security, the debate on the relevance of strategic national food grain reserves is likely to continue for some time. In the context of this thesis, it is important to recognize that the Bangladesh government although applying some neo-liberal policies in the agricultural field never abandoned its commitment to a national food reserve policy. The rationale for maintaining a central role for the state through the mechanism of the PFDS will be discussed below. As will be demonstrated the fact that, the commitment to the PFDS cannot simply be reduced to an ideological commitment to an interventionist policy.

Differing from traditional analysis of the PFDS, I raise a question—is the PFDS being used as a means of regime survival rather than promoting food security by using state resources? In other words, I am interested to investigate the politics of the PFDS, with special reference to its political use. This question is worth examining, as the PFDS is a well-known state mechanism for generating entitlement for promoting food security. By examining the politics of the PFDS, I am particularly interested to investigate two main problems concerning its various programmes—the problems of targeting errors and leakage errors. In order to understand the politics of the errors of the PFDS, two questions are noteworthy to examine—what are the linkages between these errors and policy design and implementation by the neopatrimonial regimes? Is this linked, if there is any linkage, with the strategy of regime survival through patronage politics?

This section proceeds in six further sub-sections. In the next section, I critically expound the genesis, development, reforms and current situation of the PFDS. The second part of the chapter attempts to conceptualize the political economy of targeting errors and leakage errors of the PFDS. It then discusses the origin of targeting errors of the PFDS. This section suggests that the political elite of Bangladesh has always been using the PFDS as a means of regime survival rather than promoting food security. Section four explicates the origin of leakages. This section examines whether leakages are connected with the politics of neopatrimonial regimes. It then deals with the SSN programmes, poverty reduction strategy and food security. It finally discusses the role of the state in creating entitlement in Bangladesh using the budgetary allocation of the PFDS.

The Public Food Distribution System: Its Origins, Reforms, and Policy issues

What is the Public Food Distribution System?

The PFDS is a traditional government mechanism through which it seeks to cater to the foodgrain needs of different consumer groups—mainly the poor—and in so doing control foodgrain marketing through market intervention, support producers as well as consumers through enforcing floor and ceiling prices and managing disasters by providing relief. The PFDS is basically supported by government budgetary resources, food aid and financial assistance from the donor community. More specifically, it aims to achieve three different basic goals: (a) enforcing floor and ceiling prices to support producers as well as consumers; (b) managing disasters; and (c) targeting distribution to alleviate poverty and promoting food security. In order to achieve these goals, it has two basic functionalities/mechanisms: (1) collecting foodgrains to manage a public stock; and (2) distribution of those foodgrains. The former one can be divided in three main categories—domestic procurement, import, and food aid. To explain the PFDS, first I will explain these three categories of the government's procedures of collection of foodgrains, and then its distribution mechanism. It is important to examine the sources of public foodgrains and their distribution system by the government as the aim of this discussion is to understand the leakage and significance of the PFDS.

The domestic procurement system was introduced by the British government to stabilize the foodgrain market and to supply the ration shop, which was continued in East Pakistan until 1971 though on a very small scale. In the first two years after Independence, domestic procurement was ignored by the government because of the large influx of food aid. This state inability or inertia with respect to strengthening food stocks through internal procurement is considered as one of the main reasons for the failure of the government to prevent famine in 1974 (for example, see Alamgir 1980).[3] However, under the pressure of severe food shortages, a compulsory procurement scheme was launched in 1974-5. But it not only failed due to the administrative weakness of the government, but also encouraged hoarding by means of creating panic. As a consequence of the failure of domestic procurement and its impacts in foodgrain markets, successive governments were very careful about it. As a result, since 1975-6, internal procurement has become a major policy of the government. The rationale behind this was that even a modest quantity of stocks procured internally acts as a valuable underpinning of the PFDS. In 1994, after a series of policy reforms, Bangladesh liberalized trade policy to permit imports by private traders, which has become a major component of its stabilization policy (Rashid et al. 2008: 13). However, to minimize any emergency needs during disasters, the Government of Bangladesh still maintains modest amounts of security reserve via internal procurement. The National Food Policy 2006 (NFP 2006: 8) stated that in order to handle uncertainties of import arrival and emergency off-take requirements, the government has decided to maintain a public stock of one million tonnes of foodgrains.

In addition to domestic procurement, two other main components of the PFDS are, (a) external procurement or public import of foodgrains; and (b) food aid. In order to avoid repetition of the points I have already made in Chapter 4 and 5, I will not discuss these two other important components of the PFDS.

The Origin and Evolution of the PFDS: A Critical Review

The PFDS of Bangladesh has its influences in British colonial rule and then Pakistan's tradition of government intervention in foodgrain markets. The birth of this policy was a policy choice to mitigate a manmade crisis, the Bengal famine of 1943. A massive change in food policy, particularly public intervention in food management, was introduced in British India due to the great Bengal Famine of 1943. Mukerjee (2010) blames British policy for creating a devastating famine. In the words of Bose (1990), the famine struck Bengal 'amidst plenty'. Considering the famine as 'manmade', Islam (2007: 422) argues that 'the famine was due to the negligence of the government, gross administrative inefficiency and implementation of wrong policies'. As a result of the political impact of the famine, the British administration focussed on ensuring a steady flow of supplies at 'reasonable' prices to consumers through domestic production supplemented by imports whenever production suffered a setback. Besides, rationing systems of foodgrains to the civilian population were introduced, especially in urban areas, so that the priority areas like wartime industries and soldiers in the cantonments were not adversely affected. Not surprisingly, several studies show that during the famine of 1943, landless, particularly agricultural, labourers suffered most (for instance, see Ó Gráda 2009: 159-84). In a recent study, Mukerjee (2010: 151-67) also demonstrates that the plight of famine in villages was huge. Despite the sufferings of rural life, the targeting was designed for urban people and particularly focussed on soldiers who were already better off than millions of malnourished Indians. Therefore, it would not be wrong to claim that the creation of the PFDS and its targeting was by the regime and for the regime, not for famine sufferers.

Throughout the Pakistan period, the targeting was never aimed to reach the rural destitute to mitigate hunger. In the form of food rationing, the objective of Pakistan's traditional government intervention was to mitigate seasonal price swings in *the major urban centres* that resulted from arbitrage failure, brought on by inadequate infrastructure (Rashid et al. 2008: 12). Until 1971, Bangladesh was a part of Pakistan and shared the same policies, which were continued in the early years after Independence. The early policy of the Government of Bangladesh wholeheartedly accepted the historical root of urban-based channelling. However, the Government of Bangladesh was compelled to consider the PFDS after the devastating impact of the famine in 1974. In the 1970s, there was a large influx of food aid and an associated upsurge in public distribution. During the latter half of the 1970s, the PFDS handled almost twice as much foodgrain as during the latter half of the 1960s. A total of 13-15 per cent of all foodgrains consumed in the country passed through this system, which employs more people than any other government department (Franda 1982: 201-2). Thus, with the traditional mechanism of a foodgrain distribution system, the large influx of food aid played a vital role in shaping the early food policy of Bangladesh. Later, because of heavy leakages as well as targeting errors identified by donors and international agencies, reforms shifted the orientation of public policy from rationing to poverty alleviation programmes through SSN schemes.

In the following discussion, I will show that, similar to the British colonial design of the PFDS, it was not designed to feed the hungry poor in Bangladesh after Independence. Under the PFDS of the British administration, rationing of foodgrains to the civilian population, especially in urban areas, was introduced so that the priority areas like wartime industries and soldiers in the cantonments were not adversely affected. In Bangladesh, its major purpose was to provide government workers, the police, the military, and other 'priority' sectors with payment in kind, as a means of protecting them against the erosive effects on their real income of seasonal and year-to-year fluctuations in food prices (ibid.: 202). The PFDS dispenses foodgrains through a variety of targeted consumption groups. In order to show the target groups of the PFDS, in the following discussion, I categorize its major channels.

(a) *Major Channels of the PFDS in the 1970s*

The priority group within the system is a category called Statutory Rationing (SR), which covered the entire population of the major urban centres. Until 1973, this system included the four principal towns, Dhaka, Narayanganja, Chittagong and Khulna. It was later extended to two more towns with the inclusion of Rajshahi and Rangamati. Almost every one residing in these cities was entitled to a ration card, but food was distributed first to certain 'priority categories' in both urban and rural areas, which included members of the armed services, the police, all government employees, students, and employees of large companies. According to one estimate, in 1980 these categories (SR, 23 per cent and priority categories, 31 per cent) accounted for a total of 54 per cent of food distribution through the PFDS (ibid.).

In addition to SR, there was another rationing system called Modified Rationing (MR), which covered certain categories of the urban and rural population outside the SR areas. MR is the system of distribution in which a listed article is sold to consumers through an appointed dealer against rural ration cards or permits duly issued by a competent authority. The population in each area is graded into classes A, B, C, and D. Each class is categorized according to the local taxes paid by a person, which is taken as a proxy for the family income level of the person. Among the four classified income categories, Category A was considered the poorest group; persons in this group are, in fact, designated as too poor to pay taxes and usually were favoured in the administrative rules of distribution. However, in 1989 under policy reforms, the Modified Rationing System was replaced by the Rural Rationing System, which was then suspended in 1991.

Apart from the SR and MR systems of distribution, there are a number of channels still operating public foodgrains under the PFDS. These are: Food For Work (FFW), relief programmes, the Vulnerable Group Feeding (VGF) Programme. FFW was introduced in 1975 as a channel of food distribution to the rural poor. This programme was undertaken with the objective of providing food as well as employment to the rural landless labour in the lean/dull season of the year. Since its inception, in the words of Franda (ibid.: 203), 'FFW programmes have acquired a reputation for greater honesty than some of the older relief schemes, primarily because international agencies have established elaborate procedures for measuring the amount of earth to be moved before the initiation of a canal-digging or road-building project, and then measuring the amount actually moved after the project's completion'.

Because of its good reputation and relatively smaller leakage rates, this scheme is still a reliable programme of the PFDS. However, in subsequent sections, I will show how public corruption is embedded in this programme, resulting in misappropriation of resources.

Under the relief programme, food is distributed to the destitute during periods of emergency, such as flood, famine or any other natural disasters. This programme gained its provenance after the liberation war, when a massive amount of relief supplies were distributed to the poor. Forty years later after Independence, this programme is still important in maintaining emergency operations, as the country is highly disaster-prone as well as having large levels of poverty.

The Vulnerable Group Feeding (VGF) programme is another important distribution channel of PFDS. Its objective is to provide food to certain high-risk groups. The vulnerable groups include destitute women, particularly in rural areas, and in some areas, pregnant and lactating mothers with their children. In 1975, the WFP initiated this programme under which each member of the vulnerable groups were provided a monthly wheat ration of 31.25 kg for their households.

(b) *Major Channels of the PFDS in the 1980s: 'Preparatory Phases of Food Policy Reforms'*

In 1978, as a consequence of the policy recommendations of donors, the Planning Commission of Bangladesh advocated phasing out rationing subsidies. Throughout the 1980s, experiments and abolition of some selected PFDS channels took place. Ali et al. (2008: 106) describes the period (1978-91) as 'preparatory phases of food policy reforms'. In the 1980s, foodgrains was distributed through more than a dozen ration channels. Interestingly, although this new policy downsized the rationing subsidies, it did not withdraw channels targeted to the 'better-off' population.

In the early 1980s, the objective of the VGF was redefined and was renamed Vulnerable Group Development (VGD). This programme was aimed to achieve self-reliance for poor women—to reflect the change in orientation from relief to development. The development focus came in the form of training in skills needed for poor women to become self-reliant, encouragement of monthly cash savings, and integrating VGD food distributions and training with support and management from nongovernmental organizations (Atwood et al. 2000: 155).

(c) *Major Channels of the PFDS in the post-Reform Period: Policy Reforms with Keeping 'Better off Group'*

Throughout the 1980s and 1990s, significant changes have been made under the various initiatives of the food policy reforms, which basically reduced the number of PFDS channels as well as its volume (see Islam 2012). Under these reforms a number of the pro-poor programme—which were important to generate entitlements such as rural rationing and other subsidies—were either abolished or reduced. According to a study, between the mid-1980s and the mid-2000s, the share of public distribution in market supply shrank from 13 per cent to 5.2 per cent (Chowdhury, Farid & Roy

2010: 23). In other words, this liberalization is the handover of the responsibility of the state to the mercy of the 'invisible hand', i.e. the market. However, since the reform process started, Bangladesh has developed a wide range of SSN programmes which possess a wealth of institutional diversity (Ali et al. 2008: 107). The main difference between the PFDS and SSN programmes is that, while the aim of the former was exclusively to promote food security, the latter is basically oriented towards development efforts, such as training, education and infrastructural programmes. In other words, under the SSN programmes, hunger and food security receive less attention than the development programmes.

As a result of various food policy reforms, at present, there are two major channels of the PFDS—non-monetized distribution channels and monetized distribution channels. Food For Work, Test Relief, Vulnerable Group Feeding Programme, Vulnerable Group Development and Gratuitous Relief (GR) are distributing under the banner of non-monetized channels; while Emergency Operation (EP), Other Priorities (OP), Large Employers (LE) and Open Market Sales (OMS) are operating through monetized channels. A FAO/WFP (2008: 33) crop and food supply assessment mission estimates that approximately 6.1 million households or 30.5 million individuals (based on an average household size of 5) were receiving assistance from the above-mentioned programmes during the fiscal year of 2007-8.[4] Not surprisingly, although the major rationale behind the food policy reforms was reducing its target errors and leakage errors, channels targeted at better-off people, such as the EP, OP and LE, remained unchanged.

The Political Economy of Targeting Errors and Leakage errors

What is a Targeting Error?

In order to provide subsidized food in reducing hunger and malnutrition, the PFDS is a well-known mechanism in Bangladesh which operates through various ration channels, with different degrees of subsidization. However, since the inception of the PFDS, it has been observed that several targeted channels serve relatively well-off segments of the society. For instance, in the period of FY 1985-90, only 45 per cent of government foodgrain resources were distributed through channels targeted towards the poor (World Bank 1992: 61). Beneficiaries of the other 55 per cent of the foodgrain were people in better-off groups: government employees in certain districts, government and parastatal employees, military and security forces, and workers in large industries (in industries with 50 or more workers), through four different channels, such as statutory rationing, other priorities, essential priorities, and large employers, respectively. Thus, in order to make the targeted food distribution to the pro-poor, throughout the 1980s and early 1990s, the food policy of Bangladesh has gone through a number of reforms. As a consequence, a recent survey (BBS 2011) indicates that SSN programmes are reasonably well-targeted. A humongous chunk of 43.4 per cent of beneficiaries of SSN programmes live in poverty, compared with 27.5 per cent of the population not included in SSN programmes. However, available data also indicates that the problem of targeting errors still persists in the PFDS.

In order to ensure food security to the vulnerable sections of the poor, pro-poor targeting is necessary. As one of the early studies of the World Bank (1992) of Bangladesh's food sector suggests, for the welfare of the poor, untargeted interventions to reduce the price of rice in domestic markets have the most far-reaching consequences. Hence, untargeted interventions can be supplemented with mechanisms for targeting specific groups with food and/or income transfers to enhance their food security. Several issues are important in pro-poor targeting. First, programmes such as VGD require targeting the poor within communities, rather than central actions to target poor areas. Second, some programmes such as the FFW programme could be well-targeted with reference to the disparities in the regional incidence of poverty (this is currently a nationwide programme and does not allocate its resources, considering the poverty map of the country). Third, regimes purposefully target the non-poor, such as the police and military for political reasons. Fourth, there are anomalies in the selection process in various PFDS programmes. Thus, targeting errors happen when a programme fails to target the poor within the community, some programme fail in targeting the community, and for political reasons when regimes appease the urban middle class and purposefully include the non-poor in their aegis.

Hence, targeting errors refer to the channels of the PFDS which are targeted at better-off groups rather than the hardcore poor and, therefore, food subsidies go to well-off segments of the society, not to the hungry poor. Targeted programmes are necessary for generating entitlements to the poor, but without the appropriate target, there is a risk that the pro-poor nature of spending on these programmes would be, likely turn to pro-rich.

What is a Leakage Error?

Leakage is another important problem of the subsidized food-based programmes in Bangladesh—all programmes suffer a considerable 'leakage' of resources, meaning 'resources not being used for the purpose for which they were intended' (ibid.: 64). According to a study of Ahmed et al. (2003: 2):

> . . . in any Public Food Distribution System, there are incentives and opportunities for the unauthorized diversion of food; for sale in the open market, and other redirections and use. To the extent that such leakage occurs, the government and the food aid donors incur the cost while the benefits accrue, not to the intended or targeted consumers, but to those who gain access to and misappropriate resources. . . . Depending on the rules and operation of a particular Public Food Distribution System, leakage may occur at several points in the distribution system.

A number of sources (World Bank 1977, 1979, 1992; Adam 1998 and more recently Ahmed et al. 2004, 2006; Ahmed et al. 2003; IFPRI 2004, 2007) identifies the PFDS of Bangladesh as a system of targeting errors and leakage errors and shows the extent, nature and consequences of leakages. To different extents, these leakages occur in every stage of the PFDS. Some common types of leakages are as follows:

- During food discharge at harbours, foodgrain losses are a common occurence, including pilferage (see Ahmed et al.) 2004;
- The expenditure for PFDS procurement is particularly vulnerable to leakages as it provides the greatest opportunity for rent-seeking behaviour. Both government officials and private agents are involved in these leakages (Adams 1998);
- Local officials receive less foodgrains than the actual allocated quantity when the movement of PFDS foodgrains from one Local Supply Depot (LSD) to another LSD occurs;
- Estimating leakage due to short rations (beneficiaries receive less than their full entitlement) is high;
- Leakages occur due to undercoverage (when the actual number of beneficiaries is less than the officially determined number for whom food was allocated);
- Union Parishad (UP) members, politicians and public officials sell foodgrains and then make payments by cash to the programme beneficiary.

Thus, leakage is the aggregate disappearance of food resources from any channels of the PFDS other than the losses such as transit and storage, which happens in any stage of the PFDS through various forms of anomaly. By discussing all kinds of leakages, in this study, I show leakage as the outcome of rent-seeking, public corruption and poor governance. In other words, I argue that the term targeting error and leakage errors as they appear in various literature/reports is misleading in the political sense (rather than economic), as it is really purposeful manipulation.

It is imperative to note that conventional accounts of the PFDS of Bangladesh only focus on the degree of targeting errors and leakage errors. In addition to the technical problems of the system suggested by conventional studies, my purpose is to unearth the structural causes of the targeting errors and leakage errors. In doing so, I employ the framework developed in Chapter 3 of this thesis. Historically, targeting errors are the purposeful outcome of regimes in order to avoid political unrest, and its main goal is 'regime survival' by using the state's resources through the PFDS. In the present context, I suggest that despite a number of food policy reforms, targeting errors still exist because of the 'partial reform syndrome' of the neopatrimonial regime. Similarly, the notion of rent-seeking and public corruption explicate the underlying reasons of the leakages of the PFDS.

The Origin of Targeting Errors: Political Gain through Appeasing the Middle Class and Donors?

Since its inception the political elites of Bangladesh have always used the PFDS as a means of regime survival rather than promoting food security. Historically, political unrest is a common feature in Bangladesh and, therefore, every regime wants to maximize its security in various ways—using the state's resources such as the PFDS is one of them. In this section, I show that initially, for the British colonial government, the purpose of the PFDS was only to appease the urban middle class, while the Pakistani as well as Bangladeshi governments used it for two purposes. In order to mitigate the two major challenges of the regime's stability successive governments simultaneously appeased the urban middle class as well as the donor community through the PFDS.

Appeasing the Middle Class: The Politics of Urban-based Channelling of the PFDS

The historical origin and development of the PFDS suggests that before introducing the Food for Work and Vulnerable Group Development Programmes in 1974 and 1975 respectively, the purpose of the mechanism was only to feed the urban middle class which, to some extent, indirectly helped in price stabilization. It is noteworthy to examine why the target group of the PFDS was the urban middle class, not the hungry poor. The following factors suggest that the aim of political gain played a pivotal role in targeting the middle class. First, the great Bengal famine of 1943, a manmade famine, was the result of a great administrative failure of the British Raj (see Bose 1990; Islam 2007; Ó Grada 2009; Mukarjee 2010). As noted earlier, this famine occurred in the Indian province of Bengal, where the middle class were the main activists of the Indian Independence movement. So it was the aim of the British administration to satisfy the middle class to prevent further outbursts of anti-British sentiment. Second, targeting in urban areas was introduced so that priority areas like wartime industries and soldiers in the cantonments were not adversely affected. The government responded to the need of industrial labour as it was required to keep industries going as part of war requirements. Third, according to the Famine Enquiry Commission, 'the Government of Bengal, consciously or unconsciously, allowed the needs of the rural areas to be outweighed by those of Calcutta and particularly its big business' (as cited in Molla 1990: 6). No evidence suggests that the purpose of targeting was to stabilize the price, or to feed the genuinely vulnerable group of famine sufferers in Bengal. Thus, there was neither a lack of efficiency of the rationing system, nor a wrong targeting, but rather feeding poor people was not the purpose of the PFDS. The purpose of this targeting was to appease a particular group of middle class/lower middle class citizens for the political agenda of the British Raj and the Government of Bengal.

The Government of Pakistan also mainly targeted the urban middle class under the PFDS. With very little exception, Pakistan never had a democratic government. The military rulers of Pakistan were never concerned with the issue of social distribution or the widespread hunger of the nation. Rather, the main concern of the military dictators of the country were to keep the middle class happy by providing rations and any other forms of appeasement so as to avoid political unrest.

For the first few years after Independence, Bangladesh followed the PFDS channels originated by Pakistan. But in 1974, food policy reforms took place with the introduction of Food for Work, followed by the Vulnerable Group Development (VGD) Programme in 1975. Several factors contributed to these changes of the distribution channels: (1) the Awami League, the first government of Bangladesh, had a long history of rights-based movements against socio-economic inequality, with popular support at the grassroots level. Thus the party had commitments to pro-poor distribution and to feeding the poor; (2) Bangladesh received a large influx of food as food aid soon after its independence, which raised the importance of rethinking distribution channels policy; (3) the donors soon realized the inefficiency of the rationing system and advocated a progressive shift towards a pro-poor policy of in-kind distribution programmes; (4) a better public food operating system was in demand as the country was going through a crisis due to a series of bad harvests and the aftermath of war damage. However, the Awami League was not successful in changing the urban middle class-based PFDS channels, mainly because of the government's immediate challenge to prevent any urban unrest. After the Awami League regime, successive regimes ensured their security by giving the responsibility of food policy to donors and keeping urban-based PFDS channels unchanged. Islam (2012: 232) shows that food policy reforms during the 1980s and 1990s did not downsize or abolish any urban-based channels of the PFDS. A report of the food division, Ministry of Food and Disaster Management, suggests that (rice) rationing allocated to the members of armed police battalions and Dhaka metropolitan police were found on the black market, which demonstrates that 'this is additional for their necessity, which can be considered as their extra income' (*Prothom-alo*, 19 January 2011). Similarly, in an interview with BBC Bangla (radio), Abdur Razzak, Food and Disasters Management, Minister of Bangladesh, candidly admitted that it has been a practice in the last 30 years that most of the beneficiaries (members of the military, police, security forces and government employees who are entitled rations) sell their rice/wheat ration and then buy better quality (preferable) rice from the market (BBC Bangla 2011). Despite the fact that the PFDS channels such as WP, OP, LE are not serving food-insecure people, the successive regimes of Bangladesh never took the initiative to change or abolish these programmes, even though ones such as rural rationing had already been abolished.

Thus, it would be wrong to claim that the shortcomings of the early design of the PFDS were due to leakages or that it was incorrectly targeted. In fact, this policy design was a deliberate outcome to achieve the maximum political benefits for regime survival. Food insecurity was never the main concern of the system, as poor people were never a potential threat to the government. Like in Bangladesh, it has been observed in the 1970s that in most of the least-developed countries food distribution policies reflected urban influence and interests rather than rural interests. As Michael Lipton (1980: 25) suggests, food supplies are structured to please the greedy, not to feed needy.

Appeasing Donors: In Search of Legitimacy through Partial Reform of the PFDS

My previous discussion clearly shows that the early design of PFDS was not to feed to the poor but rather to ensure regime survival by feeding the urban middle class. Why then did successive regimes go through a series of food policy reforms, particularly in the 1980s and early 1990s?

The chronology of food policy reforms in Bangladesh suggests that donors played a key role in those reforms with rigorous studies and discovered both targeting errors and leakage errors of the PFDS, which led to the prescribing of new policies and implementing all of their recommendations (Montgomery 1983; Shahadat Ullah 1988; IFPRI 1993; Chowdhury & Haggblade 2000). Initially, a proposal of subsidy reduction was implemented in 1981, after the 1979 drought—an almost famine-like situation. As Chowdhury, Farid & Roy (2010) suggest, food policy change in Bangladesh was the outcome of the policy paper of the World Bank known as *Food Policy Issues* (World Bank 1979). It is important to note that it happened when the then military ruler, General Ziaur Rahman, was seeking legitimacy through Western support to stabilize his own power. It is to be noted that Zia's action was motivated by a new foreign policy orientation in which he turned away from the Awami League's close friendship with India and some communist countries. Mimicking the footsteps of General Ayub, Ziaur sought to develop economic and political ties with the West, as well as with the oil-rich Islamic Gulf states and other Muslim countries, including Pakistan (see Ali 2010; Milam 2009; Ziring 1992). He was rewarded only after confirming that his regime 'intended to introduce such further economic reforms as subsidy reduction, agricultural taxation, and import liberalization' (World Bank 1976). As a result, while the Mujib regime was suffering serious economic crisis and failed to import foodgrains due to a shortfall in the balance of payments, Zia proudly declared that 'money is not a problem'. To consolidate the power by implementing economic reforms, successive regimes wholeheartedly followed Zia's footsteps, realizing that international support is a prerequisite for regime survival (see Quadir 2000). Not surprisingly, later under the leadership of Sheikh Hasina, the Awami League also joined the reformers, club for similar purposes (see Nuruzzaman 2006).

Islam (2012) examines the chronology of food policy reforms in Bangladesh. As a consequence, the Government of Bangladesh downsized the PFDS and abolished a number of programmes such as Rural Rationing. Displaying the 'partial reform syndrome' by appeasing donors, various regimes ensured their own security to survive in an unstable political environment in Bangladesh; regimes also maintained local support by not reducing programmes designed for urban better-off people such as EP, OP and LE. As noted, EP provides for public employees in the armed forces, paramilitary border forces, police and Ansars (para-police). EP accounts for the majority of food subsidies each year. OP provides for the employees of the civil defence forces and other strategically influential agencies. While the neopatrimonial regimes benefited by appeasing donors and the urban middle class (the two potential threat groups for various corrupt regimes of Bangladesh), donors were satisfied by integrating a peripheral economy through food market liberalization. It may be noted that by liberalizing/allowing private imports of foodgrains (and some inputs), the role of the government in the domestic food market was downsized (in both procurement and distribution).

The Origin of Leakage Errors: Regime Survival through Politically Motivated Projects?

A study of Murgai and Zaidi (2005) points out that any definitive conclusions about the 'pro-poor' nature of spending on programmes of the PFDS are clouded by the survey findings which suggest that a large share of total resources devoted to these programmes disappear before reaching their intended beneficiaries. In other words, despite a number of food policy reforms which basically downsized the role of Government in creating entitlements, leakages are still widespread in various programmes of the PFDS. In a personal interview, former agricultural secretary and then advisor of the caretaker Government of Bangladesh suggests that in order to control leakages, a strong monitoring system is needed. He adds politically motivated projects, political favour, and the involvement of the Members of Parliament (MPs) in the system further intensify the existing leakages (IvGoB9). Hence, it would not be unfair to claim that the targeting errors and/or leakage errors of the PFDS or SSN programmes are deeply connected with the political culture of the state and its administrative structure. Programmes of the PFDS can be abolished, downsized or transformed into SSN programmes and leakages will remain high unless the nature of the state changes. In this section, first I explain leakages based on existing literature and then I will recount my field-level experiences in order to examine the linkage between leakages and regime interests.

Conventional Accounts about Leakages in the PFDS

One of the key elements of the analytical framework developed in Chapter 3 is rent-seeking behaviour. In order to examine the operation of food subsidy systems in Bangladesh, two political economy concepts, rent-seeking lobbies and rent-seeking bureaucrats/agents, have been found to be useful in providing a partial, but not complete, explanation of why this system has failed to benefit the rural poor (see Adams 1998). In Bangladesh, Adams (ibid.) identified two rent-seeking lobbying groups for food subsidies: rice mill owners and the military/police. Rice millers received rents from the continued operation of the mill gate contracting system, and the military/police received benefits by successfully resisting all efforts to describe their food subsidy channels. Adams (ibid.) further shows that the policy process is dominated by a number of government officials and their agents who are able and willing to 'sell' their access to public goods—in this case, subsidized food—in return for material gain. He explains how government officials/food distribution agents work for personal gain with businessmen and how it affects the food subsidy system of Bangladesh. Both rent-seeking lobbies and rent-seeking bureaucrats/agents are the government implementing authorities of the PFDS. But it was the implementing authorities—procurement officials in the Ministry of Food, rice mill owners and ration shop dealers—who benefited the most from government efforts to improve the nutritional status of the rural poor (ibid.).

As noted earlier, because of the leakage of the PFDS, which is the result of patronage politics of the neopatrimonial state, the Government of Bangladesh has emphasized the SSN programmes. However, I will demonstrate that the government expenditure for the PFDS and SSN programmes is particularly vulnerable to leakage into the hands of the non-poor due to the rent-seeking tendencies of politicians and officials. Before addressing my own arguments based on my field-level data, I will first draw on existing literature about the problems of leakage errors.

A BRAC study (2006) of the evolution of government policy on safety nets and education in Bangladesh during the 1990s forms the basis for a discussion of accountability and corruption in each sector. In fact, there is a widespread impression abroad that leakages and corruption from the Social Safety Nets and other Public Expenditure Programmes have been extensive and highly debilitating (BRAC 2006). A number of studies (Ahmed et al. 2004; World Bank 2004, 2006; IFPRI 2007; Khatun, Rahman & Nabi 2009) note the leakage of various SSN programmes. Despite a series of food policy reforms, leakage errors still persist. Thus it is imperative to examine the problem in the context of policy implementation, with special reference to weak state capacity and poor state governance.

A number of studies analyze the governance and institutional weakness of Bangladesh as a reason for leakage in the PFDS and SSN programmes. A study of the World Bank (2006b) has argued against the devolution of programmes authority to local government on the ground that local capacities of administration and monitoring are too weak to prevent either leakages or inefficient targeting. Based on a *union*[5]-level analysis of the relations and practices among the elites in rural north-west Bangladesh. Bode (2007) states that powerful agents build political networks and alliances that they use to gain access to public resources. In turn, these resources are deployed to build support within local constituencies which provide opportunities for personal gain. Thus, Bode (ibid.) suggests that the structures and processes constitute a powerful constraint on their effectiveness, as many government policies including Social Safety Nets are implemented through the unions. It is important to understand that local councils or Union Parishads have limited resources, little revenue-raising authority, and virtually no influence on the use of resources by the central government in the Parishads' own areas. Instead, Union Parishads are dominated by the district and sub-district (*upazila*) bureaucracies, and exercise practically unilateral control in the uses to which funds are put in the hiring and disciplining of staff (GHK 2004). These weak-structured local councils of Bangladesh, which exemplify poor governance, are also dominated by rent-seeking bureaucrats/agents.

Beneficiaries of Leakages: By the Regime for the Regime?

In addition to leakage errors and corruption, which is the main focus of a number of studies, I raise several issues important to understanding the weakness of the PFDS and SSN programmes. First, most of the PFDS and/or SSN programmes are currently politically motivated. These programmes are designed for the personal and/or political gain of the ruling political party and other influential people. Second, the practical implementation process of these programmes is very different from the original objectives of these programmes. For instance, my field-level data suggest that many food transfer programmes such as Test Relief (TR), are implemented in such a way that serves the interest of political elites rather than promoting food security. Originally, the purpose of TR programmes was to provide employment for the very poor through the development and maintenance of rural infrastructure. In practice, it is a cash transfer program. Political elites in cooperation with government officials use these projects for political purposes, such as maintenance work of existing roads, mosques or temples. Therefore, the target group is not able to work in these programmes due to the lack of skills required for them.

In a personal interview, a local political leader who was involved in the political use of TR when his party was in office, candidly pointed out that 'political party leaders and activists of the incumbent government usually get the opportunities of various development programmes such as TR, FFW projects (programmes). The benefits of these projects are usually distributed between the Members of Parliaments (MP), Upazilla Chairman, and their supporters, followers, and other party activists' (IvPol2). Elsewhere, I have also shown that government food subsidies through the VGF Programmes fail to reach the poor (Islam 2012). According to a local political leader (IvPol2):

> Over the years, only politicians have benefited from these types of projects which fulfil their political purposes. These politically motivated projects are the outcome of the promises made by the MPs, ministers or a powerful ruling political leader when they make a visit to any particular region/area of his/her constituency [for instance, when an MP visits any part of his/her constituency, s/he promises the supporters and voters that the government will build a school, college, madrasa, mosque, temple, road-bridge, etc.]. In the process of implementing these kinds of politically motivated projects, the government budget for programmes, such as Test Relief (TR) Food or Food for Work (FFW) or others, is diverted to the projects promised by the politicians such as a mosque or temple development project. (IvPol2)

During my field research, I learnt from a variety of sources that in 2010, the entire TR budget was allocated for the mosque and *mandir* (temple) development projects in Dhamrai Upazila of Dhaka district.[6] Although, theoretically, SSN programmes, such as TR and FFW, should provide food to the employers (known as food transfer programmes), practically, all the foodgrains allocated for them are sold from the Upazila-level warehouse before they reach the poor and then the committee pays cash to the employers instead. In the process, rent-seeking lobbies in cooperation with rent-seeking bureaucrats manipulate the entire selling mechanism. Particularly, political activists, mostly local leaders, control this business and are the monopoly buyers of these foodgrains. Committee members unwilling to sell them face huge trouble and, therefore, though the price is almost half the market price, almost every committee member sells the foodgrain allocated for their project (IvPol2).[7] It is also worth noting that the implementation committee of these projects are always dominated and controlled by the ruling political party leaders and activists; it also includes the indirect support of local administrative officials in return due to bribes and/or threats made by ruling party leaders (IvPol2).

According to available field data, 'it may be possible to implement a range of only 50-60 per cent of the work, provided that the committee members are very sincere and honest. Mostly the range of implementation of work is between 30 and 40 per cent. There are many examples where there is no implementation of the work at all' (IvPol2). For example, a senior official of TR project in the Bogra district seeking anonymity states that 'a large sum of money had been misappropriated in the district through submitting false projects and preparing fake project completion documents as per preliminary probes. A large number of development projects in Dhunat are fake' (*The Daily Star*, 16 February 2009). These projects include an earth-filling project which was taken for Chalar Bhita Natun Jame Masjid (Mosque). A local resident doctor Anil states that 'I did not see any earth-filling work in my area during the last three months, although three tonnes of wheat was allocated for a project on the maintenance work of existing bituminous pavement under TR programme' (*The Daily Star*, 16 February 2009).

Another dimension of the political misappropriation of the SSN programmes is the regional disparity of budgetary allocation. For instance, by examining the division-wide distribution of beneficiary households, a recent study suggests that the highest share of households receiving benefits from SSN programmes was in the Sylhet division (22.4 per cent) and the lowest in the Khulna division (9.5 per cent). In contrast, division-wide poverty data suggests that the percentage of people living below the poverty line was second lowest in Sylhet and third highest in Khulna (BBS

2009). SSN programmes were not undertaken with the proper consideration of regional incidences of poverty (Khatun, Rahman & Nabi 2009: 141). During 2005, the then Finance Minister, Saifur Rahman, was elected as a Member of Parliament from a constituency of the Sylhet district which had huge power over the budgetary allocation. Once he famously stated that 'every good budget is an election budget' (*The Daily Star*, 6 June 2006). So, as leader of the Sylhet division, it is not unlikely that he awarded his region by using the state resources for the purpose of electoral gain.

SSN Programmes, Poverty Alleviation and Food Security: A Critique

One of the main characteristics of the post-reform PFDS is that it greatly emphasizes SSN programmes; in particular, its food distribution system goes through SSN programmes such as FFW, VGD and VGF. The most important difference between these two programmes is that while the PFDS is exclusively designed for food security, SSN programmes mainly focus on other development issues. Interestingly, although there is a significant difference between the PFDS and SSN programmes in relation to policy origins, policy expectation and outcome of the policy; the policy-makers, policy analysts and the various documents of the Government of Bangladesh often depict the two as one and the same. For instance, in order to show the budgetary allocation of the PFDS, the budgetary allocation of SSN programmes were included.

According to Conning and Michael (2002: 375), SSN programmes can serve an important role in alleviating poverty and in promoting long-term growth by providing households with the protection that markets and informal networks may not supply. He argues that a Social Safety Net may redistribute resources toward disadvantaged groups, or sustain political coalitions to support critical structural reforms. Similarly, a World Bank study (2006b) argues that SSN programmes are the basis of Bangladesh's social protection strategy and are the mainstay of the poverty alleviation strategy.[8] Hence, although the SSN programmes are designed to alleviate poverty and will ensure food security by eliminating poverty, these programmes are not designed exclusively to promote food security. Goals such as improving the living standards of the weakest segments of the population and helping in income and consumption smoothing are important for promoting food security, but these are not designed exclusively to eliminate hunger in the short term, nor with a vision for the long term.

SSN programmes in Bangladesh can be categorized into the following five broad categories: infrastructure building programmes, education programmes, training programmes, nutrition programmes and relief programmes. As noted above, most of these programmes were designed exclusively for promoting food security; rather, all of them are 'development programmes' in essence. First, there is no doubt that these pro-poor development programmes alleviate poverty. However, one of the central arguments of this thesis is that 'development' and food insecurity must be seen differently—poverty reduction is very important but not the only way to ensure food security. Strategies for reducing poverty and hunger cannot go together as the rate of the former is very slow. Instead, Bangladesh needs to address urgent strategies for reducing food insecurity because of its high magnitude of poverty as noted in Chapter 4. Thus, development programmes like SSN are not effective in preventing the current chronic food insecurity in Bangladesh. Second, most of the SSN programmes provide money instead of food, which is not seen as the best way to deal with food insecurity.[9] For example, the Food for Education (converted to the Primary Education Stipend Programme in 2002) and Female Secondary School Assistance Programmes (FSSAP) are two very basic and established education programmes under SSN. Both of them are stipend programmes but the amount of the stipend is very small and insufficient even for the substance of very poor families. In the FSSAP, a grade six student was given only Tk 25 (less than US$0.40) as monthly stipend, and Tk 300 (approximately US $4 yearly). This monthly stipend cannot buy one kilogram of rice and, therefore, cannot play a significant role in promoting food security. In addition, although this programme is part of the SSN its 'themes' cover only 25 per cent of SSN. The remaining themes of the programme are gender (25 per cent), education for all (25 per cent), and rural services and infrastructure (25 per cent) (see FSSAP-II 2008). In other words, 75 per cent of this programme is not an SSN programme in essence. Third, women and children, the most vulnerable food-insecure group, as well as many rural poor are not competent to attend many SSN programmes because of the requirements. Fourth, these programmes do not help price stabilization as the Open Market Sale (OMS) and other programmes of PFDS do.

It is often argued that SSN programmes are much better-targeted than many other PFDS programmes, which have been abolished. However, the aim of this targeting is not to seek the pockets of food-insecure regions and, therefore, does not prioritise most vulnerable food-insecure areas. Although the main targeting strategy of these programmes is poverty alleviation, many suggest that they are not even well-targeted with respect to poverty elimination in vulnerable areas. As Sobhan (2010: 215) argues, 'the larger FFW programme is less well targeted since it is dispersed across the country without any reference to the disparities in the regional incidence of poverty'. Similarly, some other programmes such as FFE, are neither targeted in the context of regional incidence of poverty, nor focusses on chronic food insecure regions but rather promotes female or primary education across the country. Thus, by not giving special emphasis on hunger, these 'pro-poor targeted' programmes in fact exclude the hungry people and pay less attention to food security.

Budgetary Allocation: How well is the State doing in Creating Entitlement?

As stated earlier, food policy reforms took place in Bangladesh because of leakage and targeting errors. As a consequence of the reforms, the government abolished rural rationing and many other pro-poor programmes of the PFDS. In addition, many reforms have shifted the orientation of public policy from rationing to poverty alleviation programmes, and the social assistance expenditures as a percentage of GDP and public expenditures have been reduced significantly. This decline in government expenditure is so alarming that, in 2006, a World Bank study argued 'real expenditures on safety net programmes should not decline further' (World Bank 2006b: IV). In this section, my argument is that by considering the poor as no threat to political regimes throughout the timeframe of this thesis (1975-2010), various governments constantly reduced the budgetary allocation for the PFDS programmes. The exception to this occurred in 2007-8, but the budgetary allocation increased for two basic reasons—first, the sudden price hike due to a global food crisis as well as natural disasters in Bangladesh; and second, this budgetary allocation was increased by the military-backed, unpopular and non-elected caretaker government which was seeking an avenue to remain in power (the government was appointed for three months but they remained in power for two years by violating the Constitution).

As Table 6.1 indicates, during the past two decades, the size and composition of the PFDS has changed significantly. The annual volume of foodgrain distribution under various PFDS programmes declined from 2.3 million MT in the early 1990s to about 1.3 MT in the first half of the last decade (2004-5–2007-8). However, after 2007-8 the volume of annual distribution of the PFDS has increased dramatically, particularly in 2008-9 and then displayed a gradual downward trend in 2009-10.

Table 6.2, the most recent available data, shows the trend in public expenditure on targeted food programmes as a share of total development as well as public expenditure for the period of 1990-1 to 2004-5. The Table clearly indicates three basic trends of public expenditure on targeted food programmes with little fluctuation. First, until 1998-9, a peak year, the average share of targeted programmes in both development and public expenditure increased somewhat. Second, since then until 2004-5 although the total public expenditure increased, expenditure on targeted food programmes decreased rapidly. Third, the overall picture indicates a steady downward trend of the budgetary priorities to targeted food programmes.

Thus, although the state has the ability to generate entitlement, over the years, various regimes were apathetic to invest for the

TABLE 6.1: PUBLIC FOODGRAIN DISTRIBUTION IN BANGLADESH (*'000 metric tonnes*)

Programme	1989-90-1991-2	1992-3-1996-7	1997-8-2000-1	2004-5-2007-8	2008-9	2009-10
SALES CHANNELS: RATION						
Statutory Rationing (SR)	187	11	0	0	0	0
Rural Rationing (RR)	376	0	0	0	0	0
Essential Programmes (EP)	145	172	207	239	219	245.6
Other Priorities (OP)	232	11	15	19	22	21.0
Large Employees Industries (LEI)	45	17	12	12	10	15.3
Open Market Sale (OMS)	137	200	41	233	195	259.4
Fare price cards	0	0	0	13	0	6.1
Garments	0	0	0	0	0	43.1
Flour mills	235	39	10	1	0	0
Palli chake (rural mills)	96	21	0	0	0	0
Other/auction	0.0	7	0	0	0	0.1
Sub total	1,456	482	285	517	446	590.6
	63 %	33 %	16 %	38 %		
NON-SALES CHANNELS: RELIEF						
Food For Work (FFW)	471	444	628	162	395	377.4
Test Relief (TR)	153	101	109	131	368	369.0
Vulnerable Group Development (VGD)	214	167	207	220	279	272.4
Gratuitous Relief (GR)	0	30	38	45	43	37.1
Food For Education (FFE)	0	154	308	0	0	0
Vulnerable Group Feeding (VGF)	0	0	204	190	507	248.3
Other	0	64	59	90	92	68.8
Sub total	838	961	1,552	838	1,684	1,373.0
	37 %	67 %	84 %	62 %		
Total	2,294	1,443	1,837	1,355	2,130	1,963.5
	100.0 %	100.0 %	100.0 %	100 %		

Source: Author's calculation from Directorate of Food and also Shahabuddin, et al., 2009.

TABLE 6.2: TREND IN EXPENDITURE ON TARGETED FOOD PROGRAMMES AS A SHARE OF TOTAL DEVELOPMENT AND PUBLIC EXPENDITURE

Year	Expenditure on Targeted Food Programmes	Total Development Expenditure	Total Public Expenditure	Expenditure on Targeted Food Programmes as % of Total Development Expenditure	Expenditure on Targeted Food Programmes as % of Total Public Expenditure
	(1)	(2)	(3)	(1)/(2) X 100	(1)/(3) X 100
1990-1	811.81	5,269	12,579	15.4	6.5
1991-2	826.59	6,024	13,924	13.7	5.9
1992-3	641.71	6,550	15,060	9.8	4.3
1993-4	755.26	8,983	18,133	8.4	4.2
1994-5	1,293.69	10,303	20,603	12.6	6.3
1995-6	1,226.78	10,016	21,830	12.3	5.6
1996-7	1,626.95	11,041	23,576	14.7	6.9
1997-8	1,772.55	11,037	25,537	16.1	6.9
1998-9	2,180.83	12,509	29,274	17.4	7.5
1999-2000	1,929.57	15,471	33,915	12.5	5.7
2000-1	1,968.08	16,240	36,902	12.1	5.3
2001-2	1,670.24	14,090	36,782	11.8	4.5
2002-3	1,586.31	15,434	40,741	10.3	3.9
2003-4	1,659.02	16,817	45,207	9.9	3.7
2004-5	1,753.14	18,771	53,435	9.3	3.3

(Tk in crores)

Source: Ministry of Finance (various years) and also Shahabuddin 2010: 108.

hungry poor and, therefore, the aggregate budgetary allocation has decreased. On the other hand, as a result of 2007-8 food crisis, the then military-backed government increased the budgetary allocation for the PFDS. Two factors played an important role in order to facilitate increasing the amount of budgetary allocation for the PFDS: (a) the rapid unpopularity of the government posed a huge challenge to continue governing and, therefore, compelled them to allocate an increasing amount of money; (b) to seek market stabilization through public intervention after the devastating impact of sudden price hikes. Unsurprisingly, after 2009 the democratically elected government was not in the midst of a popularity crisis like its predecessor military-backed government and, therefore, the regime gradually started to decrease the aggregate budgetary allocation.

This section draws three different but interrelated conclusions. First, it demonstrates that since the very onset of the PFDS in Bangladesh, it has always been politically motivated. Second, the neopatrimonial state is generally less interested in promoting food security through the PFDS, which reflects its trend of budgetary allocation. And third, my discussion shed light on the weakness of SSN programmes in promoting food security.

MARKET MANAGEMENT/REGULATION IN BANGLADESH: POLITICS, RHETORIC AND REALITY

To promote food availability and increase food accessibility, food subsidies and food price stabilization schemes have been implemented in most nations of the world concurrently. Price stability is important for both producers and consumers since it helps maintain production incentives and ensures adequate access (Alamgir & Poonam 1991). It is particularly important in a country like Bangladesh, where food insecure people are both 'peasants' and the 'rural and urban poor'. A large number of the poor people in Bangladesh depend on markets for access to food. As Barrett (2002: 17) notes, adverse movements in terms of trade between purchased food and the goods or services they produce and sell (including wage labour) can cause entitlements failure. In 2007-8, as noted earlier, an additional 7.5 million people joined the ranks of the hungry because of high food prices in Bangladesh (see FAO/WFP 2008: 7). While several factors are responsible for high price hikes, poor market management is one of the most important ones. In pursuance of a strategy that aims to provide price stability, it is very important to ensure that the domestic market operates efficiently. In other words, efficiency is not only important for market regulation, it is important for every stage of the food security mechanism. As Maxwell (1991: 16) asserts, 'all stages in the food chain, from production to final consumption, should be efficient in a social welfare sense. Production policies should take account of dynamic comparative advantage; marketing margins should provide no more than normal profits in the long term; and consumer prices should reflect real scarcity values'.

In this part of the chapter, I attempt to investigate the role of the state in market management/regulation focusing on the rice market. The heart of this discussion is—what are the state mechanisms in pursuance of food price stabilization and how well is the state doing? I endeavour to investigate the challenges of food accessibility in Bangladesh with regard to market, market failure, and market interventions, which together can be called market management. I am particularly interested in examining the linkages between economic management, market inefficiency, challenges of food accessibility, and neopatrimonial politics. I endeavour to examine factors that may hurt market efficiency in Bangladesh, with special reference to the rice market.

I begin this part of the chapter with a brief theoretical discussion of market management and then I examine how political elites see the problem of market failure in Bangladesh and its potential remedy. It then deals with the nature of the state's response to market management. It particularly examines how successive governments have always taken some political initiatives in pursuance of market rectification. The discussion then seeks the causes of the failure of state initiatives in market management, with particular reference to the recent food crisis and the management of public foodgrain stock. In order to explore the linkage between the neopatrimonial state of Bangladesh and market failure, it finally examines extortion as a cause of market failure in Bangladesh.

Market Failure: Conceptual Clarification

Market failure is a broad concept for a variety of critiques of markets in economic terms—it refers to a series of factors that may result in pure market solutions failing to be efficient (Kay 2008: 23). Market power, externalities, public goods and information failures/imperfect information are examples of a general phenomenon called market failure. In simple terms, market failure implies the inability of some unregulated markets to allocate resources efficiently (Mankiw 2011). Incorrect price signals are likely to misallocate scarce resources, which can cause panic followed by hoarding, price hikes and, thereby, food insecurity. Thus, government actions are often necessary to manage vulnerability and address food insecurity, and are *always desirable to guide and discipline markets*, particularly during the first stages of economic and agricultural development, or in transition situations (Timmer 2008; as cited in WFP 2009: 121; emphasis added). *To guide and discipline markets* is particularly important in Bangladesh, where market failure is a common phenomenon and causes dramatic price hikes and food insecurity. Actions are necessary as the 'actions to enhance market functioning may prevent or mitigate the effects of market failures and improve households' access to food, local food availability and, in some cases, food utilization' (WFP 2009: 121). In disciplining markets, a set of action principles are proposed such as analysis, transparency, predictability, consistency and implementation (see ibid.).

As Mankiw (2011: 151) points out, 'when markets fail, public policy can potentially remedy the problem and increase economic efficiency'. If the government needs to intervene to rectify market failures, there is no doubt that the most important point is efficiency. With regard to food systems, as Timmer, Falcon and Pearson (1983: 151) suggest, 'the efficiency and economic gains potentially available from successful market coordination of a society's food system are an empirical issue, not a matter of faith or logic'. It is a matter of political choice how the elites of a particular country like to deal with the markets—it can be based on empirical and/or scientific study with an efficient implementation mechanism, or can merely be a political agenda with the rhetoric of political slogans. It is important to bear in mind that, where government intervention in a market function is deemed necessary, it may still not adequately rectify the community's needs or the market's own weaknesses because of failings in the public decision making process (Michael 2006: 124). The ability to use scientific knowledge as an input into decision making, and into the management of public affairs, is a distinguishing characteristic of modern states; although technical analysis is rarely the sole basis on which public decisions are made (Grindle 1996: 109). Akin to many other developing countries, technical knowledge is rarely used to formulate public decisions in Bangladesh, more specifically in market management, to control food price hikes. In addition, it is also imperative to remember that political choice is derived from several factors which may hurt the interest of poor. For example, the model of policy formation suggests that interest groups are the focal point of the policy process, subsuming all of the legitimate political interests of the community (Woll 1974: 53). Thus policy formulation and execution depends on the interests of the political elites. Grindle (1996: 110) notes that 'political elites appoint, promote, support, and protect technical advisors and create technical analysis units—or fail to do so—largely as a result of their own perceptions, ideas, interests, and decision making styles'.

Market Regulation in Bangladesh: Political Rhetoric?

This section aims to examine how political elites see the problem of market failure in Bangladesh and how they seek potential remedies. It will show that, since the very beginning of the nation, the political elites of Bangladesh have viewed market failure or price instability as merely a conspiracy of the political opposition. Hence, 'the blame game' gains currency rather than a real agenda for a remedy of market failure.

Like many other developing countries, the political elite of Bangladesh seek low cost foodstuffs for the interest of the regime.[10] It is particularly seen in Bangladesh, where hunger and famine have become such major issues on the public's mind that political action has become inevitable (Rahman 1995). Bangladeshi society has been highly sensitized by famine-related issues since the Bangladesh famine of 1974. As a consequence, subsequent governments and politicians are always concerned about food issues. The issue of food has gained importance as a political agenda in society, which can be understood in every national election in Bangladesh. As I discussed in Chapter 4, the issue of food is not only the major agenda of election manifestos of all the political parties, it is also the major agenda of election campaigns. According to many political analysts, food price was the key determinant factor of the landslide victory of the Awami League in the 2009 national election. They argued that price hikes of daily essentials, particularly foodstuffs, was the cause of the overthrown (BNP) government. It is also argued that the long-term caretaker government of Bangladesh (2007-8) lost their popular support, mainly, because of the price hike of daily essentials, particularly foodstuffs (Mahmud 2010).

Considering market regulation as an important mechanism to stabilizing food prices, it appears that the government is very keen to take initiatives to regulate the market. Political pressure for low cost food comes from several sources—media, civil society and political parties, particularly the opposition. Hence, the government needs to 'pretend' that they are seriously monitoring the market and taking action against all wrongdoings in the market system. While the government acts for their own interest and for political gain, it hardly helps to promote better economic management. For instance, drawing the example of television talk shows in Bangladesh, Mahmud, (*Prothom-alo*, 4 February 2010) argues that instead of making a meaningful discussion of rice price hikes, leaders and activists of the major political parties tend to make it merely a political debate, where both parties just want to show how successful they are now and were in the past.

The widespread belief in Bangladesh is that the markets are not functioning well and that speculative behaviour is driving the market price, raising the possibility of sharp price increases in the future. In this regard, the very term 'market syndication' is a buzzword in contemporary Bangladesh. Whether it is the regular inflation of daily essentials or an unexpected price hike, it is common practice in Bangladesh that the government and opposition blame each other. For example, on 12 May 2010, in her speech in national parliament, Prime Minister Sheikh Hasina accused the BNP-Jamaat alliance of hatching a conspiracy to increase the prices of essential goods. According to Hasina,

> . . . using the money they looted while in power, BNP-Jamaat alliance is spending their looted money to increase the prices of essentials. Thousands of crores of Taka are now in their hands and it does not matter to them if they spend Tk 1,000 crore for this purpose. They are not concerned with people's sufferings

due to price hike of essentials. Their only aim is to undermine the Awami League government (*The Daily Star*, 12 May 2010).

A closer look at Bangladesh's political history suggests that this stance of the government in blaming the opposition is nothing new. In 1974, Mujibur Rahman, the then Prime Minister of Bangladesh overtly states that '. . . a group of sharks, hoarders, smugglers, profiteers and black-marketeers were trading on human miseries' (*The Bangladesh Observer*, 23 September 1974). Since 1991, after returning to electoral democracy, this practice of the blame game has been the general trend of Bangladeshi politics. Since 2003-4, agflation rates in Bangladesh were increasing more than the general inflation rate. This upward trend of agflation seriously kicked in during 2007-8. However, in 2003-4, the then BNP-led, four-party alliance government also blamed 'market syndication' media and the opposition for the unexpected price hikes of essentials including foodgrains. Thus, the initiative of market regulation is merely a political agenda in Bangladesh. The purpose of this kind of initiative is to maximize political gain, rather than the rectification of markets by understanding the real causes of market failure. As a consequence, public policy fails to seek potential remedies for the problem and increase economic efficiency.

Market Regulation in Bangladesh: the Nature of the State's Response

Historically, in pursuance of market rectification, successive governments have always taken some initiatives. These initiatives or policy responses can be categorized in two major groups: (i) the offensive policy response; and (ii) the defensive policy response. In the following section, I will outline these policy responses of the government in dealing with markets. I will also address the underlying reasons of policy failure.

(i) *The offensive policy response*: Based on historical analysis it is evident that the government of Bangladesh often employs a special type of policy which I call 'the offensive policy' response, as it is based on coercion, using military, paramilitary, police and other elite forces such as the rapid action battalion (hereafter RAB). The purpose of this type of policy is to create a frightening environment so that traders cooperate with the government by selling goods regularly according to the prices fixed by the government or by simply not hoarding foodgrains. Many suggest that in the name of market rectification this is in fact a kind of harassment of the traders—a Bangladeshi economist stated 'doing business in Bangladesh is a great sin' (Faridee 2010).

For instance, at the beginning of the 1974 food crisis, district authorities in Barisal carried out a drive against hoarding by seizing rice from traders and selling it in the open market at a moderate price. Alamgir (1980: 120) suggests, 'while it provided temporary relief to the people, it "scared away" rice from the market, which naturally caused tremendous hardship to the people in that area'. In spite of the negative impact, after the famine successive governments have always employed anti-hoarding laws with the exception of the 1998 floods. Dorosh et al. (2004: 159) notes that in dealing with the 1998 floods, one of the most important successes of the government, 'perhaps, was a policy not taken. Despite pressure from some high-level officials, the Government of Bangladesh did not reinstate anti-hoarding laws, which would have seriously disrupted incentives for both domestic and international rice trade'. Policy analysts warned that invoking the provisions of the anti-hoarding laws could enable law enforcement and regulating agencies to harass private traders, extracting official and unofficial payments, ultimately resulting in higher rice prices (ibid.). In response to government initiatives against hoarding or price fixing, traders find alternative ways to continue hoarding, fearing a future scarcity of foodgrains. Either they stop selling completely to keep secret their hoarding, or they offer bribes to the members of implementing agencies such as the police and RAB, which causes further crisis. However, Bangladesh has been invoking the provisions of the anti-hoarding laws again since the beginning of 2003, when a new agflation crisis caused a price hike of foodgrains. In 2007-8, under a state of emergency, the then military-backed caretaker government attempted to address the problem of price hikes using coercion. Military, paramilitary, RAB, the police and intelligence agencies took various initiatives to control price hikes. This extreme offensive policy is seen as 'harassment' to traders and, therefore, the resulting damage is further price hikes.

In addition to invoking the provisions of the anti-hoarding laws, the government often attempt price-fixing to stabilize foodgrain prices. For example, on 20 August 2009, on the eve of Ramadan, the government fixed the wholesale prices of potato, onion, garlic and ginger to ensure stability in the essential commodity market during Ramadan. Commerce Minister, Faruk Khan, fixed the price and claimed that 'these are rational retail prices and anyone selling at more than the mentioned prices is a profiteer. The government should not spare the profiteers as they are making the market unstable'. He adds that 'we have already instructed the officials of city corporations and deputy commissioners' offices to monitor the gap between wholesale and retail prices of commodities. They should take punitive actions against the unscrupulous traders if they are found making unusual profits' (*The Daily Star*, 21 August 2009). In September 2009, as a result of the price hike of sugar, the government arrested a few top-level sugar traders/dealers for hoarding. Because of the weakness of anti-hoarding laws, charges were filed against the businessmen under special act (*Daily Prothomalo*, 9 October 2009).

Using force for the purpose of 'disciplining' or 'civilizing' the market is common in Bangladesh. Indeed, there are plenty of examples of the abovementioned initiatives to rectify markets which shows that the government 'attempts' to monitor markets for political gain, most of which do not work. While the government is very rhetorical about market regulation, weak state capacity and poor governance are clearly evident in every stage of market management. For example, on 21 March 2011, the government issued a decree *ottabossokiyo ponno biponon o poribeshok niyog adesh* (essential goods marketing and dealer recruitment order) as an official gazette which stated that dealers will be appointed within three months and the Delivery Order (DO) system would be abolished. One year and three months after this decree was issued, *Prothomalo* (29 June 2012) suggests that the process of dealer recruitment has not yet been begun.

(ii) *The defensive policy response:* This policy aims to support consumers by influencing markets based on public stocks (the ceiling price) and it also supports producers by providing incentives (the floor price). Under this policy, the government has traditionally been participating in foodgrain markets in order to reduce price fluctuations. Traditionally, public interventions in foodgrain markets through the PFDS have contributed to price stability, despite the absence of clear guidelines to reduce price variability (as cited in Ali et al. 2008: 113). According to the Department of Food, Ministry of Food and Disaster Management, adequate public stock acts as a check on the profiteering behaviour of grain traders. Particularly, it has been observed that release of grain from public stock for open market sale has a sobering and positive effect on the market (ibid.). However, since the recent food crisis in 2007-8, the objective of price stability has not been achieved through the PFDS, although during the 1990s price stability was achieved. The lack of price stability through the PFDS is simply the failure of the policy of the government, which was the outcome of food policy reforms throughout the 1990s. For example, during the 1980s, the government developed a public storage capacity of nearly 1.8 million MT for the purpose of disaster management, providing subsidized food to targeted groups and OMS. Stock was gained by both domestic procurement and imports. Domestic procurement provided incentives to producers through the minimum support price for rice and wheat. However, after the food policy reforms, food stocks were reduced from about 1.5 million MT in the 1980s to about 0.6 million MT in recent years. Therefore, the government's capacity to influence the market with such small stocks remains limited (Hossain 2010: 178). As a consequence of the relatively small stock, this policy option of the government failed to make any positive impact in the market.

Efficiency Matters: Why do the State Initiatives Fail?

Why does the government fail to take necessary initiatives to regulate the market in a manner that can potentially remedy the problem and increase economic efficiency? Why have most of the state's initiatives never been successful in market management? What are the main causes of sudden price hikes? I attempt to answer these questions in order to explicate the role of the state in market management in Bangladesh. My discussion of this section relies on four tools of my central analytical framework—weak state capacity, poor governance, rent-seeking and public corruption.

As it links the production and consumption sectors, marketing can contribute several objectives for a food system as a whole, such as efficient economic growth, a more equal distribution of incomes, nutritional well-being and food security. These objectives can be achieved through the efficiency with which it communicates signals of scarcity and abundance to decision makers (Timmer, Falcon & Pearson 1983: 151). It is argued that the labels 'middleman' and 'speculator' almost universally carry negative connotations or actual opprobrium (ibid.). Similarly, in Bangladesh, 'market syndication' is another pejorative label. I have argued in Chapter 4 that market syndication is a special form of market power where a buyer, seller or a small group of them has the ability to influence power. It is the responsibility of the state to crackdown on syndication and to regulate middlemen and/or speculators. In doing so, rent-seeking and public corruption are the major challenges to the state. While rent-seeking and public corruption are inherently associated with capitalism and exist in most societies (developed or developing countries), the efficiency differs. In pursuance of the strategies to manage price stability, it is efficiency that matters, which increases the gap between developed and developing countries. Efficiency is particularly important for a country like Bangladesh, where the market is significantly affected by the prices of global market and the production of its own foodgrains. The Bangladesh state seeks price stability by providing guaranteed floor and ceiling prices for major products. In doing so, a strong administrative capacity as well as a strong state monitoring mechanism is required. In the following discussion, I examine how and what the state is doing in ensuring market stability, with particular reference to the 2007-8 food crisis management strategies of the government.

Throughout the late 1980s and early 1990s, the PFDS underwent many reforms. In the process, although the PFDS was significantly downsized in several key issues, its role in enforcing floor and ceiling prices remained unchanged in the early 1990s, considering its necessity for price stabilization. Later, public stocks of cereals in Bangladesh significantly decreased (see figure 6.1), therefore, the ability of the state to play a significant role in price stabilization decreased dramatically. Here, it is imperative to note that two important trends need to be taken into account when considering levels of stocks—population growth and production growth. While, over the years, both population as well as total domestic agricultural production has increased significantly, and the aggregate number of poor has not decreased, the per capita figure of public stock levels have been dramatically decreasing (see Figure 6.1).

The Ministry of Food and Disasters Management and its special wing for food, the Department of Food, believe that a healthy public stock acts as a check on the undue profiteering behaviour of grain traders (Ali et al. 2008: 113). In a personal interview, one prominent former state official argued that 'there is no alternative of adequate public stock to influence the market' (IvGoB5). Parti-

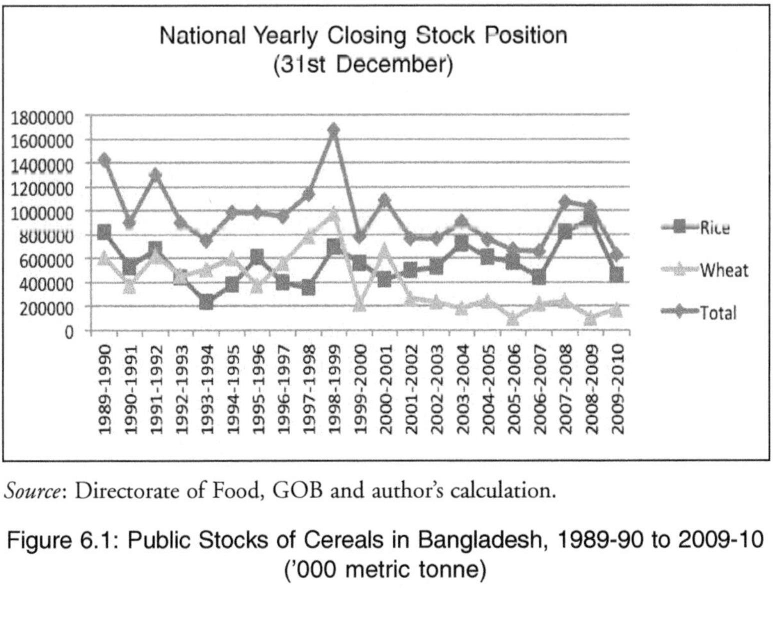

Source: Directorate of Food, GOB and author's calculation.

Figure 6.1: Public Stocks of Cereals in Bangladesh, 1989-90 to 2009-10 ('000 metric tonne)

cularly after recent experience of the sudden price hike, many suggest that a healthy public stock is required for managing food price stability.[11] For example, based on the experience of the recent food crisis in Bangladesh, Hossain (2010: 179) suggests:

> Because of limited stocks the government could increase the allocation by only 10 per cent during 2007-8 compared to the previous year. The amount allocated during July 2007 to May 2008 was only 1.43 million tonnes. This amount did not have an impact in market. The estimated national consumption is about 27 million MT of which 12 million MT is transected in the market. The government allowed the para-military force to operate Open Market Sales (OMS) of essential commodities including rice at subsidized prices to urban consumers. But the OMS also did not have a significant effect in containing the price rises due to their low amount in relation to demand.

In other words, it was the failure of the government to influence the market because of its relatively small stocks of foodgrain. Despite high imports in 2008, rice prices rose sharply in Bangladesh, which shows that 'information' can be very influential on markets.[12] Under these circumstances, farmers, millers, traders and even consumers reportedly responded to 'information' such as inadequate public stocks, global food price hikes and export bans by India and other rice-producing countries. Most importantly in this situation, public confidence in the government's ability to stabilize food consumption was absent.

Questioning the efficacy for seeking better macroeconomic benefits while the state reduced public stocks has not kept any avenues open to mitigating emergency crises. In addition to downsizing public stocks, which is important for price stability, the operation of public procurement—which has traditionally supported farmers by ensuring floor prices for foodgrain production—has also been reduced. The creation of market syndication, middlemen, and speculation is also the result of this small amount of public stock.

The effective government storage capacity (warehouses) in Bangladesh is less than 1.2 million tonnes although officially it is 1.7 million tonnes, of which some are inedible. With regard to 12 million MT transected rice market in Bangladesh, this is not adequate storage for the purpose of market stabilization, as well as food-based safety nets and emergency relief. Furthermore, rice cannot be stored in these warehouses for more than six months. In contrast, wheat can be stored for a long time. However, a reduction in wheat-based food aid in recent years has increased the amount of rice in store and thus the need to 'roll over' the stock (Shahabuddin et al. 2009). In an interview, a prominent former government official argued that at the end of 2006 and in 2007 he wrote to the Food Ministry several times to import wheat as an alternative to rice, as the rice price was already quite high in the global market. He also wrote to the then Chief Advisor (CA) of the Caretaker Government (CG) through his personal secretary. However, according to him, at the beginning of the crisis (in 2007-8) no decision was made (IvGoB5). In relation to the storage capacity and quality, he states:

> [While I was in office] I personally wrote to the ministry that the government has to increase the storage capacity. And warehouses have to be built in a manner so that foodgrains can be stored for approximately 3-4 years. Although the conditions of the present warehouses are much better than those of the old warehouses, they still need to be improved. I noticed that bad weather easily affects the stock because of the poor quality of storage. For example, a special type of silo is now being used in warehouses which cannot protect the quality of stock from even a little rain. I argued that this structure should be changed and suggested the building of concrete floors instead of silt floors. These can be cost-effective and stock will not deteriorate.

Similarly, explaining the bad impact of the present floor system of the warehouses, a field-level food inspector also suggests that it is important to modernize warehouses in Bangladesh for the better conservation of foodgrains (IvGOB7).

In a personal interview, a former state official who served a long time as a Director General (DG) of food argued that there is no alternative to adequate stocks for managing food price stability in Bangladesh, and making adequate stocks a high-priority policy is the need of the hour (IvGoB5). In an interview with the daily *Prothom-alo* (5 December 2010), an eminent Bangladeshi food policy expert also suggests that at present the government has the capacity to stock 1.2 to 1.5 million MT, and that this stock should be increased to 2.5 to 3 million MT to influence the market price.

In a personal interview, a rice trader goes a step further, 'the government must have the ability to know the precise amounts of its demands for each particular season. Based on the demands, it is important to manage necessary stocks, or more . . . in order to manage price stability in any crisis healthier stock is the only solution. Harassing us [traders] is not a solution' (IvRTrd12). A better policy must envisage long-term requirements focussing on stock capacity. Not only has the government failed to realize that without adequate stock it would not be able to regulate markets; but it has also not kept any scope for the future increase of stocks to mitigate challenges.

In addition to the poor quality of warehouses that hampers the stocks, poor governance also challenges the appropriate levels of stock. The Food Department of Bangladesh is generally known as one of the most corrupt public sectors where many irregularities/anomalies are often legitimized by the law. For example, one per cent losses of stocks released from the warehouses of stocks has always been the norm. A former official suggests that 'one per cent is huge and unnecessary . . . this rule was made when we had no warehouses . . . while I was in charge, I attempted to change this policy but I failed to do so because of huge pressure from the stakeholders' (IvGoB5). He adds that the Food Department needs radical change in relation to its administrative structure, policy-making and staff. Another prominent state official who worked as both Secretary of the Food and Disasters Ministry and also served as DG food argues that 'if the government is really sincere about ensuring food security, they must stop corruption. Have you ever heard that any staff member of the Food Department or the Upazila Nirbahee Officer (UNO) or Chairman lost his/her job for wrongdoing or corruption? There is no fear of punishment for corruption at all' (IvGOB8). He adds that this corruption is not only the matter of a single department but rather it is mostly interdepartmental. Under the Upazila (sub-district) administration, food officers cannot do anything themselves, they do it along with the Chairman and/or the UNO (IvGOB8).

While the purpose of public stocks is price stabilization, it is important to manage them with efficiency. Stocks alone cannot ensure price stability, efficient use of the stock is required in order to influence the market. For example, in order to maintain a floor price for farmers, the domestic procurement programme needs to be arranged in a timely and efficient manner. In order to reduce foodgrain prices to protect consumers when prices go high, timely and very precise OMS programmes are necessary. While there is no doubt that both domestic procurement and OMS is vital for encouraging domestic production and promoting price stability, the outcome of these programmes is questioned. The faulty designs of the current procurement system prevent it from having an impact on prices (IvGoB4; IvGoB5; IvGOB8; Ali et al. 2008: 113; also see, Dorosh & Shahabuddin 1999). Using two political economy concepts, rent-seeking lobbies and rent-seeking bureaucrats/agents, Adams (1998) shows that food subsidy systems in Bangladesh failed to benefit the rural poor. He suggests that 'it is the PFDS' use of procurement pricing for rice that provides the greatest opportunity for rent-seeking behaviour by implementing authorities—both government officials and private agents—in Bangladesh'. Because of the flaws of the current procurement system it does not benefit the target group, i.e. farmers, instead the main beneficiaries include traders, millers and Ministry of Food officials. As a result, as Rahman notes, 'there appears to be serious lapses in the management of the millgate contracting (system), with huge quantities of missing (rice) stock and consequent losses to the government' (Rahman 1992: 41; Adams 1998: 77). Similarly, a study of the World Bank (as cited in Adam 1998: 78) estimated that about 1.6 billion Taka (US$40.3 million) could be saved if all rice procurement in Bangladesh was done through competitive tenders rather than millgate contracting. Until now, the situation has remained unchanged. For example, in 2010 the government grossly failed in meeting the procurement target of 1.2 million tonnes of *boro* rice. Mondal, a former Food Secretary of the Government of Bangladesh, pointed out that 'this was basically a management failure' (*The Daily Star*, 7 August 2010).

Adequate stock is important but it is imperative to bear in mind that it is only one factor that influences the market; it is not possible to influence the market without its proper and timely use.

Available data indicates that over the years the size of the OMS operations remains negligible, particularly throughout the 1990s. The size of the operation was recently increased after the food crisis of 2007-8. However, due to inadequate supply in relation to demand, unplanned operation and poor governance, the OMS did not have a significant effect in containing the price rises. While my earlier discussion focusses on the weak state capacity of Bangladesh in managing food price stabilization due to inadequate stocks, in the following discussion, I will draw upon two other factors that deter the possible outcome of the OMS operation as a means of price stabilization—unplanned operation and poor governance.

Since the early 1980s, OMS programmes have been used to reduce foodgrain markets for consumers when prices go high and caused transitory food insecurity, particularly for low income households. In addition to the negligible size of the operation, lack of planning is another important reason why this programme failed to make a significant impact on the recent surge in rice prices, particularly since the 2007-8 crisis. By examining the nature of the structure, recruitment of dealers and the operational areas of the OMS, it is clear that the programme is basically targeting a particular group of people for political gain—it is not designed in a manner so that people can easily buy low cost foodgrains. For example, out of a total of 540 OMS truck dealers, 250 are employed in Dhaka city. The rest of the truck dealers are employed in adjutant districts of Dhaka (Nayanganja, Gazipur, Narshindhi) and other divisional district cities (see DG Food 2011). Within the city, however, most of the places used as selling venues are inconvenient for the poor buyers. In an interview with *Prothom-alo*, H.Z. Rahman, a former Commerce Advisor of the Caretaker Government, pointed out that 'there is a problem with the OMS selling process. The OMS trucks can be seen in Dhanmondi area [a very affluent part of the capital city]. The number of poor people living in this area is very few. Poor people will not come here from other parts of the city to buy rice' (see *Prothom-alo*, 10 October 2010).

According to OMS policy, an individual can buy a maximum of 5 kg of rice at a fixed price per day from the dealers, who start selling at 9 a.m. and continue until 6 p.m., six days a week. However, because of the inconvenient location of the OMS trucks it is often not economically viable for the poorest of the poor to buy rice from OMS centres. In some centres there is a long queue and in some there are no buyers at all. Therefore, to make OMS operations meaningful, a massive rectification of the system is necessary.

It is often argued that 'the rice sold at OMS centres is of such a low quality that it is only usable as poultry feed. It is actually a mixture of particles (*khud*) of different varieties of rice full of husks and grits. The rice seems to have lost its original colour and emits a bad odour' (*The Daily Star*, 6 May 2011). In response to this very common allegation, a rice trader argues that this is often the policy of the OMS dealers to show and sell some low quality rice in order to avoid selling at the fixed price (IvRTrd12). However, sometimes even this low quality rice may not be found due to corruption and, therefore, many poor people leave the OMS centres empty-handed. *The Daily Star* investigation reveals that the dealers prepare fictitious lists of potential buyers and sell the OMS rice on the black market where each kilogram of rice yields a profit of at least Tk 5.50. The report adds,

> [T]he Food Department officials, who are 'strictly monitoring' the dealers during and after the sale, are also enjoying benefits from the theft. . . . During a spot visit at the City Bhaban intersection around 9.30 a.m. on 18 October, a dealer, who identified himself as Wahed Ali, was found commencing the day's OMS sale showing 1.5 metric tonnes of rice already sold to 300 people. Asked for an explanation, Wahed Ali and the food inspector, who identified himself as Sardar Akbar Ali, offered this correspondent tea [bribe] and expressed their helplessness to comment on that. Meanwhile, according to the register, the duty inspector for that day was Amirul Islam. . . . A quarter kilometre from Barnali Mor, another dealer Mostak Ahmed was also found starting the day showing 1.5 metric tonnes of rice sold to 300 consumers. Food inspector MA Hannan at that time arrived on the spot on a rickshaw. Informed about the matter, the inspector expressed surprise saying, 'I don't know how it is possible as I left the spot half-an-hour before yesterday's closing and today he is yet to start the sale' (31 October 2010).

Selling rice in the black market is profitable and, therefore, OMS dealers bribe monitoring officers, is a practice known as 'commission' (*The Daily Star*, 31 October 2010). The reason OMS dealers are not punished for any wrongdoing is patronage politics. For example, a report of a daily newspaper notes that in Khulna city, 25 out of 31 dealers have been appointed allegedly on political consideration, and they have little experience in business or in dealing with rice, and do not have a registered shop in the city (*The Daily Star*, 22 March 2010).

Extortion and Market Failure: Exploring the Role of The State

'Today extortion has increased so wildly that, even if the government sincerely wants to, they will not be able to control the current unbridled price hike of daily essentials'.

Personal Interview, IvPol2

Here I examine extortion as a cause of a market failure in Bangladesh. I show that market failure in Bangladesh is the result of institutional failure which is the ultimate outcome of the patronage politics of neopatrimonial regimes. It is not only that the state cannot provide institutional and infrastructural facilities to support the markets, but rather it also allows 'state-sponsored' illegal activities such as extortion that hurts the mechanism of market management/regulation. As a result, price stabilization attempts by the state fail. In other words, this section attempts to clarify the linkage between market management, the neopatrimonial state and price stabilization.

A study of Olken and Barron (2009) demonstrates that market structure affects the level of illegal payments. The market structure has a substantial impact on the amount of bribes charged. Not surprisingly, this study of 'the simple economics of extortion' is closely relevant to the market structure of Bangladesh, where bribes and other forms of extortion are common practice. In light of the study of Olken and Barron, it can be seen that various types of extortion significantly affect the market structure—an important reason behind market failure—which subsequently causes the price hike of daily essentials in Bangladesh, including foodgrains. Here, my discussion aims to provide a systematic analysis to understand the underlying causes of market failure.

In 2009, the Minister for Food and Disaster Management, Abdur Razzak, openly admitted that 'extortion causes price hike'. In a public meeting, he stated that 'I don't know whether it would be wise for me, as a minister, to tell you the story of extortion. . . . I came to know from various sources that a truck owner received only Tk 7,000 for a trip from Jessore to Mymensingh although the trip was pre-settled at Tk 28,000. The rest of Tk 21,000 had to be paid as extortion' (*The Daily Star*, 17 August 2009; *Prothom-alo*, 17 August 2009). He admits that more than 70 per cent of transportation costs are actually extortion.

As a result of reckless extortion, farmers are deprived as they get very little for their produce; it also affects the consumers as the prices of foodgrains go up. A vegetable trader from Tangail, a constituency of the Food Minister, admits that they deprive the farmers and fleece consumers to make profit after paying the extortionists. Because of extortion the prices of commodities differ significantly between the villages and cities, and even within cities. For example, according to the Food Minister, in Gazipur, on the way to Dhaka, a truck needs to pay extortion sums in two different places within fifteen minutes of each other (*Prothom-alo*, 17 August 2009). Consequently, the price goes up within this short distance.

The Finance Minister of Bangladesh, Abul Mal Abdul Muhit, sees extortion as one of the major challenges that deter economic prosperity and development in Bangladesh. He states that Bangladesh will be a happy and prosperous country if stability can be maintained and extortion controlled in the next ten years (*Prothom-alo*, 17 August 2009). The statements by government ministers suggest that extortion is the result of opportunistic behaviour but this view fails to get to the reality of the situation. The state fails to control various illegal activities such as extortion due to patronage politics. While it is the responsibility of the government to support the markets by providing better institutions and infrastructure, the ruling elite and government institutions are responsible for the extortion. For example, the Food Minister suggested that truck drivers need to bribe weigh station attendants located in Manikgang for heavy loads (*Prothom-alo*, 17 August 2009). A report of Sharmin, a news journalist of ETV, clearly visualizes the poorly-kept secret of extortion by the police (see Sharmin 2012). My field-level data suggests that the reason for the state failure to control this extortion is that the beneficiaries of this money range from local political leaders and government officials (police constables, soldiers, weigh attendants) to top-level politicians, as well as top-level government officials (e.g. senior police officers). Drawing on the case of the Daulatdia ferry terminal extortion, a report of *The Daily Star* notes that toll collection has its apparently in the 'silent support' of none other than Shipping Minister, Shahjahan Khan. According to the report, 'the gang, comprised of ruling party leaders and activists, police and staff of Bangladesh inland water transport corporation, illegally realizes around Tk 5 lakh from vehicles every-day' (*The Daily Star*, 22 July 2012). In September 2010, at a view-exchange meeting with the newly appointed Inspector General of Police (IGP), the FBCCI (Federation of Bangladesh Chambers of Commerce and Industries) Director, Mojibor Rahman Khan, candidly stated 'extortion is taking place openly on the highway in assistance with police' (*The Daily Star*, 17 September 2010). Thus, extortion which causes price hikes has its linkages with public corruption, weak state capacity and patronage politics in Bangladesh.

CONCLUSION

This chapter investigates two aspects of food accessibility—the state-sponsored, direct-entitlement generation mechanism and market regulation for price stability. The chapter demonstrates that food accessibility is still deeply problematic for the poor segment of the population. The challenges of food accessibility are linked with the nature of the state's particularly weak capacity, poor governance, rent-seeking behaviour, corruption and partial reform.

Given the socio-economic conditions and widespread poverty in Bangladesh, this chapter argues that the state patron entitlement generation is still important in Bangladesh in order to ensure food accessibility for the vulnerable sections of the population. Traditionally, the PFDS generated entitlement in Bangladesh through various projects and programmes. By focussing on three key weaknesses of the PFDS, this chapter shows that projects and programmes of the PFDS are under severe challenges—(a) it is a highly politically-motivated system which extensively damages its humanitarian goals; (b) the state is disinclined to promote food security through the PFDS which reflects its trend of budgetary allocation; and (c) SSN programmes are not entirely appropriate for promoting food security, particularly to the vulnerable sections of the poor. This chapter shows that since the beginning of the PFDS in Bangladesh, it has always been politically motivated. Its historical origin, development, and current practice suggest that the purpose of this program is to help regime survival by using state resources rather than promoting food security. I suggest that this policy is derived from the necessity of regime survival. It appeased the urban middle class through various urban-based channels of the PFDS; and also successive regimes appeased donors through various reforms recommended by the donors, and it purposefully fostered target errors and leakage errors through politically-motivated projects and programmes. Thus, while the leakage errors and target errors are widely seen as the problem of governance, I contend that this is the mechanism of regime survival with the distribution of opportunities among various actors.

On the other hand, considering the impact of sudden price hikes as an important impediment of entitlement generation, this chapter seeks to explore the state mechanisms/initiatives of market regulation necessary for price stabilization. I argued that market regulation in Bangladesh is merely a political agenda. Because of political pressure, in order to ensure low cost food for the middle and lower-middle classes, neopatrimonial regimes 'pretend' that the government is seriously monitoring the market, taking necessary initiatives for the sake of price stabilization. The purpose of this kind of initiative is more to maximize political gain rather than market rectification by understanding the real causes of market failure. As a consequence, public policy fails to seek a potential remedy for the problem and increase economic efficiency. I have argued that, historically, in pursuance of market rectification, successive governments have always taken some political initiatives, which I categorized into two main types. The first type is based on coercion, using military, paramilitary, police and other law enforcement agencies which is detrimental for the market rather than a remedy. The second strategy is influencing the market based on public stock. In other words, public intervention in the foodgrains market through the PFDS. Drawing upon the recent food crisis of 2007-8, I have shown the policy failure of the government with regard to the strategy of market influence. My discussion reveals that the government mechanism of public intervention in foodgrain markets fails for several reasons, including weak state capacity and poor governance. In addition, rent-seeking behaviour and public corruption provides meaningful insights in order to grasp state failure in public intervention. This chapter has shown that the market structure has a substantial impact on the amount of bribes, extortions and other form of illegal payments charged. In other words, it is not only that the state cannot provide institutional and infrastructural facilities to support the markets, but rather it also allows illegal activities which hurt the complete market mechanism, which is the inevitable outcome of the patronage politics of a neopatrimonial government.

NOTES

1. This term I borrowed from a public lecture of Dipesh Chakrabarty (2009) where he describes Indian Modernity as 'Once Colonial, Now Global'.
2. See Lilliston and Ranallo (2012) for an interesting collection of papers on this theme.
3. Alamgir (1980: 119) suggests that after the good harvest of the 1973-4 winter rice crop, the government made a half-hearted attempt to procure winter rice but it was a failure. As we see later, in the light of the development of severe famine during 1974, the failure of the government to procure a substantial quantity of Aman rice from surplus farmers turned out to be an important factor in accentuating the suffering of the people.

4. The 6.1 million estimate includes a relatively small Case for Work component; estimated at 370,000 participants.
5. Union Parishad is the bottom tier of the local Government of Bangladesh.
6. A number of reports of daily newspaper also suggests similar story. For example, '*TR er name tree-mukhi protarona* (triangle cheats in the name of TR)', an article of the daily *Prothom-alo* (Dhaka, 11 November 2011) suggests that wheat allocated for development works under the TR programme in Patia upazila under Chittagong district for Sree Loknath Mandir had been allegedly misappropriated as there is no such *mandir* in that region. Similarly, there were a number of institutions which received allocations for TR programmes meant for maintenance, which also did not exist. The report further suggests that money from these allocated TR programmes was spent for the UP Chairman election in favour of a candidate who is a supporter of the local MP of the ruling party. Also see, '*TR er chal attosat Awami League netader* (Awami League leaders embezzled TR rice!)' in *Prothom-alo*, 3 May 2011; '*Club o school er nam vangiye TR er taka attosat* (Money of TR embezzled in the name of club and school)' in *Prothom-alo*, 23-24 August 2011.
7. A report of the influential Bengali daily *Prothom-alo* (16 August 2011) also demonstrates the way in which a powerful syndicate, consisting of the leaders and activists of the ruling political party, control the business of rice and wheat of different TR and FFW programmes in the Kustia district. It also shows the misappropriation of various TR programmes.
8. This study further argues that 'numerous safety net programmes have been implemented, aimed at helping different groups within the population cope with adverse shocks that are either idiosyncratic or aggregate in nature. These programmes are intended to (i) improve the living standards of the weakest segments of the population (as defined economically, socially, by gender, by location, and by religion), (ii) help in income and consumption smoothing for households that have been impacted with negative shocks, and (iii) prevent and mitigate the impact of economic and natural shocks. Successive governments have recognized the importance of well-functioning safety nets, both for groups that are chronically poor and for those at risk of falling into poverty. Well-functioning safety nets also provide the transient poor an opportunity to climb out of poverty'.
9. In response to a question (Rasul & Thapa 2004: 345), all farmers mentioned that if they earn some income from a small amount of surplus paddy (in this case, SSN benefits), it is mostly utilized for buying non-food items, including clothes and other daily necessities. Another research find-

ing (Ahmed, Quisumbing & Hoddinott 2007) suggests that as income increases, beneficiaries' preference for food declines, indicating that the poorest households prefer only food as the transfer.

10. In the context of African markets and states, with special reference to the food sector, Bates (1981: 30) notes that in almost all developing countries, political pressures for low cost food comes from two main sources—urban workers and employers who, when their workers are faced with high cost food, are forced to pay higher wages. Bates (ibid.) adds that 'governments must appease the urban worker; but as major employers and as the sponsors of industry, governments share the interests of those who pay the wage bill. To appease consumers while pursuing their own interests, governments, therefore, join with workers and industry in seeking low cost food'.
11. There are two main types of literature which suggest the impact of public stocks in relation to price stabilization in Bangladesh. Studies of Ravallion (1985; 1990) and Osmani (1991) suggest the positive aspects of adequate public stock for price stabilization. According to Ravallion (1990: 259-60), '. . . price stabilization may have an important role in anti-hunger policies, . . . Public buffer stocks are the traditional instrument for this purpose . . . when this [public foodgrain stock] is believed to be low, the traders expect future prices to be high'. Similarly, Osmani (1991) argues that greater public confidence in the government's ability to stabilize food consumption was an important reason why Bangladesh was able to avoid further famines in 1979 and 1984. In contrast, Goletti (2000) questioned the efficacy of price stabilization and its economic benefits. He argues that 'the microeconomic benefits of price stabilization in Bangladesh are small, the effects on poverty negligible, and the possible macroeconomic benefits of price stability unknowable. At the same time, the need for government price stabilization has diminished' (ibid. 2000). Drawing upon the case of the 1998-9 floods of Bangladesh, del Ninno et al. (2001) conclude that private sector imports rather than public stock levels contributed to meeting foodgrain availability requirements. As part of the policy recommendation, the study of the World Bank (1979) cited optimal national stocks as equal to 1.5 million MT as of 1 July of every year and 1.2 million MT as of 15 November of every year. Security stocks equal to 600,000 tonnes were considered 'appropriate'. According to Ahmed et al. (2004), the current national food security stock level of 800,000 metric tonnes appears to be high. A stock of 600,000 metric tonnes of wheat and rice (300,000 metric tonnes each) would be cost-effective. The study adds that stock levels greater than this increase total PFDS costs because of quality deterioration,

higher transit costs and storage losses, and suboptimal use of its administrative structure (ibid.).

12. Ravallion (1990: 260) points out that Bangladesh's rice markets demonstrate how influential information can be on markets. An important part of that information is the level of the government's foodgrain stock, itself determined by the government's past procurement efforts, food aid and imports. When this is believed to be low, traders expect future prices to be high. But they don't have rational expectations; it was found that their *ex post* forecasting errors are generally and quite strongly correlated with *ex ante* information.

CHAPTER 7

Conclusion

The central aim of this book was to understand the political and economic dimensions of food security in Bangladesh. The book has critically examined the role of the state in meeting the challenges of food security and demonstrates that hunger and food insecurity in Bangladesh are deeply embedded in the nature of the state itself and in the political institutions that link the state and society. In this concluding chapter of the study, I first briefly revisit the objectives of this thesis. I then summarize the argument of the study, consider the implications of the study with comparative possibilities, and finally attempt to provide directions for additional research.

In examining the politics of food security in Bangladesh with special reference to food availability and accessibility, this thesis had two primary objectives. The first and foremost objective of the study was to provide a detailed empirical study of the state's role in promoting food security in Bangladesh, focussing on two important aspects of food security: food availability and food accessibility. In doing so, I questioned the ability, intention, and outcome of food availability and accessibility under the auspices of the Bangladesh state which exhibits neopatrimonial tendencies. I was particularly interested in critically examining the issue of food security in relation to the inherent nature of the state in policymaking and effective policy implementation. The case study, therefore, has sought to make a critical analysis of the challenges, difficulties, and outcomes of food availability and accessibility which emanate from a neopatrimonial state.

Considering the fact that national governments make policies that determine food security and insecurity, a second goal of this thesis was to seek to understand the nature of the Bangladesh state. My initial understanding was that to investigate the structural causes of hunger, it was imperative to examine the missing dimensions of *stateness* that includes state institutions, scope of state functions, etc. I have argued that it is imperative to explore the nature of the state as the state is not only an important, active economic and social development actor, but it is also vital because the state is the fundamental actor whose role is to protect its citizens by providing goods and services by using the economic resources of their own society and allowing markets to flourish by monitoring through rules and institutions. To that end, poverty, hunger, food insecurity, etc., are closely linked with the nature of the state. Thus, to examine the politics of food security in Bangladesh, the centre of my attention was to investigate the role of the state with special reference to the process of policymaking and the policy implementation mechanism.

Using the five analytical elements of the central framework of the study, throughout this thesis, I have critically investigated the role of the state. Each of the analytical elements provides a clear understanding about the state's failure to carry out its projects and programmes in order to promote food security. To that end, I have shown that the root cause of hunger is deeply embedded in the nature of the state. In this thesis, my discussion firstly has illustrated the nature of the Bangladesh state and how that systematically erodes the state's capacity to carry out development including food security. I have then looked at the challenges of food availability and accessibility in Bangladesh and how the government responds to those challenges.

The historical trend of the Bangladesh polity suggests that the political leadership has always struggled to monopolize state power, whether it is a populist authoritarian, military autocratic or democratically elected regime. Successive regimes have always sought to accumulate power in specific core offices of the state, and usually within the executive branch. In the process of power accumulation, regimes systematically weaken state institutions and the centralized decision making process. Until 1990, the core characteristics of the various regimes of Bangladesh were that they all practised an authoritarian and paternalistic mode in running the administration. Although the nature of the patrimonial rule changed after the multi-party election in 1991, the authoritarian and paternalistic attitude of regimes remains unchanged. Since 1991, regimes have practised 'patrimonial' power within a 'legal-rational' domination as the degree of bureaucratic institutionalization is now deeply entrenched. By examining this new form of state authoritarianism, I suggest that the contemporary Bangladesh state is a neopatrimonial state. Under this new arrangement, regimes survive through patronage politics, and the political manipulation of state resources shape policy outcomes. In doing so, the political elites of Bangladesh create networks (by using the traditional patron-client structure of the society) and alliances, relying on *exchanges* to meet their objectives. In this regard, state elites use elements of the state and political system to mediate these exchanges—regimes use various state apparatus for personal or sectoral interests, not for societal interests. With a particular focus on the period of the 'democratic' era, my discussion in Chapter 3 demonstrates that successive regimes in Bangladesh have used various state institutions as a tool and mechanism in order to monopolize state power which has eventually helped them to establish personal rule under a democratic framework.

As a consequence of patronage politics in the neopatrimonial state of Bangladesh, I have shown in Chapter 3 that rent-seeking and public corruption are widespread and reforms necessary for better governance have fallen into the trap of the 'partial reform syndrome'. Moreover, there is a distinct indication of poor governance and weak state capacity to formulate policies and implement them. My investigation in Chapter 3 has shown that the Bangladesh state neither has the capacities to penetrate society, nor to regulate social relationships, nor to extract resources, and it also cannot appropriate or use resources in determined ways. In this sense, the Bangladesh state is a weak state. However, I have argued that this systematic regression of the capacity of the Bangladesh state is closely linked with the neopatrimonial politics of Bangladesh. The fact is that patronage politics which are the outcome of neopatrimonial regimes are the main factors that weakens the state's capacity in Bangladesh. While a weak state is a state that fails to perform a number of activities, the failure of performance is a purposeful outcome of regimes in the neopatrimonial Bangladesh state. In this respect, because of patronage politics and pay-off or exchange-based rule, regimes 'do not'—and not 'cannot'—perform a number of activities and fail to carry out development programmes. For instance, while administrative capacity is essential for an effective state, my discussion has demonstrated how the actions of successive regimes of Bangladesh have undermined the quality of the bureaucracy. As a result, over the years, Bangladesh has observed a noticeable decline in the quality of the civil service.[1] Although political leaders, such as the Prime Minister, occasionally express frustrations about the incompetence of the civil service, the fact is that this incompetence is the outcome of the hiring and promotion policies of the successive regimes of Bangladesh.

Systematic regression of the state's capacity in Bangladesh along with its pre-colonial inheritance has resulted in weak links between the state and society. Hence, the state has failed to reach the society and thus has been incapable of making policies and implementing them in the interests of society. The fact that political elites in Bangladesh use the state's apparatus as a tool for the personalization of state power results in the systematic decline of institutional capacity. In other words, the poor capacity of the Bangladesh state is the direct consequence of the formal policies and informal practices of neopatrimonial regimes. On the one hand, as noted earlier, reforms necessary for increasing institutional capacity, such as strengthening the Anti-Corruption Commission, are not being implemented by formal policies; on the other hand, informal practices, such as recruiting and promoting those in the bureaucracy based on reward for personal connections and loyalty to political leaders are important factors impairing administrative capacity.

Given the nature of the Bangladesh state, the numerous challenges of promoting food security in Bangladesh have been shown in Chapter 4 of this thesis. Two of them are noteworthy. First, I have shown that both food availability and accessibility in Bangladesh are under serious threat. The supply side or the availability of food includes some factors which are involved with agri-governance, environmental degradation, and stagnation of new technological development—inadequate policy attention and the lack of investment of the state have further exacerbated the situation. Moreover, there is also uncertainty in terms of trade and food aid being able to mitigate the shortfall in production. The moot question that arises is thus is the road ahead blocked in relation to further production to meet the increasing future demands? I have shown that the present nature of the state not only shows its weak ability to overcome existing challenges, but it is also unable to deal with future challenges in a scientific manner. Second, the problem of food accessibility is another major challenge for thousands of the hungry poor. With a particular focus on the entitlement approach, I have shown several challenges of food accessibility in Bangladesh—poverty, the increasing amount of urban poverty, intra-household disparity of food, impact of sudden price hikes, etc. With the existing crises in ensuring food accessibility, this chapter has shown that the only way to promote food accessibility to the chronically hungry poor is state-generated entitlement. However, I have argued that, over the years, the Bangladesh state has gradually withdrawn from its role of promoting food accessibility through entitlement generation.

In Chapter 5, a critical investigation of the role of the Bangladesh state in promoting food availability has shown the institutional incapacity of the state in a range of important sectors which are vital for ensuring food availability. The state's inability has been observed in promoting agriculture in order to boost domestic production; over-reliance on importing foodgrains rather than promoting domestic production; failure in timely imports of foodgrains; dependency on food aid despite its uncertainty; and faultiness in promoting food availability.

Drawing on the political economy of the budgetary allocation and budget-making process in Bangladesh, I have shown that the state is gradually decreasing its role in promoting agricultural growth. In addition to the trend of the gradually decreasing budgetary allocation in the agriculture sector, the state has also not been doing 'enough' and/or is unable to take the necessary measures to promote agricultural growth in a manner that can promote food availability. A critical examination of the underlying changes that have taken place in Bangladesh's agriculture sector in the past few decades suggests that the state failure in promoting the agriculture sector is mainly because of weak state capacity and poor governance, and that the extent of its role is also shrinking. In other words, the poor state performance in economic management, particularly in the agriculture sector, has clearly been observed. I have shown that as a result of patronage politics which is the inevitable outcome of a neopatrimonial regime, rent-seeking, public corruption, poor governance and weak state capacity seriously jeopardize the state's initiatives in developing and implementing agricultural development policy. Moreover, due to the neopatrimonial nature of the state, reform initiatives also fall into the trap of interest politics which I label as the partial reform syndrome. In consequence, the state's initiatives in the development agenda for agriculture such as the fertilizer subsidy and/or its distribution failed to provide meaningful support to poor farmers. Thus, by demonstrating poor economic management, weak state regulation and monitoring, partial reforms and the state's incapacity to develop and implement appropriate policy, I have argued that the state has left the farmers virtually on their own.

In addition to domestic food production, as Bangladesh is a food-deficit country, international trade and food aid still play a vital role in ensuring food availability. In this regard, I have shown four major challenges for the effective import of foodgrains into Bangladesh in order to promote food availability by means of international trade. First, there are uncertainties with regard to foodgrain imports which are focussed on the global rice market. Second, the government decision making mechanism in Bangladesh is very slow—there is a lack of infrastructural capacity for a strong early warning system which is particularly crucial in Bangladesh as the main reason for fluctuation in food availability is natural disaster such as flood and drought. I have shown the failure of the state in providing an appropriate statistical service which is essential for the scientific decision making necessary for food availability. Third, because of patronage politics and poor governance, there is an 'absence' of effective state regulation and monitoring of private sector traders and, therefore, it more often does harm rather than provide a steady supply of foodgrains. And fourth, the chapter has shown that for the steady supply of foodgrains, although some emphasize the necessity of mobilizing the TCB, the fact remains that, because of rent-seeking, public corruption and administrative inefficiency, this government institution is incapable of undertaking effective imports. By highlighting these four main failures of the state, I suggest that international trade is not a safe means of ensuring food availability in the neopatrimonial state of Bangladesh.

As was noted in Chapter 5, historically, Bangladesh has been one of the largest food aid recipient countries, and in the peak food aid year of 1987-8, food aid constituted 12 per cent of its cereal availability. However, historical experience suggests that the country has failed to manage food aid during its major crises such as in 1974 and 2007-8. Moreover, with considerable growth in agricultural production as well as progress in other sectors, including economic growth, the importance of food aid has been seriously eroded. As a consequence, I raised the question of whether food aid could result in disincentive effects in rice and wheat production in contemporary Bangladesh. However, the truth is that as a large segment of poor people still live below the poverty line, state intervention is required to support the nutritional status of these hardcore poor. In the process, I have shown the failure of the Bangladesh state to reach the intended real beneficiaries of the various food aid-based programmes. Expenditure for food aid-based programmes is vulnerable to leakage to the non-poor due to rent-seeking, widespread corruption, poor governance and institutional incapacity. In this regard, the necessity as well as the reliability of food aid in promoting food availability in Bangladesh demands further inquiry.

Similar to the state's inability to effectively plan and carry out policies that can promote food availability, the state's incapacity has also been evident in promoting food accessibility in Bangladesh. In Chapter 6, my main argument was that policies adopted by the neopatrimonial Bangladesh state are broadly politically motivated and, therefore, do not promote food accessibility to the hungry poor. Focussing on two major factors of food accessibility, namely entitlement creation and effective market regulation for price stabilization, I have shown that the policy formulation mechanism is predominantly based on the interests of small ruling elites and it is, therefore, unable to carry out any meaningful projects or programmes that can promote food security. Moreover, I have argued that because of several factors such as weak state capacity, poor governance, rent-seeking, corruption and partial reform, which are the inevitable outcome of the patronage politics of neopatrimonial regimes, the Bangladesh state cannot implement the policies necessary for ensuring food access for the very poor segments of the poor.

I have argued in Chapter 6 that, given the socio-economic conditions and widespread poverty, the state's patronage of entitlement generation is important in Bangladesh in order to ensure food accessibility for the vulnerable sections of the population. Traditionally, the Public Food Distribution System (PFDS) generates entitlement in Bangladesh through various projects and programmes. By examining in detail three key weaknesses of the PFDS, I have shown three major limitations of the projects and programmes of the PFDS. These are—first, most of these projects and programmes are highly politically motivated which extensively damage its humanitarian goals; second, the state is disinclined to promote food security through the PFDS which reflects its trend of declining budgetary allocation; and third, I raise the question whether SSN programmes are appropriate for promoting food security particularly to the vulnerable section of the poor.

I have shown that, from the very outset of the PFDS in Bangladesh it has always been politically motivated. Its historical origin, development and current practice suggest that the purpose of this programme is to help regime survival by using state resources rather than promoting food security. I have revealed that this policy is derived from the necessity of regime survival. Successive regimes appease the urban middle class through various types of urban-based channelling of the PFDS. They also appease donors through various reforms recommended by donors, and purposefully fosters 'target error' and 'leakage error' through politically motivated projects and programmes. Thus, while 'leakage error' and 'target error' are widely seen as the problem of governance, my discussion in Chapter 6 has clearly shown that this is the mechanism of 'regime survival' through the distribution of state resources among the various political actors.

Considering the impact of sudden price hikes as an important impediment to entitlement generation, my discussion in Chapter 6 also sought to explore the state mechanisms/initiatives of market regulation that are necessary for price stabilization. In other words, given the neopatrimonial nature of the state, I have examined the challenges of food accessibility in Bangladesh in relation to markets, market failures and market interventions which, in other words, can be called market management. I have shown that market regulation in Bangladesh is merely a political agenda. Because of the political pressure for political purposes and in order to ensure low cost food for middle class or lower middle class people, neopatrimonial regimes need to 'act' and/or 'pretend' that the government is seriously monitoring the market, taking the necessary initiatives for the sake of price stabilization. The purpose of this kind of initiative is more to maximize political gain rather than to regulate the markets through understanding the real causes of market failures. In consequence, public policy fails to seek potential remedies for the problem and fails to increase economic efficiency. I have argued that historically because of political reasons, in pursuance of market rectification, successive governments have always taken political initiatives which I categorized into two main types. The first type is based on coercion—using military, paramilitary, police and other law enforcement agencies which is damaging for the market rather than a remedy, as I have shown in Chapter 6. The second strategy is influencing the market based on the use of public stock; in other words, public intervention in the foodgrain markets through the PFDS. Using the recent food crisis of 2007-8 as an illustration, I have then shown the policy failure of the government with regard to the strategy of market influence. My discussion has revealed that the government mechanism of public intervention in the foodgrain market fails for several reasons, above which are the weak state capacity and poor governance of the Bangladesh state. In addition, rent-seeking behaviour and public corruption provide meaningful insights in order to grasp the state's failure in public intervention. I have also shown that the market structure in Bangladesh has a substantial impact on the amount of bribes, extortion, and other forms of illegal payments charged. In other words, it is not only that the state cannot provide institutional and infrastructural facilities to support the markets, but rather that it also allows illegal activities which hurt the complete market mechanism. This, I argue, is the inevitable outcome of the patronage politics of a neopatrimonial government.

In order to understand the political and economic dimensions of food security, throughout this thesis, I have used five political economy approaches—rent-seeking, public corruption, the partial reform syndrome, weak state capacity and poor governance. I have shown that because of the neopatrimonial nature of the state each of these concepts are deeply entrenched within the state's functions and scope. This has substantial impact on development policy making as well as on implementation mechanisms for food policy. By making a thorough empirical study of the politics of food security in Bangladesh, I have shown that: (a) rent-seeking and public corruption are deeply embedded in food and agricultural governance; (b) like many other development reform agendas ranging from privatization (market-based reforms) to administrative reforms for good governance, 'the partial reform' which suits the interests of ruling elites only just sees the light of the day and, therefore, the reform agenda can neither improve land distribution nor improve the PFDS in Bangladesh; and (c) weak state capacity and poor governance are also evident in every stage of food and agriculture policy, from policymaking to policy implementation, and have fatally eroded a variety of development agendas including food security.

Not surprisingly, although this study draws on the Bangladesh case, it does not mean that the findings here do not have implications that extend beyond the case study of this thesis. It is likely that this thesis has implications for the developing world, particularly in Africa, South America, and in many Asian countries, which exhibit neopatrimonial regimes or neopatrimonial tendencies of regimes (for a discussion on personal rule, neopatrimonialism, and regime typologies in contemporary world politics, see Guliyev 2011). The implications can be summarised as follows:

Firstly, despite the risk of generalization, many of the countries in Africa, South America and Asia which exhibit neopatrimonial regimes or neopatrimonial tendencies are poor and many of them are food insecure. In order to explore the problems of the food security mechanisms of these nations, the existing literature mainly focusses on corruption without examining the problem in detail. By going underneath the surface, I have argued that corruption is an important point to begin with but it is not the only point in understanding the complex mechanism of food security politics. It is imperative to remember that corruption is merely the outcome of neopatrimonial regimes. Under the neopatrimonial regime, the general conditions which I have shown such as patronage politics and the elite's interest in policymaking and implementation are far deeper than only poor governance and/or corruption-based studies of the food security problem. In other words, this study rejects the simplistic argument that corruption is the only underlying factor behind the poor policymaking process and the weakening of policy implementation mechanisms resulting in the state's failure to promote food security for its hungry citizens. Rather, this thesis argues that poor governance is the inevitable and deliberate outcome of the patronage politics of a neopatrimonial state. I argue that without understanding the nature of the state or its politics, the explanation that identifies poor governance and/or corruption is partial or incomplete. Moreover, as Van de Walle (2001) argues, most accounts which focus on political corruption are journalistic. He argues (2001: 281) that 'the public policy literature has rarely seriously addressed the impact of political corruption on policy making'. Thus, the given framework of this study can pave the way to avoiding the 'journalistic approach' of food security analysis and can seriously address food security challenges.

Secondly, chronic hunger is a serious problem in most of Africa. However, in addressing food insecurity and hunger, the academic literature pays little attention to the institutional aspects, that is, state capacity, state-society relationship, nature of the state, institutional effectiveness, etc. This study of the Bangladesh case, has demonstrated that hunger and food insecurity are deeply embedded in the nature of the state. In making this argument. The thesis has shown that the state's responses and activities and the ways in which it interacts with the food and agricultural market, agricultural development strategy and activities, farming and non-farming subsidies, and entitlement generation through the Public Food Distribution System are all politically motivated and purposefully designed for the interests of the state's elites rather than the poor. Thus, the analytical framework of the present study can be useful for many nations in Africa or in any other parts of the world whose politics are of a neopatrimonial nature and thus can explore those nations' responses in dealing with strategies of food aid, food production, trade and its distribution mechanisms.

Thirdly, one of the key analytical elements of this study is the partial reform syndrome. Using this analytical element, I have shown that the PFDS, land reform, administrative effectiveness for policy implementation, etc., have fallen into the trap of the partial reform syndrome in Bangladesh, resulting in persistent state failure in making and implementing appropriate policies necessary for ensuring food security. Although this framework is very useful in understanding the problem of African economics and political crises which became visible in the work of Van de Walle (2001), so far, the academic literature on food security has not used this as the analytical tool in neopatrimonial African states. Hence, I believe that this approach could pay dividends in other countries particularly in Africa which suffer from both the neopatrimonial tendencies of their regimes as well as food insecurity.

By revealing the root causes of hunger and food insecurity in the resource-poor country of Bangladesh whose state is neopatrimonial in nature, I suggest that the given framework of this study could also be useful for examining the situation of food insecurity in other food-insecure countries in other regions of the world.

NOTE

1. Referring to a leaked cable (WikiLeaks) from the US embassy in Bangladesh, *The Daily Prothom-alo* (18 September 2011) reports that after coming back into office in 2009, the Prime Minister, Sheikh Hasina, had noted a marked decline in the quality of civil servants between her 1996-2001 government and now. For example, according to Rizvi, the PM's advisor, the PM and top World Bank officials agreed to collaborate on a comprehensive programme to develop a social safety net for Bangladesh's poor. The PM instructed her government to work with the World Bank on this initiative and was dismayed to discover recently that Government of Bangladesh inertia had stalled the project. Rizvi added that it was not that the bureaucrats were unwilling or unsupportive but rather that they were incompetent.

APPENDIX 1

Interviewee Codes (Anonymized)

Interviews of this study were conducted under the UNSW 3.2 (a) ethics approval by the Arts, Humanities & Law Human Research Ethics Advisory Panel. In compliance with the UNSW's code of practice on research ethics, I agreed that any information that was obtained in connection with this study through interviews and that could be identified with interviewees would remain confidential and would be disclosed only with the permission of interviewees, except as required by law. With the permission of interviewees, I only discussed and published the results of the interviews as part of this study of the politics of food security in Bangladesh. Moreover, to prevent any interviewee from any potential for harm, it was my aim that in this thesis or any other publication, information would be provided in such a way that she/he cannot be identified. Therefore, in order to ensure confidentiality of interviewees, in this instance, no details have been given.

Code	Organization/Profession/Department	Date Interviewed
IvGoB1	State official, Ministry of Agriculture, GOB	12 August 2010
IvPol2	Political activist and foodgrain traders	14 August 2010
IvNGO3	NGO staff (UBINIG)	18 August 2010
IvGoB4	Former Secretary, Ministry of Food and Disasters Management, GOB	23 August 2010
IvGoB5	Former Directorate of Food, Ministry of Food and Disaster Management, GOB	17 September 2010
IvCS6	Prominent civil society member, economist and political analyst	18 September 2010
IvGOB7	State official, Ministry of Food and Disaster Management, GOB	25 September 2010
IvGOB8	Former Secretary, Ministry of Food and Disaster Management, GOB	7 October 2010
IvGoB9	Former Secretary, Ministry of Agriculture, and Former Advisor of Caretaker government, GOB	10 October 2010
IvCSPol10	Prominent civil society member, political activist, political analyst, and professor of economics	8 August 2010
IvEcn11	Author, political analyst, and professor of economics	22 August 2010
IvRTrd12	Rice trader	1 September 2010
IvFmr13	Small farmer	20 September 2010
IvSeedtrd14	Seed trader	15 September 2010
IvPolprf15	Political analyst, and professor of political science	10 November 2010
IvCS16	Prominent civil society member, activist, and author	19 October 2010

APPENDIX 2

Glossary of Key Bengali Terms Used

Aman	Monsoon season rice crop, grown mainly in lowland
Aus	Early summer or pre-monsoon rice crop
Bazaar	Marketplace
Boro	Winter season rice crop
Char	River land (silt sandbars formed in rivers), often shifting when rivers change course
Chita	Paddy grains containing no pith. In other words, whole paddy grains without or with only partially formed rice kernels inside the husk
Dalal	Literally, tout; an intermediary
Hat	Weekly or biweekly market
Gram	Village
Godowns	Warehouses
Haor	A form of lake or a wetland ecosystem
Hartal	A strike action that shut down all commercial and disrupt government activity which could be regional or nationwide. Usually violent in nature, and physically enforced by patrols from the group or organisation that called the *hartal*. Generally, the political opposition calls the *hartal* against the government actions and/or policies
Kharif	Monsoon season
Khas	State-owned land (this land has either been newly formed by changing river courses, or is confiscated from landowners in breach of land reform legislation)
Khud	Particles of rice (a mixture of rice grains comprising mostly particles of rice)
Manga	A famine-like situation due to the scarcity of food and lack of the people's access to income, particularly in the lean season (also known as the hungry season). In the north-western part of Bangladesh, in a particular time of the year, this seasonal food insecurity is caused by unemployment and income deficit

Mastaans	Local gangsters, leader or hoodlums
Matabbar	Literally, village leader or a village elite
Mazar	Tomb or mausoleum
Palli rationing	Rural rationing (this was a programme under the Public Food Distribution System of Bangladesh which was abolished in 1992)
Parishad	Council
Rajneeti	Politics
Union Parishad	Union council is the smallest/bottom tier of administrative units formed by a number of villages. In other words, it is a bottom tier of the local government units in Bangladesh
Samaj	Local residential community in Bangladesh, literally, 'society'
Sarkar	Government
Taka	Bangladesh currency (Tk), approximately US$1.00 = Tk 81.94 (13 June 2012)
Thana	Previously referred/known as subdistricts, literally, 'police station'
Unnayan	Development
Upazila	New sub-district (a district is divided into sub-districts), which is the second lowest tier of the local administration system in Bangladesh
Upazila Nirbahi	Chief administrator of an Upazila
Zila	District

Bibliography

Abbott, P.C., C. Hurt & W.E. Tyner, *What's Driving Food Prices*, Oak Brook: Far Foundation Issue Report, 2008.

Acemoglu, D., S. Johnson & J.A. Robinson, *The Colonial Origins of Comparative Development: An Empirical Investigation*, Cambridge, MA: National Bureau of Economic Research (NBER), Working paper no. 7771, 2000.

——, 'Reversal of Fortune: Geography and Institutions in Making of the Modern World Income Distribution', *Quarterly Journal of Economics*, 2000, 117(4): 1369-1401.

Acemoglu, D. & J. Robinson, *Why Nations Fail: The Origins of Power, Prosperity, and Poverty*, New York: Crown Business, 2012.

Adams, R.H., 'The Political Economy of the Food Subsidy System in Bangladesh', *The Journal of Development Studies*, 1998, 35(1): 66-88.

ADB, *People's Republic of Bangladesh: Developing Innovative Approaches to Management of Major Irrigation Systems*, Dhaka: Asian Development Bank, 2009.

Ahluwalia, I.J. & W. Mahmud, 'Economic Transformation and Social Development in Bangladesh', *Economic and Political Weekly*, 2004, 39(36): 4009-11.

Ahmad, E., *Military Rule and the Myth of Democracy*, Dhaka: University Press Limited, 1988.

Ahmad, K. & S.M.Q. Hasanuzzaman, 'Agricultural Growth and Environment', in R. Faruquee (ed.), *Bangladesh Agriculture in the 21st Century*, Dhaka: University Press Limited, 1998.

Ahmed, A.U., A.R. Quisumbing & J.F. Hoddinott, *Relative Efficiency of Food and Cash Transfers in Improving Food Security and Livelihoods of the Ultra-Poor in Bangladesh*, Washington D.C. : International Food Policy Research Institute, 2007.

Ahmed, A.U., S. Rashid, M. Sharma & S. Zohir, *A Study on Food Aid Leakage in Bangladesh*, Washington D.C.: International Food Policy Research Institute, 2003.

——, *Food Aid Distribution in Bangladesh: Leakage and Operational Performance*, Washington D.C.: International Food Policy Research Institute, 2004.

Ahmed, F., S. Barua, M. Mohiduzzaman, N. Shaheen, M.A. Bhuyan, B.M.

Margetts & A.A. Jackson, 'Interactions between Growth and Nutrient Status in School-Age Children of Urban Bangladesh', *The American Journal of Clinical Nutrition,* 1993, 58(3): 334-8.

Ahmed, I., 'Governance and Flood: Critical Reflections on the 1998 Deluge', *Futures,* 2001, 33(8-9): 803-15.

Ahmed, I. & S. Khan, 'BNP's Polls Manifesto Pledges Abundant, but Specific Target Issuing', *The Daily Star,* 15 December 2008, p. 14.

Ahmed, N., *The Parliament of Bangladesh,* Aldershot: Ashgate, 2002.

——, 'From Monopoly to Competition: Party Politics in the Bangladesh Parliament (1973-2001)', *Pacific Affairs,* 2003, 76(1): 55-77.

Ahmed, R., 'Liberalization of Agricultural Input Markets in Bangladesh: Process, Impact and Lessons', *Agricultural Economics,* 1995, 12(2): 115-28.

——, *Retrospects and Prospects of the Rice Economy of Bangladesh,* Dhaka: University Press Limited, 2001.

Ahmed, R., S. Haggblade & T.E.E. Chowdhury (eds.), *Out of the Shadow of Famine: Evolving Food Markets and Food Policy in Bangladesh,* London: John Hopkins University Press in association with IFPRI, 2000.

Ahmed, S., *Bangladesh: Past and Present,* New Delhi: A. P. H. Publishing Corporation, 2004.

Ahmed, Z., 'Soils are "Hungry", May "Eat" Fertiliser, and Become Intoxicated', *New Age,* 11 February 2009.

Akram, T., 'A Theory of Ineffective Privatization', in R. Sobhan (ed.), *Privatization in Bangladesh: An Agenda in Search of a Policy,* Dhaka: University Press Limited, 2005.

——, 'Ineffective Privatization of Public Enterprises: The Case of Bangladesh', in R. Sobhan (ed.), *Privatization in Bangladesh: An Agenda in Search of a Policy,* Dhaka: University Press Limited, 2005.

Aktaruzzaman, 'Food Security and Containing Price Inflation', in CPD, *Development with Equity and Justice: Immediate Tasks for the Newly Elected Government,* Dhaka: Centre for Policy Dialogue (CPD), 2009.

Akter, N., *Alternative Agriculture in Bangladesh: A Study of UBINIG, CDA, and PROHIKA Programs,* Dhaka: Bangladesh Rural Advancement Committee (BRAC), 1997.

Alam, S.M.S., *The State, Class Formation and Development in Bangladesh,* Lanham: University Press of America, Inc., 1995.

Alamgir, M., *Famine in South Asia: Political Economy of Mass Starvation,* Cambridge, Manchusetts: Oelgeschlager, Gunn & Hain, 1980.

Alamgir, M. & P. Arora, *Providing Food Security for All,* Rome: International Fund for Agriculture Development by IT Publications, 1991.

Alavi, H., 'The State in Post-Colonial Societies: Pakistan and Bangladesh', *New Left Review*, 1972, (July-August): 59-81.

——, 'The State in Crisis', in H. Gardezi & J. Rashid (eds.), *Pakistan: The Roots of Dictatorship*, London: Zed Press, 1983.

Alesina, A., S. Ardagna & F. Trebbi, *Who Adjusts and When? The Political Economy of Reforms,* IMF Staff Papers, 53 (Special Issue), 2006.

Ali, A., 'Livelihood and Food Security in Rural Bangladesh: The Role of Social Capital', PhD Thesis, The Netherlands: Wageningen University, 2005.

Ali, A.K.M.S., I. Jahan, A. Ahmed & S. Rashid, 'Public Food Distribution System in Bangladesh: Successful Reforms and Remaining Challenges', in S. Rashid, A. Gulati & R.J. Cummins (eds.), *From Parastatals to Private Trade: Lesson from Asian Agriculture,* Baltimore: The John Hopkins University Press (Published for the International Food Policy Research Institute), 2008.

Ali, A.M., 'Population Pressure, Environmental Constraints and Agricultural Change in Bangladesh: Examples from Three Agroecosystems', *Agriculture, Ecosystems and Environment,* 1995, 55(2): 95-109.

Ali, A.M.M.S., 'Development Dogma and Death of Farmers', *New Age,* 26 May 2005.

Ali, S.M., *Understanding Bangladesh,* London: Hurst & Company, 2010.

Alston, J.M., P.G. Pardey & M.J. Taylor, *Agricultural Science Policy: Changing Global Agendas,* Baltimore: Johns Hopkins University Press, 2001.

Anwar, M.K., 'Food Security and Containing Price Inflation', *Development with Equity and Justice: Immediate Tasks for the Newly Elected Government,* Centre for Policy Dialogue (CPD), Dhaka, 2009.

Aron, J., 'Growth and Institutions: A Review of the Evidence', *World Bank Research Observer,* 2000, 15(1): 99-135.

Asaduzzaman, M., Q. Shahabuddin, U.K. Deb & S. Jones, *Input Prices, Subsidies and Farmers' Incentives,* Dhaka: BIDS, 2009.

Asian Human Rights Commission, *Bangladesh: Government Food Subsidy Fails to Reach the Poor Due to Corruption,* viewed 17 September 2011, <http://www.humanrights.asia/news/hunger-alerts/AHRC-HAG-004-2011 >.

Atwood, D.A., A.S.M. Jahangir, H. Smith & G. Kabir, 'Food Aid in Bangladesh: From Relief to Development', in R. Ahmed, S. Haggblade & T.E.E. Chowdhury (eds.), *Out of the Shadow of Famine: Evolving Food Markets and Food Policy in Bangladesh,* Baltimore and London: IFPRI and The Johns Hopkins University Press, 2000.

Awokuse, T.O., 'Food Aid Impacts on Recipient Developing Countries: A Review of Empirical Methods and Evidence', *Journal of International Development,* 2011, 23(4): 493-514.

Azmat, F., 'Reforms in the Bangladesh Agriculture Input Sector: Room for Complacency?', *Contemporary South Asia*, 2009, 17(4): 379-98.

Azmat, F. & K. Coghill, 'Good Governance and Market-Based Reforms: A Study of Bangladesh', *International Review of Administrative Sciences*, 2005, 71 (4): 625-38.

Babbie, E., *The Practice of Social Research*, 12th edn., Belmont, CA: Wadsworth, 2010.

Bach, D.C., 'Patrimonialism and Neopatrimonialism: Comparative Trajectories and Readings', *Commonwealth and Comparative Politics*, 2011, 49(3): 275-94.

BAL, *Election Manifesto of Bangladesh Awami League 2008*, Bangladesh Awami League, viewed 8 June 2012, <http://www.albd.org/english/index. php?option=com_content&view=article&id=177&Itemid=113>.

Bala, B.K. & M.A. Hossain, 'Food Security and Ecological Footprint of Coastal Zone of Bangladesh', *Environment, Development and Sustainability*, 2010, 12(4): 531-45.

Ball, R. & C. Johnson, 'Political, Economic and. Humanitarian Motivations for PL 480 Food Aid: Evidence from Africa', *Economic Development and Cultural Change*, 1996, 44(3): 515-37.

Banerjee, A.V. & E. Duflo, *Poor Economic: A Radical Rethinking of the Way to Fight Global Poverty*, New York: Public Affairs, 2011.

Banyan, 'In the Name of the Father: An Obsession with Bangladesh's Past May Explain its Prime Minister's Growing Intolerance', *The Economist [blogs]*, 2011, viewed 14 August 2011, <http://www.economist.com/node/21525908>.

——, 'Bangladesh Looks Back: Misusing the Past', *The Economist [blogs]*, 2011, viewed 26 July 2012, < http://www.economist.com/blogs/banyan/2011/08/bangladesh-looks-back?page=3>.

Barakat, A., 'Political and Economic Scenario of Bangladesh: Where to Go, Where are we Going?', paper presented to the *National Seminar on Economic, Social and Political Situation in Bangladesh*, organized by the Bangladesh Federation of Chambers of Commerce and Industry, Dhaka, 2003.

Barman, D.C., M.G. Rahman & T. Siddiqui, *Democracy Report for Bangladesh*, International Institute for Democracy and Electoral Assistance for Bangladesh, 2001.

Barrett, C.B., 'Does Food Aid Stabilize Food Availability?', *Economic Development and Cultural Change*, 2001, 49(2): 335-49.

——, 'Food Security and Food Assistance Programs', in A.G.R.B. Gardner (ed.), *Handbook of Agricultural Economics*, vol. 2B, Amsterdam: Elsevier, 2002.

——, 'Measuring Food Insecurity', *Science,* 327 (12 February 2010): 825-8.

Barrett, C.B. & P.A. Dorosh, '"Farmers" Welfare and Changing Food Prices: Nonparametric Evidence from Rice in Madagascar', *American Journal of Agricultural Economics,* 1996, 78(3): 656-69.

Barrett, C.B. & D.G. Maxwell, *Food Aid After Fifty Years,* London: Routledge, 2005.

Bates, R., A. Grief, M. Humphreys & S. Singh, *Institutions and Development,* Cambridge, Manchusetts: Harvard University Center for International Development working paper no. 107, 2004.

Bates, R.H., *Markets and States in Tropical Africa: The Political Basis of Agricultural Policies,* Berkeley: University of California Press, 1981.

BBC Bangla, *OMS-e Chal Bikrite Oniyom (Anomalies in Selling OMS Rice),* London, British Broadcasing Corporation, Bengali Service, viewed 1 June 2011, <http://www.bbc.co.uk/bengali/multimedia/2011/04/110425_mb_bd_ricetheft.shtml?s>.

BBS, *Statistical Yearbook of Bangladesh, 1995,* Dhaka: Bangladesh Bureau of Statistics, Ministry of Planning, Government of Bangladesh, 1996.

——, *Bangladesh National Nutritional Survey 1995-6,* Dhaka: Bangladesh Bureau of Statistics, Ministry of Planning, Government of Bangladesh, 1997.

——, *Census of Agriculture 2005,* Dhaka: Bangladesh Bureau of Statistics, Ministry of Planning, Government of Bangladesh, 2005.

——, *Agricultural Sample Survey of Bangladesh 2005,* Dhaka: Bangladesh Bureau of Statistics, Ministry of Planning, Government of Bangladesh, 2006.

——, *Preliminary Report of Agri Census, 2008,* Dhaka: Bangladesh Bureau of Statistics, Ministry of Planning, Government of Bangladesh, 2008.

——, *Updating Poverty Maps of Bangladesh,* Dhaka: Bangladesh Buruea of Statistics and the World Bank in Collaboration with World Food Programme (WFP), 2009.

——, *Report on Welfare Monitoring Survey 2009,* Dhaka: Bangladesh Bureau of Statistics, Ministry of Planning, Government of Bangladesh, 2010.

——, *Preliminary Report on Household Income and Expenditure Survey, 2010,* Dhaka: Bangladesh Bureau of Statistics, Ministry of Planning, Government of Bangladesh, 2011.

——, *Population Census 2011,* Dhaka: Bangladesh Bureau of Statistics, Ministry of Planning, Government of Bangladesh, 2011.

bdnews24, 'A Monopolistic Force is Controlling the Market', *bdnews24.com,* 2011, viewed 7 January 2012, <http://world.bdnews24.com/details.php?id =154337&cid=4 >.

Begum, M.A.A. & B. Manos, 'Impacts of Fertilizer Pricing Policy in Bangladesh: A Multicriteria Analysis', *Agricultura Tropica Et Subtropica*, 2005, 38(2): 6-18.

Behrman, J., 'Intrahousehold Allocation of Nutrients and Gender Affects: A Survey of Structural and Reduced Form Estimates', in S.R. Osmani (ed.), *Nutrition and Poverty*, Oxford Oxford University Press, 1990.

Bello, W., 'How to Manufacture a Global Food Crisis', *Development*, 2008, 51(4): 450-55.

Benson, T., *Study of Household Food Security in Urban Slum Areas of Bangladesh, 2006*, Washington D.C.: Final Report for World Food Programme-Bangladesh, by International Food Policy Research Institute, 2007.

Bertocci, P.J., 'Bangladesh in the Early 1980s: Praetorian Politics in an Intermediate Regime', *Asian Survey*, 1982, 22(10): 988-1008.

Bhagwati, J., 'Getting Corruption Right', *Project Syndicate*, vol. 2011, 2010, viewed 17 August 2011, <http://www.project-syndicate.org/commentary/bhagwati7/English >.

Blair, H., 'Participation Public Policy, Political Economy and Development in Rural Bangladesh', *World Development*, 1985, 13(12): 1231-47.

BNP, *Election Manifesto 2008*, Bangladesh Nationalist Party (BNP), viewed 15 December 2011, <http://bangladeshnationalistparty-bnp.org/content.aspx?tablename=webitem2&id=18&child=null&parentid=null>.

Bode, B., *In Pursuit of Power: Local Elites and Union-Level Governance in Rural Northwestern Bangladesh*, Dhaka: CARE Bangladesh, 2007.

Bogason, P. & M. Zolner (ed.), *Methods in Democratic Network Governance*, New York: Palgrave Macmillan, 2007.

Bose, S., 'Starvation Amidst Plenty: The Making of Famine in Bengal, Honan and Tonkin, 1942-45', *Modern Asian Studies*, 1990, 24(4): 699-727.

BRAC, *Corruption and Accountability in the Social Sectors*, Dhaka: BRAC University Center for Governance Studies and BRAC Research and Evaluation Division, 2006.

——, *The State of Governance in Bangladesh 2009: Entitlement, Responsiveness, Sustainability*, Dhaka: Institute of Governance Studies, BRAC University, 2010.

——, *Bangladesh Agriculture & Food Security: Hybrid Rice and Maize Varieties*, Bangladesh Rural Advancement Committee (BRAC), 2012, viewed 8 June 2012, <http://www.brac.net/content/bangladesh-agriculture-food-security-hybrid-rice-and-maize-varieties>.

Bradsher, K. & A. Martin, 'World's Poor Pay Price as Crop Research is Cut', *New York Times*, 18 May 2008.

Brammer, H., 'Floods in Bangladesh: Geographical Background to the 1987 and 1988 Floods', *The Geographical Journal*, 1990, 156(1): 12-22.

Bratton, M. & N. Van deWalle, 'Neopatrimonial Regimes and Political Transitions in Africa', *World Politics*, 1994, 46(4): 453-89.

——, *Democratic Experiments in Africa: Regime Transitions in Comparative Perspective*, Cambridge: Cambridge University Press, 1997.

Brinkerhoff, D.W. & A.A. Goldsmith, *Clientelism, Patrimonialism and Democratic Governance: An Overview and Framework for Assessment and Programming*, Cambridge, Manchusetts: Abt Associates Inc., 2002.

BRRI, *Bangladesh Rice Research Institute (BRRI)*, viewed 23 March 2011, <http://www.brri.gov.bd/success_stories/index.htm>.

Budd, E., *Democratization, Development and the Patrimonial State in the Age of Globalization*, Lanham/Oxford: Lexington Books, 2004.

Burkle Jr., F.M., 'Globalization and Disasters: Issues of Public Health, State Capacity and Political Action', *Journal of International Affairs*, 2006, 59(2): 241-65.

Callaghy, T.M., *The State-Society Struggle: Zaire in Comparative Perspective*, New York: Columbia University Press, 1984.

Cathie, J., *The Political Economy of Food Aid*, New York: St. Martin's Press, 1981.

Chabal, P. & J.P. Daloz, *Africa Works: Disorder as Political Instrument*, Oxford: International African Institute in Association with James Currey, 1999.

Chakrabarty, D., *Indian Modernity: Once Colonial, Now Global*, online video (YouTube), viewed 22 June 2012,<http://www.youtube.com/watch?v=9ABmMC6zC8I>.

Chang, H.J., *Globalisation, Economic Development and the Role of the State*, London: Zed Books, 2003.

Chowdhury, A., 'Politics, Society and Financial Sector Reform in Bangladesh', *International Journal of Social Economics*, 2002, 29(12): 963-88.

Chowdhury, A. & W. Mahmud, 'Bangladesh', in A. Chowdhury & W. Mahmud (eds.), *Handbook on the South Asian Economics*, Cheltenham: Edward Elgar Publishing Limited, 2008.

Chowdhury, M., *Matia Criticises World Bank*, bdnew24.com, 2010, viewed 21 June 2012, <http://www.bdnews24.com/details.php?id=165850&cid=2>.

Chowdhury, N., 'Seasonality of Foodgrain Price and Procurement Programme in Bangladesh since Liberalization: An Explanatory Study', *Bangladesh Development Studies*, 1987, 15(1): 105-28.

Chowdhury, N., N. Farid & D. Roy, *Food Policy Liberalization in Bangladesh: How the Government and the Markets Delivered?*, Washington D.C.: IFPRI, 2006.

Chowdhury, N., N. Farid & D. Roy, 'Food Market Liberalization in Bangladesh: How Well Did the Government and the Markets Deliver?', in A. Ganesh-Kumar, D. Roy & A. Gulati (ed.), *Liberalizing Foodgrains Markets: Experi-*

ences, Impact, and Lesson from South Asia, New Delhi: Oxford University Press, 2010.

Chowdhury, O.H., 'Review of Rural Nutrition', in M. Asaduzzaman & K. Westergaard (eds.), *Growth and Development in Rural Bangladesh: A Critical Review*, Dhaka: University Press Limited, 1993.

Chowdhury, T.E.E. & S. Haggblade, 'Dynamic and Politics of Policy Change', in R. Ahmed, S. Haggblade & T.E.E. Chowdhury (eds.), *Out of the Shadow of Famine: Evolving Food Markets and Food Policy in Bangladesh*, Baltimore, London: The John Hopkins University Press, published for IFPRI, 2000.

Clapham, C., 'Clientelism and the State', in C. Clapham (ed.), *Private Patronage and Public Power: Political Clientelism in the Modern State*, London: Frances Pinter, 1982.

Clapham, C., *Third World Politics: An Introduction*, London: Croom Helm, 1985.

Clapp, J., *Food*, London: Polity, 2012.

Clapp, J. & D.A. Fuchs (ed.), *Corporate Power in Global Agrifood Governance*, Cambridge, Manchusetts: MIT, 2009.

Clay, E., 'The 1974 and 1984 Floods in Bangladesh: From Famine to Food Crisis Management', *Food Policy*, 1985, 10(3): 202-6.

Clay, E.J., S. Dhiri & C. Benson, *Joint Evaluation of European Union Programme Food Aid: Synthesis Report*, London: Overseas Development Institute, 1996.

Clay, E.J., N. Pillai & C. Benson, *Food Aid and Food Security in the 1990s: Performance and Effectiveness*, London: Overseas Development Institute, 1998.

Coates, J.C., P. Webb, R.F. Houser, B.L. Rogers & P. Wilde, 'He Said, She Said: Who Should Speak for Households about Experiences of Food Insecurity in Bangladesh?', *Food Security*, 2010, 2010(2): 81-95.

Coelli, T., S. Rahman & C. Thirtle, 'Technical, Allocative, Cost and Scale Efficiencies in Bangladesh Rice Cultivation: A Non-Parametric Approach', *Journal of Agricultural Economics*, 2002, 53(3): 607-26.

Collier, P. & C. Pattillo, *Reducing the Risk of Investment in Africa*, Basingstoke: Macmillan, 2000.

Conning, J. & M. Kevane, *Why Isn't There More Financial Intermediation in Developing Countries?*, UNU-WIDER (United Nations University—World Institute for Development Economics Research), Discussion paper no. 2002-28, 2002.

Cox, R., 'Gramsci, Hegemony and International Relations: An Essay in Method', in S. Gill (ed.), *Gramsci, Historical Materialism and International Relations*, Cambridge: Cambridge University Press, 1993.

CPD, *Development with Equity and Justice: Immediate Tasks for the Newly Elected Government*, Dhaka: Centre for Policy Dialogue (CPD), 2009.

Crouch, C., *The Strange Non-death of Neoliberalism*, Cambridge: Polity, 2011.

Curtis, D., M. Hubbard & A. Shepherd (eds.), *Preventing Famine: Policies and Prospects for Africa*, New York: Routledge, 1988.

Dasgupta, S., C. Meisner & M. Huq, 'A Pinch or a Pint?: Evidence of Pesticide Overuse in Bangladesh', *Journal of Agricultural Economics*, 2007, 58(1): 91-114.

Datta, S., 'Political Violence in Bangladesh: Trends and Causes', *Strategic Analysis*, 2005, 29(3).

Deb, U., M. Hossain & S. Jones, *Rethinking Food Security Strategy: Self-Sufficiency or Self-Reliance*, Dhaka: BIDS, 2009.

Deb, U.K., N. Khaled, M.A. Amin & A. Nabi, 'Climate Change and Rice Production in Bangladesh: Implications for R&D Strategy', paper presented to the *Special Conference on 'Climate Change and Bangladesh Development Strategy: Domestic Tasks and International Cooperation'*, 2009.

del Ninno, C., P.A. Dorosh & K. Subbarao, 'Food Aid, Domestic Policy and Food Security: Contrasting Experiences from South Asia and Sub-Saharan Africa', *Food Policy*, 2007, 32(4): 413-35.

del Ninno, C. & P.A. Dorosh, 'Averting Food Crisis: Private Imports and Public Targeted Distribution in Bangladesh after the 1998 Flood', *Agricultural Economics*, 2001, 25(2-3): 337-46.

Devarajan, S., 'South Asian Surprises', *Economic and Political Weekly*, 2005, 40(37): 4013-15.

Devereux, S., *Theories of Famine*, New York: Harvester Wheatsheaf, 1993.

Devereux, S. & J. Edwards, 'Climate Change and Food Security', *IDS Bulletin*, 2004, 35(5): 22-30.

Devereux, S. & S. Maxwell, *Food Security in Sub-Saharan Africa*, London: ITDG, 2001.

DG Food, *OMS Information*, Directorate General of Food, Food Division, Government of Bangladesh, 2011, viewed 1 February 2012, <http:// www. dgfood.gov.bd/oms_information.php>.

Dorosh, P., N. Farid, R. Amin & M.A. Aziz, 'Policy Response to Producion Shocks: The 1997-8 Aman Shortfall and the 1998 Flood', in P. Dorosh, C. del Ninno & Q. Shahabuddin (eds.), *Food Policy in the 1998 Floods and Beyond: Towards Comprehensive Food Security in Bangladesh*, Dhaka: University Press Limited and International Food Policy Research Institute, 2004.

Dorosh, P. & Q. Shahabuddin, *Price Stabilization and Public Foodgrain Distribution: Policy Options to Enhance National Food Security*, Dhaka: Food Management and Research Support Project, Ministry of Food, Government of the People's Republic of Bangladesh, 1999.

Dorosh, P.A., 'Trade Liberalization and National Food Security: Rice Trade between Bangladesh and India', *World Development*, 2001, 29(4): 673-89.

Eckhardt, C., *Micronutrient Malnutrition, Obesity and Chronic Disease in Countries Undergoing the Nutrition Transition,* IFPRI FCND discussion paper 213, 2006.

Eggleston, R., 'Determinants of the Levels and Distribution of PL 480 Food Aid: 1955-79', *World Development*, 1987, 15(6): 797-808.

Eide, A., 'Freedom from Hunger as a Basic Human Right: Principles and Implication', in P. Pinstrup-Andersen & P. Sandøe (eds.), *Ethics, Hunger and Globalization: In Search of Appropriate Policies*, Dordrecht: Springer, 2007.

Eisenstadt, S.N., *Traditional Patrimonialism and Modern Neopatrimonialism*, London/Beverly Hills/CA: Sage Publications, 1973.

EM-DAT, Frequency of Disasters in Bangladesh, 2011, viewed 4 October 2011, <http://www.emdat.be/database/country%20profile>.

Esmark, A. & P. Triantafillou, 'Document Analysis of Network Topography and Network Programmes', in P. Bogason & M. Zolner (eds.), *Methods in Democratic Network Governance*, New York: Palgrave Macmillan, 2007.

Evans, D.H., 'Bangladesh: An Unsteady Democracy', in A. Shastri & A.J. Wilson (eds.), *The Post-Colonial States of South Asia: Democracy, Development and Identity*, New York: Palgrave, 2001.

FAO, 2021, *The State of Food Security and Nutrition in the World 2021: Transforming Food Systems for Food Security, Improved Nutrition and Affordable Healthy Diets for All*, Rome: FAO. https://doi.org/10.4060/cb4474en

FAO, *World Food Conference: Appraisal of Prospective Food Deficits and Food Aid Needs,* Rome: Food and Agriculture Organization of the United Nations, 1974.

——, *Selected Indicators of Food and Agriculture Development in Asia-Pacific Region, 1989-99,* Rome: Food and Agriculture Organization of the United Nations, 2000.

——, *The Right to Food Guidelines: Information Papers and Case Studies,* Rome: Food and Agriculture Organization of the United Nations, 2006.

——, *Food Security: Policy Brief*, 2006, viewed 15 November 2012, <ftp://ftp.fao.org/es/esa/policybriefs/pb_02.pdf>.

——, *The State of Food Insecurity in the World 2008: High Food Prices and Food Security-Threats and Opportunities,* Rome: Food and Agriculture Organization of the United Nations, 2008.

——, *The State of Food Insecurity in the World: Economic Crises: Impacts and Lessons Learned,* Rome: Food and Agriculture Organization of the United Nations, 2009.

——, *Country Responses to the Food Security Crisis: Nature and Preliminary*

Implications of the Policies Pursued, Initiative on Soaring Food Prices, Rome: FAO, 2009.

——, *The State of Food Insecurity in the World: Addressing Food Insecurity in Protracted Crises,* Rome: Food and Agriculture Organization of the United Nations, 2010.

——, *The State of Food Insecurity in the World: How Does International Price Volatility Affect Domestic Economies and Food Security?,* Rome: Food and Agriculture Organization of the United Nations, 2011.

FAO/WFP, *FAO/WFP Crop and Food Supply Assessment Mission to Bangladesh,* Rome: Food and Agriculture Organization of the United Nations and the World Food Programme, 2008.

FAOSTAT, *Bangladesh Overview*, Food and Agriculture Organization of the United Nations, 2012, viewed 8 June 2012, <http://faostat3.fao.org/home/ index.html#VISUALIZE_BY_AREA>.

Farida, A., 'Budget for Agriculture: Promoting Unsuitable Technologies and Ignoring Farmers', 2010, *Opinion,* bdnews24.com<http://opinion. bdnews 24.com/2010/06/18/budget-for-agriculture-promoting-unsuitable-technologies-and-ignoring-farmers/>.

——, 'Introducing GE Rice!', *Opinion,* 2010, bdnews24.com, 28 November 2011, bdnews24.com, <http://opinion.bdnews24.com/2010/10/05/in-troducing-our-very-own-ge-rice/>.

Faridee, R., '*Babsha Kora Moha Pap* (Doing Business is a Great Sin)', *Prothom-alo,* 9 October 2010.

Faruk, O., 'Food Security and Containing Price Inflation', in CPD, *Development with Equity and Justice: Immediate Tasks for the Newly Elected Government,* Dhaka: Centre for Policy Dialogue, 2009.

Federico, G., *Feeding the World: An Economic History of Agriculture, 1800-2000,* New Jersey: Princeton University Press, 2005.

FFYP (Fifth Five Year Plan), *The Fifth Five Year Plan, 1998-2002,* Dhaka: Planning Commission, Ministry of Planning, Government of Bangladesh, 1998.

Flick, U., *An Introduction to Qualitative Research,* London/New Delhi/Thousand Oaks: Sage, 2002.

Fogel, R.W., *The Escape from Hunger and Premature Death, 1700-2100: Europe, America, and the Third World,* New York: Cambridge University Press, 2004.

Foster, P., *The World Food Problem: Tackling the Causes of Undernutrition in the Third World,* Boulder, Colorado: Lynne Rienner, 1992.

FPMU (Food Planning and Monitoring Unit), *Bangladesh Food Situation Report,* 83, Dhaka: Food Division, Ministry of Food and Disaster Management, 2010.

Franda, M., *Bangladesh: The First Decade,* New Delhi: South Asian Publishers Pvt Ltd in association with Universities Field Staff International, 1982.

FSI , 'The Failed States Index 2012', *Foreign Policy*, 2012, viewed 2 July 2012, <http://www.foreignpolicy.com/failed_states_index_2012_interactive>.

FSNSP, *Preliminary Results: The Food Security Nutritional Surveillance Progra,* Round 4: February-May 2011, Dhaka: Helen Keller Internation in association with BBS, European Union, and BRAC University, 2011.

FASSP-II, *Project at-a-glance, Female Secondary School Assistance Project-II,* 2008, viewed 7 November 2011, <http://web.worldbank.org/external/projects/main? pagePK=64283627&piPK=73230&theSitePK=40941& menu PK=228424&Projectid=P044876>.

Fukuyama, F., *State-Building: Governance and World Order in the Twenty-First Century*, London: Profile Books Ltd, 2004.

Gauri, V. & J. Galef, 'NGOs in Bangladesh: Activities, Resources, and Governance', *World Development*, 2005, 33(12): 2045-65.

George, S., *How the Other Half Dies: The Real Reasons for World Hunger*, New York: Penguin, 1991.

GHK, 'Local Governance and Service Delivery to the Poor: Bangladesh Case Study', paper presented to the *Manila Workshop on Local Government Pro-Poor Service Delivery*, Manila, 9-13 February 2004.

GOB, *National Food Policy 2006*, Dhaka: Ministry of Food and Disaster Management, Government of the People's Republic of Bangladesh, 2006.

——, *Bangladesh Climate Change Strategy and Action Plan 2008*, Dhaka: Ministry of Environment and Forests, Government of Bangladesh (GoB), 2008.

——, *National Food Policy Plan of Action (2008-2015),* Dhaka: Food Planning and Monitoring Unit (FPMU), Ministry of Food and Disaster Management, GOB, 2008.

——, *National Agriculture Policy 2010*, Dhaka, Ministry of Agriculture, Government of the People's Republic of Bangladesh, 2010.

Gobo, G., 'Sampling, Representativeness and Generalizability', in C. Seal, G. Gobo, J.F. Gubrium & D. Silverman (eds.), *Qualitative Research Practice*, London: Sage, 2004.

Goletti, F., 'Price Stabilization and the Management of Public Foodgrain Stocks in Bangladesh', in R. Ahmed, S. Haggblade & T.E.E. Chowdhury (eds.), *Out of the Shadow of Famine: Evolving Food Markets and Food Policy in Bangladesh*, Baltimore/London: The Johns Hopkins University Press (published for the International Food Policy Research Institute), 2000.

Gregory, P.J., J.S.I. Ingram & M. Brklacic, 'Climate Change and Food Security', *Philosophical Transactions B*, 2005, 360 (1463): 2139-48.

Griffin, K., A.R. Khan & A. Ickowitz, 'Poverty and the Distribution of Land', *Journal of Agrarian Change*, 2002, 2(3): 279-330.

Grindle, M.S., *Challenging the State: Crisis and Innovation in Latin America and Africa*, New York: Cambridge University Press, 1996.

Gujarati, D.N., *Basic Econometrics*, 4th edn., International edn.: Mc Graw Hill, 2003.

Guliyev, F., 'Personal Rule, Neopatrimonialism, and Regime Typologies: Integrating Dahlian and Weberian Approaches to Regime Studies', *Democratization*, 2011, 18(3): 575-601.

Haeften, V., Roberta & P. Moses, *USAID Office of Food for Peace: Bangladesh Food Security Country Framework FY 2010- FY2014,* Washington D.C.: Food and Nutrition Technical Assistance II Project (FANTA-2), Academy for Educational Development (AED), 2009.

Halim, M.A. & K.U. Ahmed, 'Foreign Affairs: Safeguarding National Interest', in H. Zafarullah (ed.), *The Zia Episode in Bangladesh Politics*, New Delhi: South Asian Publishers, 1996.

Haque, A.N.M.N., 'Wanted a Truly Pro-people Budget', *The Daily Star*, 7 May 2005.

Harris, R., *Political Corruption: In and Beyond the Nation State*, New York: Routledge, 2003.

Hartmann, B. & J.K. Boyce, *Needless Hunger: Voices from a Bangladesh Village*, Revised, San Francisco: Institute for Food and Development Policy, 1982.

——, *A Quiet Violence: View from a Bangladesh Village*, London: Zed Books, 1990.

Hay, C. & M. Lister, 'Introduction: Theories of the State', in C. Hay, M. Lister & D. Marsh (eds.), *The State: Theories and Issues*, New York: Palgrave MacMillan, 2006.

Hayami, Y. & V.W. Ruttan, *Agricultural Development: An International Perspective*, Baltimore: John Hopkins University Press, 1985.

Headey, D., 'Rethinking the Global Food Crisis: The Role of Trade Shocks', *Food Policy*, 2011, 36(2): 136-46.

Hellman, J.S., 'Winners Take All: The Politics of Partial Reform in Postcommunist Transitions', *World Politics*, 1998, 50(2): 203-34.

Herrmann, M. & D. Svarin, *Environmental Pressures and Rural-Urban Migration: The Case of Bangladesh*, 2009, viewed 26 January 2012, <http://mpra.ub.uni-muenchen.de/12879/>.

Hirst, P., 'Democracy and Governance', in J. Pierre (ed.), *Debating Governance: Authority, Steering and Democracy*, Oxford: Oxford University Press, 2000.

Hollist, W.L. & F.L. Tullis, *Pursuing Food Security: Strategies and Obstacles in Africa, Asia, Latin America, and the Middle East*, Boulder: L. Rienner Publishers, 1987.

Hossain, G., *General Ziaur Rahman and the BNP: Political Transformation of a Military Regime*, Dhaka: University Press, 1988.

Hossain, M., *Agriculture in Bangladesh: Performance Problems and Prospects*, Dhaka: University Press Limited, 1991.

——, *The Impact of Shallow Tubewells and Boro Rice on Food Security in Bangladesh*, Washington D.C.: International Food Policy Research Institute (IFPRI), 2009.

——, 'The 2007-8 Surge in Rice Prices: The Case of Bangladesh', in S. Ahmed & H.G.P. Jansen (eds.), *Managing Food Price Inflation in South Asia*, Dhaka: University Press Limited, 2010.

Hossain, M. & A. Bayes, *Rural Economy and Livelihoods: Insights from Bangladesh*, Dhaka: AH Development Publishing House, 2009.

Hossain, M. & U. Deb, 'Food Security and Containing Price Escalation: Facts and Implication for Policy', in CPD, *Development of Bangladesh with Equity and Justice: Immediate Tasks for the New Government*, Dhaka: Centre for Policy Dialogue, 2009.

Hossain, M., A. Janaiah & M. Husain, 'Hybrid Rice in Bangladesh: Farm-Level Performance', *Economic and Political Weekly*, 2003, 38(25): 2517-22.

Hossain, M., F. Naher & Q. Shahabuddin, 'Food Security and Nutrition in Bangladesh: Progress and Determinants', *Electronic Journal of Agricultural and Development Economic*, 2005, 2(2): 103-32.

Hossain, S., *Urban Poverty in Bangladesh: Slum Communities, Migration and Social Integration*, London: I.B. Tauris, 2010.

Hossain, S.M.A., 'The Development of Farming Systems Research in Bangladesh', in S. Haque, A.A. Rahman & G.R. Conway (eds.), *Environmental Aspects of Agricultural Development in Bangladesh*, Dhaka: University Press Limited, 1990.

Hossain, S.M.A. & M.A. Kashem, 'Agronomic Management to Combat Declining Soil Fertility in Bangladesh', Paper presented in the *6th Biennial Conference of the Bangladesh Society of Agronomy*, Dhaka, 29 July 1997.

Huda, M.N., *Why Quality Seed?: Reality and Vision*, Dhaka: GTZ Office, 2001.

Human Right Watch, *Bangladesh: Elite Force Tortures, Kills Detainees*, 2006, viewed 25 November 2011, http://www.hrw.org/news/2006/12/13/bangladesh-elite-force-tortures-kills-detainees.

Husain, A.M.M., M. Hossain & A. Janaiah, *Hybrid Rice Adoption in Bangladesh: Socio-economic Assessment of Farmers' Experiences*, BRAC Research Monograph Series no. 18, Dhaka: BRAC, Bangladesh, 2001.

IEG (Independent Evaluation Group), *Bangladesh: Country Assistance Review*, The World Bank, 2010, viewed 20 April 2011, <http://lnweb90. worldbank.org/oed/oeddoclib.nsf/DocUNIDViewForJavaSearch/609C127BFF0A89B1852567F5005D6129>.

IFPRI, *Summery of Research Output: Working Papers and Manuscripts*, Washington D.C: International Food Policy Research Institute, Mimeo, 1993.

——, *Relative Efficacy of Food and Case Transfers in Improving Food Security and Livelihoods in Ultra Poor in Bangladesh,* Washington D.C.: International Food Policy Research Institute, 2007.

IGS, *The State of Governance in Bangladesh 2006: Knowledge, Perceptions, Reality,* Report (IGS); December 2006, Dhaka: Centre for Governance Studies and BRAC Research and Evaluation Division, BRAC University, 2006.

IMF, *The IMF's Approach to Promoting Good Governance and Combating Corruption: A Guide,* 2002, viewed 22 June 2012, <http://www.imf.org/external/np/gov/guide/eng/index.htm>.

INFS, *Bangladesh National Nutrition Survey, 1995-6,* Dhaka: Bangladesh Institute of Nutrition and Food Science, University of Dhaka, 1998.

Isenman, P. & H. Singer, 'Food Aid: Disincentive Effects and their Policy Implications', *Economic Development and Cultural Change,* 1977, 25(2): 205-37.

Islam, M.M., 'The Great Bengal Famine and the Question of FAD Yet Again', *Modern Asian Studies,* 2007, 41(02): 421-40.

Islam, M.S., 'Political Violence in Bangladesh', in A. Riaz & C.C. Fair (eds.), *Political Islam and Governance in Bangladesh,* New York: Routledge, 2011.

Islam, N., *Development Strategy of Bangladesh,* New York: Pergamon Press, 1978.

——, 'What was it About the 1974 Famine?', *Scholars Journal,* 2005, viewed 9 June 2012, <http://www.scholarsbangladesh.com/nurulislam1.php>.

IvCS6, 'Interviewed', Mohammadpur, Dhaka, 18 September 2010, (See Appendix 1.)

IvCS16, 'Interviewed', Dhanmondi, Dhaka, 19 October 2010. (See Appendix 1.)

IvCSPol10, 'Interviewed', Jahangirnagar University, Dhaka, 8 August 2010. (See Appendix 1.)

IvEcn11, 'Interviewed', Jahangirnagar University, Dhaka, 22 August 2010. (See Appendix 1.)

IvFmr13, 'Interviewed', Sharifbag, Dhamrai, Dhaka, 20 September 2010. (See Appendix 1.)

IvGob1, 'Interviewed', Dhamrai, Dhaka, 12 August 2012. (See Appendix 1.)

IvGoB4, 'Interviewed', Uttara, Dhaka, 23 August 2010. (See Appendix 1.)

IvGoB5, 'Interviewed', Baily Road, Iskaton, Dhaka, 17 September 2010. (See Appendix 1.)

IvGoB7, 'Interviewed', Agargaon, Dhaka, 25 September 2010. (See Appendix 1.)

IvGOB8, 'Interviewed', Gulshan, Dhaka, 7 October 2010. (See Appendix 1.)

IvGOB9, 'Interviewed', Dhanmondi, Dhaka, 10 October 2010. (See Appendix 1.)

IvNGO3, 'Interviewed', Shaymoly, Dhaka, 18 August 2010. (See Appendix 1.)

IvPol2, 'Interviewed', Islampur, Dhamrai, Dhaka, 14 August 2010. (See Appendix 1.)

IvPolprf15, 'Interviewed', Jahangirnagar University, Dhaka, 10 November 2010. (See Appendix 1.)

IvRTrd12, 'Interviewed', Dhamrai, Dhaka, 1 September 2010. (See Appendix 1.)

IvSeedtrd14 'Interviewed', Dhamrai, Dhaka, 15 September 2010. (See Appendix 1.)

Jahan, R., *Pakistan: Failure in National Integration*, London: Oxford University Press, 1972.

Jahan, R., *Bangladesh: Promise and Performance*, London: Zed Books, 2000.

——, 'Why are we Still Continuing with a "Viceregal" Political System?', *The Daily Star: 13th Anniversary Special*, 2004, viewed 22 July 2012, <http://www.thedailystar.net/suppliments/anni2004/demo_01.html>.

——, *Bangladesh Politics: Problems and Issues*, Dhaka: University Press Limited, 2005.

Jalal, A., *Democracy and Authoritarianism in South Asia*, UK: Cambridge University Press, 1995.

Jamil, I., *Administrative Culture in Bangladesh*, Dhaka: AH Development Publishers, 2007.

Jannuzi, F.T. & J.T. Peach, 'Bangladesh: A Strategy for Agrarian Reform', in R.L. Prosterman, M.N. Temple & T.M. Hamstad (eds.), *Agrarian Reform and Grassroots Development: Ten Case Studies*, Boulder: Lynne Rienner Publishers, 1990.

Jayne, T.S., J. Strauss, T. Yamano & D. Molla, 'Giving to the Poor?: Targeting of Food Aid in Rural Ethiopia', *World Development*, 2001, 29(5): 887-910.

Karim, C.S., 'Budget: Some Thoughts on Agriculture', *Opinion*, bdnews 24.com, Dhaka, 2010, viewed 12 June 2011, <http://opinion.bdnews 24.com/2010/06/11/some-thoughts-on-agriculture/>.

Karim, R., 'Party Constitutions: Rarely Followed', *The Daily Star*, Dhaka, 17 July 2003.

Kaufmann, D., *Rethinking Governance: Empirical Lessons Challenge Orthodoxy*, Washington DC: World Bank, 2003.

Kaufmann, D., A. Kraay & M. Mastruzzi, *Governance Matters IV: Governance Indicators for 1996-2004*, Washington DC: World Bank Policy research paper no. 3630, 2005.

Kay, A., 'Economism and Public Policy', in P. Kennett (ed.), *Governance, Globalization and Public Policy*, Glos & Massachusetts: Edward Elgar Publishing, 2008.

Khan, A.A., *Friendly Fires, Humpty Dumpty Disorder and Other Essays: Reflections on Economy and Governance in Bangladesh*, Dhaka: University Press Limited, 2010.

Khan, A.A. & M.H. Khan, Interview on Public Administration in Bangladesh, Interviewed by Rassel Mahmud, BBC Bengali Service [radio], 23 June 2012, 16:55 [broadcasted], viewed 5 July 2012, http://www.bbc.co.uk/bengali/multimedia/2012/06/120623_mk_civil_service.shtml.

Khan, M.A., 'Corruption a Serious Roadblock in Eradicating Poverty', *The Daily Star*, 24 October 2009.

Khan, M.H., 'Class, Clientelism and Communal Politics in Contemporary Bangladesh', in K.N. Panikkar, T.J. Byres & U. Patnaik (eds.), *The Making of History: Essays Presented to Irfan Habib*, New Delhi: Tulika, 2000.

——, 'Introduction', in M.H. Khan & J.K. Sundaram (eds.), *Rents, Rent-Seeking and Economic Development: Theory and Evidence in Asia*, Cambridge and New York: Cambridge University Press, 2000.

——, 'Markets, States and Democracy: Patron-client Networks and the Case for Democracy in Developing Countries', *Democratization*, 2005, 12(5): 704-24.

——, 'Prodhan Montreer Nironkhush Khomota, Badal ki Darkar? [The Absolute Power of the Prime Minister, Change Needed?]', *Prothom-alo,* 3 November 2009.

Khan, M.M., 'State of Governance in Bangladesh', *The Round Table*, 2003, 92(1): 391-405.

Khan, S.A., *The State and Village Society: The Political Economy of Agricultural Development in Bangladesh*, Dhaka: University Press Limited, 1989.

Khan, Z.R., 'Leadership, Parties and Politics in Bangladesh', *The Western Political Quarterly*, 1976, 29(1): 102-25.

——, 'Aspirations and Realities: Parliaments and Democratic Culture', in S.S. Andaleeb (ed.), *Political Culture in Bangladesh: Perspectives and Analysis: Selections from the Journal of Bangladesh Studies*, Dhaka: University Press Limited, 2007.

Kimmons, J.E., K.G. Dewey, E. Haque, J. Chakraborty, S.J.M. Osendarp & K.H. Brown, *Low Nutrient Intakes Among Infants in Rural Bangladesh are Attributable to Low Intake and Micronutrient Density of Complementary Foods Program in International Nutrition,* Department of Nutrition, University of California, Davis and ICDDRB: Centre for Health and Population Research, Dhaka, Bangladesh, 2005.

Knack, S. & P. Keefer, 'Institutions and Economic Performance: Cross-Country Tests Using Alternative Institutional Measures', *Economics and Politics*, 1995, 7(3): 207-27.

Kochanek, S.A., *Patron-Client Politics and Business in Bangladesh*, New Delhi/Thousand Oaks/London: Sage, 1993.

——, 'The Rise of Interest Politics in Bangladesh', *Asian Survey*, 1996, 36(7): 704-22.

——, 'Governance, Patronage Politics, and Democratic Transition in Bangladesh', *Asian Survey*, 2000, 40(3): 530-50.

Kohli, A., 'Introduction', in A. Kohli, C.I. Moon & G. Sørensen (eds.), *States, Markets, and Just Growth: Development in the Twenty-first Century*, New York: United Nations University Press, 2003.

——, *State-Directed Development: Political Power and Industrialization in the Global Periphery*, New York: Cambridge University Press, 2007.

Kukreja, V., 'Democracy and Authoritarianism in Bangladesh', in V. Kukreja & M.P. Singh (eds.), *Democracy, Development and Discontent in South Asia*, New Delhi/ Thousand Oaks/ London/ Singapore: Sage, 2008.

Lambsdorff, J.G., 'How Corruption Affects Productivity', *Kyklos*, 2003, 56(4): 457-74.

Lewis, D.J., 'NGOs, Donors, and the State in Bangladesh', *Annals of the American Academy of Political and Social Science*, 1997, 554 (November 1997): 33-45.

Lewis, D., *Bangladesh: Politics, Economy and Civil Society*, New York: Cambridge University Press, 2011.

Lien, M.E., 'The Politics of Food: An Introduction', in M.E. Lien & B. Nerlich (eds.), *The Politics of Food*, Oxford: Berg Publishers, 2004.

Lifschultz, L., *Bangladesh: The Unfinished Revolution*, London: Zed Books, 1979.

Lifschultz, L. & K. Bird, 'Bangladesh: Anatomy of a Coup', *Economic and Political Weekly*, 1979, 14(49): 1999-2014.

Lilliston, B. & A. Ranallo (eds.), *Grain Reserves and the Food Price Crisis: Selected Writings from 2008-12*, Washington D.C.: Institute for Agriculture and Trade Policy, 2012.

Lio, M. & M.C. Liu, 'Governance and Agricultural Productivity: A Cross-National Analysis', *Food Policy*, 2008, 33(6): 504-12.

Lipton, M., 'Urban Bias and Food Policy in Poor Countries', *Development Digest*, 1980, 4(18): 25.

Løvendal, C.R., M. Knowles, N. Horii, *Understanding Vulnerability to Food Insecurity: Lessons from Vulnerable Livelihood Profiling*, Rome: The Food and Agriculture Organization of the United Nations, 2004.

Madeley, J., *Food for All: The Need for a New Agriculture*, London/New York: Zed Books, 2002.

Mahmud, W., 'Bangladesh: Structural Adjustment and Beyond', in W. Mahmud (ed.), *Adjustment and Beyond: The Reform Experience in South Asia*, Basingstoke,

UK: Palgrave-Macmillan in association with International Economic Association, 2001.

——, 'Bangladesh', in A. Chowdhury & W. Mahmud (eds.), *Handbook on the South Asian Economies*, Cheltenham, UK and Northampton, Massanchusetts, USA: Edward Elgar Publishing, 2008.

——, 'Chaler Dam o Nirbachonee Protisruti (Rice Price and the Electoral Commitment)', *Prothom-alo*, 4 February 2010.

Mahmud, W., S. Ahmed & S. Mahajan, *Economic Reforms, Growth and Governance: The Political Economy Aspects of Bangladesh's Development Surprise*, Washington DC, 2008.

Majumdar, B.A., 'Fair Elections are Not Enough', *The Daily Star*, 11 March 2006.

Mallick, D. & M. Rafi, 'Are Female-Headed Households More Food Insecure?: Evidence from Bangladesh', *World Development*, 2010, 38(4): 593-605.

Maloney, C., *Behaviour and Poverty in Bangladesh*, Dhaka: University Press Limited, 1986.

Maniruzzaman, M., 'Party Politics and Political Violence in Bangladesh: Issues, Manifestation and Consequences', *South Asian Survey*, 2009, 16(1): 81-99.

Maniruzzaman, T., 'Bangladesh in 1974: Economic Crisis and Political Polarization', *Asian Survey*, 1975, 15(2): 117-28.

——, 'Administrative Reforms and Politics within the Bureaucracy in Bangladesh', 1979, 17(1): 47-59.

——, *The Bangladesh Revolution and its Aftermath*, Dhaka: University Press, 2003.

Mankiw, N.G., *Principles of Economics*, Mason: South-Western Cengage Learning, 2011.

Mann, M., *The Sources of Social Power: A History of Power from the Beginning to AD 1760*, vol. 1, Cambrdige: Cambridge University Press, 1986.

——, 'The Autonomous Power of the State: Its Origins, Mechanisms and Results', in J.A. Hall (ed.), *States in History*, Oxford: Basil Blackwell, 1986.

Marcus, R.R., 'Marc the Medici?: The Failure of a New Form of Neopatrimonial Rule in Madagascar', *Political Science Quarterly*, 2010, 125(1): 111-31.

Matin, I. & D. Hulme, 'Programmes for the Poorest: Learning from the IGVGD Programme in Bangladesh', *World Development*, 2003, 31(3): 647-65.

Matin, N. & M. Taher, 'The Changing Emphasis of Disasters in Bangladesh NGOs', *Disasters*, 2001, 25(3): 227-39.

Matthews, R.C.O., 'The Economics of Institutions and the Sources of Economic Growth', *The Economic Journal*, 1986, 1996(4): 903-18.

Mauro, P., 'Corruption and Growth', *The Quarterly Journal of Economics*, 1995, 110(3): 681-712.
Maxwell, S., 'National Food Security Planning: First Thought from Sudan', in S. Maxwell (ed.), *To Cure All Hunger: Food Policy and Food Security in Sudan*, London: International Technology Publication, 1991.
——, 'Food Security: A Post-Modern Perspective', *Food Policy*, 1996, 21(2): 155-70.
Maxwell, S. & R. Slater, 'Food Policy Old and New', *Development Policy Review*, 2003, 21(5-6): 531-53.
Maxwell, S.J. & H.W. Singer, 'Food Aid to Developing Countries: A Survey', *World Development*, 1979, 7(3): 225-46.
May, T., *Social Research: Issues, Methods and Process*, 3rd edn., Buckingham: Open University Press, 2001.
McDonald, B.L., *Food Security*, Cambridge: Polity Press, 2010.
McGrew, A., 'Globalization', in S. Hall, D. Held & A. McGrew (eds.), *Modernity and its Futures*, Cambridge: Polity, 1992,
McHenry, D.F. & K. Bird, 'Food Bungle in Bangladesh', *Foreign Policy*, 1977, (27): 72-88.
Medard, J.F., 'Corruption in the Neo-Patromonial States of Sub-Saharan Africa', in A.J. Heidenheimer & M. Johnston (eds.), *Political Corruption: Concepts and Contexts*, New Brunswich, New Jersey: Transaction Publishers, 2002.
Mellor, J.W., 'Food Price Policy and Income Distribution in Low-Income Countries', *Economic Development and Cultural Change*, 1978, 27(1): 1-26.
Meuser, M. & U. Nagal, 'Expert Interviews: Vielfach Erprobt, Wening Bedacht. Ein Beitrag zur Qualitativen Methodendiskussion', in D. Garz & K. Kraimer (eds.), *Qualitativ-empirische Sozialforschung*, Opladen: Westdeutscher Verlag, 1991.
Michael, E.J., *Public Policy: The Competitive Framework*, Melbourne: Oxford University Press, 2006.
Migdal, J.S., *Strong Societies and Weak States*, Princeton, New Jersey: Princeton University Press, 1988.
——, 'The State in Society: An Approach to Struggles for Domination', in J.S. Migdal, A. Kohli & V. Shue (eds.), *State Power and Social Forces: Domination and Transformation in the Third World*, New York: Cambridge University Press, 1994.
Milam, W.B., 'Bangladesh and the Burdens of History', *Current History*, 2007, 106(699): 153-60.
——, *Bangladesh and Pakistan: Flirting with Failure in South Asia*, New York: Columbia University Press, 2009.

Ministry of Finance, *Bangladesher Oprokkasha Orthoneetir Akar: Ekti Orthonoitik Bislation,* Dhaka: Economic Relations Department (ERD), Government of Bangladesh, 2011.

Mirza, M.M.Q., 'Global Warming and Changes in the Probability of Occurrence of Floods in Bangladesh and Implications', *Global Environmental Change,* 2002, 12(2): 127-38.

Mo, P.H., 'Corruption and Economic Growth', *Journal of Comparative Economics,* 2001, 29(1): 66-79.

Mohsin, A. & M. Guhathakurta, 'The Struggle for Democracy in Bangladesh', in Z. Hasan (ed.), *Democracy in Muslim Societies: The Asian Experience,* New Delhi: Sage, 2007.

Molla, M.G., *Politics of Food Aid: Case of Bangladesh,* Dhaka: Academic Publishers, 1990.

Montgomery, R., *Open Market Grain Sales as a Public Policy Instrument for Moderating Food Price Fluctuations in Bangladesh, Mimeo,* Dhaka, U.S. Agency for International Development (USAID), 1983.

——, 'The Bangladesh Floods in Historical Perspective', *Disasters,* 1985, 9(3): 163-72.

Muhammad, A., 'Globalisation and Economic Transformation in a Peripheral Economy: The Bangladesh Experience', *Economic and Political Weekly,* 2006, 41(15): 1459-64.

Muhith, A.M.A., 'On Good Governance', *Journal of Bangladesh Studies,* 2006, 8(1): 1-28.

——, *Budget Speech, 2010-11,* Dhaka, Ministry of Finance, Government of People's Republic of Bangladesh, 2010.

Mujeri, M.K., *Poverty Trends and Agricultural Growth Linkages,* Dhaka: Food Management and Research Support Project, Ministry of Food, Government of the People's Republic of Bangladesh, 2000.

Mukerjee, M., *Churchill's Secret War: The British Empire and the Ravaging of India during World War II,* New York: Basic Books, 2010.

Murgai, R. & S. Zaidi, 'Effectiveness of Food Assistance Programs in Bangladesh', *Journal of Developing Societies,* 2005, 21(1-2): 121-42.

Murphy, S., 'Foreword', in Ben Lilliston & Andrew Ranallo (eds.), *Grain Reserves and the Food Price Crisis: Selected Writings from 2008-12,* Minneapolis: Institute for Agriculture and Trade Policy, 2012.

Mwennda, A.M. & R. Tangri, 'Patronage Politics, Donor Reforms, and Regime Consolidation in Uganda', *African Affairs,* 2005, 104(416): 449-67.

NAP, *National Agriculture Policy 2010,* Dhaka: Ministry of Agriculture, Government of Bangladesh, 2010.

Nath, D.K., 'Combating the Price Spiral', *The Daily Star,* 13 January 2011.

Neuman, W.L., *Social Research Methods: Qualitative and Quantitative Approaches*, London: Allyn and Bacon, 2000.

Neumayer, E., 'Is the Allocation of Food Aid Free from Donor Interest Bias?', *The Journal of Development Studies,* 2005, 41(3): 394-411.

NFP, *National Food Policy 2006,* Dhaka: Ministry of Food and Disaster Management, Government of Bangladesh, 2006.

NFPCSP, *National Food Policy Capacity Strenghtening Programme,* Office at the Food Planning and Monitoring Unit (FPMU), Ministry of Food and Disaster Management, 2011, viewed 12 June 2011, <http://www.nfpcsp.org/agridrupal/food-planning-and-monitoring-unit>.

——, *Making the National Food Policy,* 2011, viewed 5 February 2011, <http://www.nfpcsp.org/MakingNFPwork2.htm> .

NFPPA, *National Food Policy Plan of Action (2008-2015),* Dhaka: Food Planning and Monitoring Unit (FPMU), Ministry of Food and Disaster Management, GOB, 2008.

Norris, P., 'Making Democratic Governance Work for Prosperity: The China and India Case', paper presented to the *Workshop on China and India,* Department of Economics, University of Sydney, 28 October 2011.

——, *Making Democratic Governance Work: How Regimes Shape Prosperity, Welfare, and Peace,* New York: Cambridge University Press, 2012.

NSP (National Seed Policy), *National Seed Policy 1993,* Dhaka: Ministry of Agriculture, Government of Bangladesh, 1993.

Nuruzzaman, M., 'Social Responses to Economic Reforms in Bangladesh: The Workers' and Peasants' Movements in the 1980s and 1990s', *Journal of Asian and African Studies,* 2006, 41(4): 341-57.

Odhikar, *Human Rights Report 2011,* Odhikar (Human Rights Organization), 2012, viewed 12 June 2012, <http://www.odhikar.org/documents/2011/English/Human_Rights_Report_2011.pdf>.

OECD, *The Development Effectiveness of Food Aid: Does Tying Matter?,* Paris: Organisation for Economic Co-operation and Development, 2006.

Ó Gráda, C., *Famine: A Short History,* Princeton, New Jersey: Princeton University Press, 2009.

OHCHR, *International Covenant on Economic, Social and Cultural Rights,* Office of the United Nations High Commissioner for Human Rights, 2011, viewed 8 June 2012, <http://www2.ohchr.org/english/law/cescr.htm>.

Olken, B.A. & Barron, P., 'The Simple Economics of Extortion: Evidence from Trucking in Aceh', *Journal of Political Economy,* 2009, 117(3): 417-52.

Osmani, S.R., 'The Food Problems of Bangladesh' , in J. Drèze & A. Sen (eds.),

The Political Economy of Hunger, vol. 3: *Endemic Hunger*, New York: Oxford University Press, 1991.

——, 'Realising the Right to Development in Bangladesh: Progress and Challenges', *The Bangladesh Development Studies*, 2010, XXXIII (1&2): 25-90.

Osmani, S.R. & M.A. Quasem, *Pricing and Subsidy Policies for Bangladesh Agriculture*, Dhaka: Bangladesh Institute of Development Studies, 1990.

Paarlberg, R., *Food Politics: What Everyone Needs to Know*, New York: Oxford University Press, 2010.

Pagiola, S., *Environmental and Natural Resource Degradation in Intensive Agriculture in Bangladesh*, Washington DC: Document of Agriculture and Natural Resource Operations Division, South Asia Region, World Bank, 1995.

Pardey, P.G., J.M. Alston & R.R. Piggott (eds.), *Agricultural R&D in the Developing World: Too Little, Too Late?*, Washington DC: International Food Policy Research Institute, 2006.

Parnini, S.N., 'Public Sector Reform and Good Governance: The Impact of Foreign Aid on Bangladesh', *Journal of Asian and African Studies*, 2009, 44(5): 553-75.

Patrick, S., *Weak Links: Fragile States, Global Threats and International Security*, New York: Oxford University Press, 2011.

Patton, M.Q., *Qualitative Evaluation and Research Methods*, Newbury Park: Sage, 1990.

Paul, B.K., 'Relief Assistance to 1998 Flood Victims: A Comparison of the Performance of the Government and NGOs', *The Geographical Journal*, 2003, 169(1): 75-89.

Paul, B.K. & H. Rasid, 'Flood Damage to Rice Crop in Bangladesh', *Geographical Review*, 1993, 83(2): 150-9.

Paul, T.V., 'State Capacity and South Asia's Perennial Insecurity Problems', in T.V. Paul (ed.), *South Asia's Weak States: Understanding the Regional Insecurity Predicament*, Stanford, California: Stanford University Press, 2010.

Peiris, H.H., 'Political Conflict in Bangladesh', *Ethnic Studies Report*, 1998, XVI(1): 1-75.

Persson, T., 'Do Political Institutions Shape Economic Policy?', *Econometrica*, 2000, 70(3): 883-905.

Persson, T., G. Roland & G. Tabellini, 'Comparative Politics and Public Finance', *Journal of Political Economy*, 2000, 108(6): 1121-61.

Persson, T. & G. Tabellini, *The Economic Effects of Constitutions*, Cambridge, Massachusetts: MIT Press, 2003.

Pierson, C., *The Modern State*, 2nd edn., New York: Routledge, 2004.

Pillai, N., 'Food Aid for Development: A Review of the Evidence', in E. Clay &

O. Stokke (eds.), *Food Aid and Human Security*, London: Frank Cass Publishers, 2000.

Pinstrup-Andersen, P., 'Agricultural Research and Policy for Better Health and Nutrition in Developing Countries: A Food Systems Approach', *Agricultural Economics*, 2007, (37): 187-98.

Pinstrup-Andersen, P. & P. Sandøe (eds.), *Ethics, Hunger and Globalization: In Search of Appropriate Policies*, Dordrecht, The Netherlands: Springer, 2010.

Pitt, M.M., M.R. Rosenzweig & M.N. Hassan, 'Productivity, Health, and Inequality in the Intrahousehold Distribution of Food in Low-Income Countries', *The American Economic Review*, 1990, 80(5): 1139-56.

Pottier, J., *Anthropology of Food: The Social Dynamics of Food Security*, Cambridge: Polity Press, 1999.

Przeworski, A., *States and Markets: A Primer in Political Economy*, Cambridge: Cambridge University Press, 2005.

Quadir, F., 'The Political Economy of Pro-Market Reforms in Bangladesh: Regime Consolidation Through Economic Liberalization?', *Contemporary South Asia*, 2000, 9(2): 197-212.

Rahman, H.Z., 'The Political Economy of Poverty-Alleviation', in H.Z. Rahman & M. Hossain (eds.), *Rethinking Rural Poverty: Bangladesh as a Case Study*, New Delhi: Sage, 1995.

Rahman, K., 'Babostapona Sonkate Rasayonik Sar (Management Crisis of Chemical Fertilizer)', in K. Rahman & R. Ahmed (eds.), *State of Agriculture in Bangladesh: Secured Food, Secured Future (Journalist's View)* Dhaka: Palok Publishers, 2009.

Rahman, M., *Public Procurement of Paddy and Rice in Bangladesh Milling and Storage Adjustment for Efficiency*, Dhaka: International Food Policy Research Institute, Bangladesh Food Policy Project, 1992.

Rahman, M. & U.K. Deb, 'Trade Liberalization, Agricultural Development and Food Security: Issues and Implications for Bangladesh', in D. Bhattacharya, M. Rahman, F. Khatun, A. Raihan & U.K. Deb (eds.), *Bangladesh in the Global Trade Regime: Labour, Environment, Agriculture, Export and Trade Negotiations*, Dhaka: Centre for Policy Dialogue and Pathak Shamabesh, 2005.

Rahman, S., 'Profit Efficiency Among Bangladeshi Rice Farmers', *Food Policy*, 2003, 28(5-6): 487-503.

Rahman, S. & G.B. Thapa, 'Environmental Impacts of Technological Change in Bangladesh Agriculture: Farmers' Perceptions and Empirical Evidence', *Outlook on Agriculture*, 1999, 28(4): 233-8.

Rao, J.M., *Food Security: A Benchmark Survey of the Literature Relevant to Bangladesh*, Dhaka: National Food Policy Capacity Strengthening Programme, Government of Bangladesh, 2007.

Rapley, J., *Understanding Development: Theory and Practice in the Third World*, Boulder: Lynne Rienner Publishers, 2007.

Rashid, S., A. Gulati & R.J. Cummins (eds.), *From Parastatals to Private Trade: Lesson from Asian Agriculture*, Baltimore: The Johns Hopkins University Press (published for the International Food Policy Research Institute), 2008.

Rasul, G. & G.B. Thapa, 'Sustainability of Ecological and Conventional Agricultural Systems in Bangladesh: An Assessment Based on Environmental, Economic and Social Perspectives', *Agricultural Systems*, 2004, 79(3): 327-51.

Ravallion, M., 'The Preference of Rice Markets in Bangladesh during the 1974 Famine', *Economic Journal*, 1985, 95(377): 15-29.

——, 'Market Responses to Anti-Hunger Policies: Effects on Wages, Prices and Emplyoment', in J. Dreze & A. Sen (eds.), *The Political Economy of Hunger*, vol. 2, New York: Oxford University Press, 1990.

Reuschmeyer, D. & P.B. Evans, 'The State and Economic Transformation: Towards an Analysis of the Conditions Underlying Effective Intervention', in P.B. Evans, D. Reuschmeyer & T. Skocpol (eds.), *Bringing the State Back*, Cambridge: Cambridge University Press, 1985.

Rhodes, R.A.W., 'The New Governance: Governing without Government', *Political Studies*, 1996, 44(4): 652-67.

Riaz, A., *God Willing: The Politics of Islamism in Bangladesh*, USA: Rowman & Littlefield Publisher, Inc., 2004.

——, *Islamist Militancy in Bangladesh: A Complex Web*, London and New York: Routledge, 2008.

——, 'Bangladesh: A "Weak State" with Multiple Security Challenges', in T.V. Paul (ed.), *South Asia's Weak States: Understanding the Regional Insecurity Predicament*, Stanford, California: Stanford University Press, 2010.

Rice, S.E. & S. Patrick, *Index of State Weakness in the Developing World*, Washington DC: The Brookings Institution, 2008.

Rodrik, D. & A. Subramanian, 'The Primacy of Institutions (And What This Does and Does Not Mean)', *Finance and Development*, 2003, 40(2): 31-4.

Rodrik, D., A. Subramanian & F. Trebbi, 'Institutions Rule: The Primacy of Institutions over Geography and Integration in Economic Development', *Journal of Economic Growth*, 2004, 9(2): 131-65.

Roy, D.K., *Governance, Competitiveness and Growth: The Challenges for Bangladesh*, Manila: ADB, 2006.

SAPRIN, *The Policy Roots of Economic Crisis and Poverty*, Dhaka: The Structural Adjustment Participatory Review International Network (SAPRIN), 2002.

Sarker, A.E., 'Administrative Reforms in Bangladesh: Three Decades of Failure', *International Public Management Journal*, 2004, 7(3): 365-84.

——, 'Patron-Client Politics and its Implications for Good Governance in Bangladesh', *International Journal of Public Administration*, 2008, 31(12): 1416-40.

Sarker, A.E. & M.H. Rahman, 'The Emerging Perspective of Goveranance and Poverty Alleviation: A Case Study of Bangladesh', *Public Organization Review*, 2006, 7(2): 93-112.

Schultz, T., 'Value of US Farm Surpluses to Underdeveloped Countries', *Journal of Farm Economics*, 1960, 421019-1030.

Scott, J., *A Matter of Record: Documentary Sources in Social Research*, Oxford: Wiley, 1990.

Scott, J.C., 'Patron-Client Politics and Political Change in Southeast Asia', *American Political Science Review*, 1972, 91-113.

Sen, A., *Poverty and Famines: An Essay on Entitlement and Deprivation*, Oxford University Press, 1981.

——, 'The Food Problem: Theory and Policy', *Third World Quarterly*, 1982, 4(3): 447-59.

——, *Development as Freedom*, New York: Oxford University Press, 1999.

——, *The Argumentative Indian: Writings on Indian History, Culture and Identity*, Great Britain: Penguin, 2005.

——, 'Quality of Life: India vs. China', *The New York Review* (12 May 2011): 44-5.

Sen, B., M.K. Mujeri & Q. Shahabuddin, 'Explaining Pro-Poor Growth in Bangladesh: Puzzles, Evidence, and Implications', in T. Besley & L.J. Cord (eds.), *Delivering on the Promise of Pro-Poor Growth: Insights and Lessons from Country Experiences*, New York: A Co-publication of Palgrave Macmillan and the World Bank, 2007.

Shahabuddin, Q., *A Disaggregated Model for Stabilization of Price in Bangladesh*, Washington D.C.: International Food Policy Research Institute, 1991.

——, 'The Right to Food: Bangladesh Perspectives', *The Bangladesh Development Studies*, 2010, XXXIII (1 & 2): 91-134.

Shahabuddin, Q., M. Asaduzzaman, E. Clay & S. Jones, *Price Support, Domestic Procurement Programme and Public Stock Management*, Dhaka: Bangladesh Institute of Development Studies (BIDS) and UK Department for International Development (DFID), 2009.

Shahadat Ullah, A.H., *Open Market Change Policy in Bangladesh: Its Performance and Prospect in Price Stabilization*. A Report prepared for the Bangladesh Ministry of Food, USAID, and International Food Policy Research Institute, Dhaka: U.S. Agency for International Development (USAID), 1988.

Shapouri, S. & M. Missiaen, *Food Aid: Motivation and Allocation Criteria*,

Report No. 240, Washington D.C.: United States Department of Agriculture Economic Research Service Foreign Agricultural Economic, 1990.

Sharma, M. & M. Zeller, 'Placement and Outreach of Group-Based Credit Organizations: The Cases of Asa, Brac, and Proshika in Bangladesh', *World Development,* 1999, 27(12): 2123-36.

Sharmin, N., *'Police? Abar Palacchhe? Kintu Keno? [Police? Fleeing? But Why?]'*, ETV news report available on YouTube, 2012, viewed 26 June 2012, <https://www.youtube.com/watch?feature=player_embedded&v=nw-ymVdm ZRg>.

Shaw, D.J., 'Food Aid in Sub-Saharan Africa: Policy Lessons for the Future', *Canadian Journal of Development Studies/Revue canadienne d'études du développement,* 2002, 23(3): 571-99.

Siddiqi, D.M., 'Political Culture in Contemporary Bangladesh: Histories, Ruptures and Contradictions', in A. Riaz & C.C. Fair (eds.), *Political Islam and Governance in Bangladesh,* New York: Routledge, 2011.

Smil, V., *Feeding the World: A Challenge for the Twenty-First Century,* Cambridge, Massachusetts: MIT Press, 2000.

——, *Enriching the Earth: Fritz Haber, Carl Bosch, and the Transformation of World Food Production,* Cambridge, Massachusetts: The MIT Press, 2004.

Smith, B.C., *Good Governance and Development,* New York: Palgrave Macmillan, 2007.

Sobhan, R., 'Politics of Food and Famine in Bangladesh', *Economic and Political Weekly,* 1979, 14(48): 1973-80.

——, *The Crisis of External Dependence: The Political Economy of Foreign Aid to Bangladesh,* Dhaka: University Press Limited, 1982.

——, *How Bad Governance Impedes Poverty Alleviation in Bangladesh,* Paris: OECD Development Centre, 1998.

——, 'Governance and Development in South Asia', in P. Panandiker (ed.), *Problems of Governance in South Asia,* Dhaka: University Press Limited, 2000.

——, 'The State of Governance in Bangladesh', in R. Sobhan (ed.), *Changes and Challenges,* Dhaka: Centre for Policy Dialogue and University Press Limited, 2001.

——, *The Political Economy of the State and Market in Bangladesh,* Dhaka, Centre for Policy Dialogue, 2002.

——, 'Structural Dimensions of Malgovernance in Bangladesh', *Economic and Political Weekly,* 2004, 39(36): 4101-8.

——, 'Food Security for Low Income Group and Hardcore Poor', in CPD, *Development of Bangladesh with Equity and Justice: Immediate Tasks for the New Government,* Dhaka: Centre for Policy Dialogue, 2009.

——, *Challenging the Injustice of Poverty: Agendas for Inclusive Development in South Asia*, New Delhi: Sage, 2010.

Stevens, C., *Food Aid and the Developing World: Four African Case Studies*, London: Croom Helm London in association with the Overseas Development Institute, 1979.

Stiglitz, J.E., 'Markets, Market Failures, and Development', *The American Economic Review*, 1989, 79(2): 179-203.

——, *Globalization and its Discontents*, New Delhi: Penguin Books India, 2002.

——, *Making Globalization Work*, New York and London: W.W. Norton & Company, 2006.

Stoker, G., 'Governance as Theory: Five Propositions', *International Social Science Journal*, 1998, 50(155): 17-28.

Stokes, B., 'Food is Different', *National Journal*, 2008, viewed 18 July 2011, <http://www.nationaljournal.com/magazine/food-is-different-20080607>.

Subbarao, K. & W.J. Smith, *Safety Nets versus Relief Nets: Towards a Medium Term Safety Net Strategy for Ethiopia*, World Bank Mimeo, 2003.

Sundaram, J.K., 'Lessons From the 2008 World Food Crisis', *Economic & Political Weekly*, 2010, XIV(12): 35-40.

Szeftel, M., 'Corruption and Spoils System in Zambia', in M. Clarke (ed.), *Corruption: Causes, Consequences, and Control*, London: Frances Printer, 1983.

Task Forces Report, *Bangladesh Development Strategies: Environment and Development*, Dhaka: University Press Limited, 1991.

Theobold, R., 'Patrimonialism', *World Politics*, 1982, 34(4): 548-59.

TIB, *Corruption in Bangladesh: A Household Survey*, Dhaka: Transparency International Bangladesh, 2005.

——, *Bangladesh Public Service Commission: A Diagnostic Study*, Dhaka: Transparency International Bangladesh, 2007.

——, *National Household Survey 2007 on Corruption in Bangladesh*, Dhaka: Transparency International Bangladesh, 2008.

Tilman, D., 'Beneficial Biofuels: The Food, Energy and Environment Trilemma', *Science*, 2009, 325(July): 270-1.

Timmer, C.P. (ed.), *Agriculture and the State: Growth, Employment, and Poverty in Developing Countries*, Ithaca, New York: Cornell University Press, 1991.

Timmer, C.P., 'Rural Changes Stimulate Rising Giants', *Science*, 2008, 321(5889): 642.

——, 'Reflections on Food Crises Past', *Food Policy*, 2010, 35(1): 1-11.

——, Falcon, W.P. & S.R. Pearson, *Food Policy Analysis*, Baltimore and London:

Published for the World Bank [by] The Johns Hopkins University Press, 1983.

UBINIG, *About UBINIG*, Policy Research for Development Alternative, 2012, viewed 8 June 2012, <http://www.ubinig.org/index.php/networkdetails/showArchive2/11/8/english>.

Uddin, A.M.F. & J.T. Haque, *Agrarian Transition and Livelihoods of the Rural Poor: The Agricultural Land Market*, Dhaka: Unnayan-Onneshan, 2009.

UN, *Report of the World Food Conference*, New York: United Nations, 1974.

UNICEF, *Understanding Urban Inequalities in Bangladesh: A Prerequisite for Achieving Vision 2021 (A Study Based on the Results of the 2009 Multiple Indicator Cluster Survey)*, Dhaka: UNICEF Bangladesh, 2010.

USAID, *Policy Determination: Definition of Food Security*, The United States Agency for International Development, 1992, viewed 18 July 2011, <http://www.usaid.gov/policy/ads/200/pd19.pdf>.

——, *Country Profile for Bangladesh (USAID Land, Tenure and Property Rights Portal)*, The United States Agency for International Development, 2010, viewed 9 June 2012, <http://usaidlandtenure.net/usaidltprproducts/country-profiles/bangladesh>.

——, *USAID: Bangladesh, Population and Health*, The United States Agency for International Development, Dhaka, Bangladesh, 2012, viewed 20 June 2012, <http://transition.usaid.gov/bd/programs/pop.html>.

Van deWalle, N., *African Economies and the Politics of Permanent Crisis, 1979-1999*, Cambridge: Cambridge University Press, 2001.

Van Schendel, W., *A History of Bangladesh*, Cambridge: Cambridge University Press, 2009.

Via Campesina, *Food Sovereignty*, 2012, viewed 15 November 2012, <http://viacampesina.org/en/index.php/main-issues-mainmenu-27/food-sovereignty-and-trade-mainmenu-38/33-food-sovereignty>.

Vivian, J., 'NGOs and Sustainable Development in Zimbabwe: No Magic Bullets', *Development & Change*, 1994, 25(1): 167-93.

Vromen, A., 'Debating Methods: Rediscovering Qualitative Approaches', in D. Marsh & G. Stoker (eds.), *Theory and Methods in Political Science*, 3rd edn., New York: Palgrave McMillan, 2010.

Wang, S., 'The Problems of State Weakness', *Journal of Democracy*, 2003, 14(1): 36-42.

Warren, C.A.B., 'Qualitative Interviewing', in J.F. Gubrium & J.A. Holstein (eds.), *Handbook of Interview Research: Context and Methods*, London: Sage, 2002.

Webb, P. & J.V. Braun, *Famine and Food Security in Ethiopia: Lessons for Africa*, London: John Wiley.

Webb, P. & K. Weinberger, *Women Farmers: Enhancing Rights, Recognition, and Productivity*, New York: Peter Lang, 2001.

Weber, M., *Economic and Society: An Outline of Interpretive Sociology*, vol. II, Berkeley, California: University of California Press, 1978.

Weber, M.T., J.M. Staatz, J.S. Holtzman, E.W. Crawford & R.H. Bernsten, 'Informing Food Security Decisions in Africa: Empirical Analysis and Policy Dialogue', *American Journal of Agricultural Economics*, 1988, 70(5): 1044-52.

Wei, S.J., 'Local Corruption and Global Capital Flows', *Brookings Papers on Economic Activity*, Washington D.C.: Brookings Institute, 2000, 31(2): 303-46,

Weiss, T.G. & R.S. Jordan, *The World Food Conference and Global Problem Solving*, New York: Praeger, 1976.

WFP, *World Hunger Series: Hunger and Markets*, Rome: World Food Programme, 2009.

White, S.C., 'NGOs, Civil Society, and the State in Bangladesh: The Politics of Representing the Poor', *Development and Change*, 1999, 30(1999): 307-26.

Wikileaks, *Loyality and Access Trump Tittles in Influencing PM*, 2011, viewed 5 June 2012,<http://www.bdnews24.com/details.php?cid=2&id=205410>.

——, *Bangladesh: Sheikh Hasina's Inner Circle: Loyal to the Core*, 2011, viewed 5 June 2012, <http://wikileaks.org/cable/2009/02/09 DHAKA 205.html#>.

Williamson, O.E., 'The New Institutional Economics: Taking Stock Looking Ahead', *Journal of Economic Literature*, 2000, XXXVIII (September): 595-613.

Woll, P., *Public Policy*, London: Winthrop Publishers, 1974.

World Bank, *Bangladesh: Current Economic Performance and Short-term Prospects*, Dhaka, 1976.

——, *Bangladesh: Food Policy Review*, Report 1764a-BD, Washington DC: World Bank, 1977.

——, *Bangladesh: Food Policy Issues*, Washington DC: World Bank. Mimeo, 1979.

——, *Poverty and Hunger: Issues and Options for Food Security in Developing Countries*, Washington DC: World Bank Policy Study, 1986.

——, *Bangladesh Food Policy Review: Adjusting to the Green Revolution*, Washington DC: World Bank, 1992.

——, *World Bank's Strategy for Reducing Poverty and Hunger: A Report to the Development Community*, Washington DC: World Bank, 1995.

——, *World Development Report 1997: The State in a Changing World*, Washington DC: World Bank, 1997.

——, *Taming Leviathan: Reforming Governance in Bangladesh*, Dhaka: World Bank, 2002.

——, *Food Assistance Programs in Bangladesh*, Washington DC: World Bank, 2004.

——, *Bangladesh Social Safety Nets in Bangladesh: An Assessment*, Report no. 33411-BD, Human Development Unit South Asia Region, World Bank, 2005.

——, *Revitalizing the Agricultural Technology System in Bangladesh*, Dhaka: World Bank Office, 2005.

——, *Bangladesh Country Environmental Analysis*, Dhaka: The World Bank Office, Dhaka, 2006.

——, *Social Safety Nets in Bangladesh: An Assessment*, Dhaka: World Bank Office, 2006.

——, *World Development Report 2008: Agriculture for Development*, Washington DC: World Bank, 2007.

——, *World Development Report 2009: Reshaping Economic Geography* Washington DC: World Bank, 2008.

——, *Worldwide Governance Indicators* 7 June 2012, 2011, viewed 9 June 2012, <http://info.worldbank.org/governance/wgi/index.asp>.

——, '*World Bank Statement on Padma Bridge*', the World Bank's Press release, 2012, viewed 29 June 2012, <http://www.worldbank.org/en/news/2012/06/29/world-bank-statement-padma-bridge>.

Wright, B.D., 'International Grain Reserves and other Instruments to Address Volatility in Grain Markets', *World Bank Research Observer*, 2012, 27(2): 79-118.

WSFS (World Summit on Food Security), *Feeding the World, Eradicating Hunger*, Rome: Food Agriculture Organization of the United Nations, 2009.

Zafarullah, H., 'Globalization, State and Politics in Bangladesh: Implication for Democratic Governance', *South Asia: Journal of South Asian Studies*, 2003, XXVI(3): 283-96.

Zafarullah, H. & A.S. Huque, 'Public Management for Good Governance: Reforms, Regimes, and Reality in Bangladesh', *International Journal of Public Administration*, 2001, 24(12): 1379-1403.

Zafarullah, H. & R. Rahman, 'The Impaired State: Assessing State Capacity and Governance in Bangladesh', *International Journal of Public Sector Management*, 2008, 21(7): 739-52.

Zafarullah, H. & N.A. Siddiquee, 'Dissecting Public Sector Corruption in Bangladesh: Issues and Problems of Control', *Public Organization Review*, 2001, 1(4): 465-86.

Zakaria, F., 'The Rise of Illiberal Democracy', *Foreign Affairs*, 1997, 76(6): 22-43.

Zaman, M.Q., 'Ziaur Rahman: Leadership Styles and Mobilization Process', *The Indian Political Science Review*, 1984, 18(2): 194-203.

Ziring, L., *Bangladesh from Mujib to Ershad: An Interpretive Study*, Karachi: Oxford University Press, 1992.

Zohir, S., *Impacts of Reforms in Agricultural Input Markets on Crop Sector Profitability in Bangladesh,* Dhaka: SAPRI/BIDS, 2001.

Zolner, M., I. Rasmusen & A. Hansen, 'Qualitative Interviews: Studying Network Narratives', in P. Bogason & M. Zolner (eds.), *Methods in Democratic Network Governance*, New York: Palgrave Macmillan, 2007.

Zug, S., 'Monga—Seasonal Food Insecurity in Bangladesh: Bringing the Information Together', *The Journal of Social Studies*, 2006 (July-September), 111: 21-39.

NEWSPAPER DOCUMENTS

'Artificial Urea Crisis Looms in Rajshahi, Black Marketing by Dealers: Lax Monitoring by Admin', *The Daily Star*, 12 September 2004.

'Attempt-to-Rape Case "Politically Motivated": Charges Against AL Lawmaker Dropped', *The Daily Star*, 25 January 2011.

'Back to Basics: An Interview with Farhad Mazhar', *Star Magazine*, 26 March 2004.

'BNP Chief's Power Consolidated Further: Changed Constitution Ensures Tarique's Eventual Leadership', *The Daily Star*, 11 December 2009.

'Businessmen see Police Link to Extortion, Drug Trade', *The Daily Star*, 17 September 2010.

'Corruption a Serious Roadblock in Eradicating Poverty', *The Daily Star*, 24 October 2009.

'Corruption, Shame and Embarrassment', *The Daily Star*, 17 March 2010.

'Crossfire Deaths: Anything but Legally Tenable', *The Daily Star*, 30 March 2010.

'Development Dogma and Death of Farmers', *New Age*, 26 May 2005, p. 11.

'Eid day Sit-in, PM Criticises Organisers: Wants to know details on Road Safety Demonstrators', *The Daily Star*, 6 September 2011.

'Embraceable You: Growing Geopolitical Interests Push India to Seek Better Relations Nearer Home', *The Economist* (London), 30 July 2011.

'Essentials' Prices Up Despite Govt. Efforts to Control', *The Daily Star*, 22 August 2009.

'Extortion at Ferry Terminal: Minister "Backer" of Toll Collection', *The Daily Star*, 22 July 2012.

'Extortion Causes Price Hike: Says Food Minister; Law Enforcers to Help Keep Market Stable', *The Daily Star*, 17 August 2009.

'Farmers Seize AED Office for Fertiliser', *The Daily Star*, 8 October 2007.

'Farmers' Fury Boils Over: They Agitate for Fertiliser, Power', *The Daily Star*, 27 February 2006.

'Faruk: First Ramadan to see TCB Goods', *The Daily Star*, 17 August 2009.

'Govt. Lets Ershad off the Hook: It Now Considers Radar Graft Case Against him Politically Motivated, Decides to Withdraw 75 More Case', *The Daily Star*, 2 March 2011.

'Govt's Market Steps may Miss Mark: NBR to Count Tk 300cr in Lost Revenue', *The Daily Star*, 16 August 2009.

'Graft Gobbles Up OMS Rice', *The Daily Star*, 31 October 2010.

'Half of TR Project Fund Gobbled Up: Fake Projects, Documents Used, Allege Officials', *The Daily Star*, 16 February 2009.

'Hasina Alleges "Slow Poisoning" in Sub-Jail', *The Daily Star*, 12 May 2010.

'If Population 14 Cr, Food in Surplus: Agriculture Minister Terms Latest Census Find Unrealistic', *The Daily Star*, 19 July 2011.

'Low Quality of OMS rice', *The Daily Star*, 6 May 2011.

'Mamun Produced in Court in Arms Case, Remanded: Pistol Found in his House', *The Daily Star*, 27 March 2007.

'Matia Backs GM Crop Research', *The Daily Star*, 30 March 2011.

'MPs Won't Give up on Duty-Free Cars: Ordinance Banning the Privilege Would Not be Made Law', *The Daily Star*, 5 February 2009.

'Niko Resources: Ottawa's Corruption Test Case', *The Globe*and *Mail* (Toronto), 25 August 2011.

'No Solution to Padma Bridge Issue Soon: WB Official for More Dialogues', *The Daily Star*, 17 November 2011.

'OMS Dealership in Khulna: Ruling Party Men Get Permit, Real Traders Deprived', *The Daily Star*, Monday, 22 March 2010.

'Padma Bridge WB-Strung: Actions of the Lead Financier Stalling Project; Govt. in Dark about Nature of Graft Allegation Raised by WB', *The Daily Star*, 30 September 2011.

'Politically Motivated Budget Won't Yield Benefit', *The Daily Star*, 6 June 2006.

'Politics, Business Behind Graft: Says ACC Chief', *The Daily Star*, 7 April 2010.

'Population No Less Than 16 Cr: Muhith', *The Daily Star*, 25 July 2011.

'Presidential Clemency: JS Body Caught in Dilemma', *The Daily Star*, 3 January 2010.

'Protect Forestlands from Land Grabbers', *The Daily Star*, 12 April 2005.

'Rationing Hardly Improves Urea Crisis in Gaibandha/People from Rangpur, Kurigram also Crowd Dealers' Shops', *The Daily Star*, 15 February 2007.

'Shake-up at the Top Echelon of Bureaucracy: Will it make Governance Dynamic?' *The Daily Star*, 21 October 2010.

'Soils are "Hungry", May "Eat" Fertiliser, and Become Intoxicated', by Zahir Ahmed, *New Age*, 11 February 2009.
'Sylhet Grassroots see Tarique Adoration', *The Daily Star*, 7 February 2010.
'The Food Grain Conundrum' by M. Abdul Latif Mondal, *The Daily Star*, 7 August 2010.
'Wanted a Truly Pro-People Budget', *The Daily Star*, 7 May 2005.
'Wholesale Prices of Essentials Fixed: Potato, Onion, Garlic and Ginger Prices set to Stabilise the Market Ahead of Ramadan', *The Daily Star*, 21 August 2009.
'Withdrawal of "Politically Motivated" Cases: Making Farce of Rule of Law', *The Daily Star*, 3 January 2011.

NEWSPAPER DOCUMENTS (BENGALI SOURCES)

Beshee Dame Chal Kinche Sorkar, *Prothom-alo*, 12 April 2011.
BNP-Awamileague-Er Shabek Shangshod o Provabshaleera e Shubidha Niyeche: Ak Bochore 644 Koti Takar Shudh Moukuf, *Prothom-alo*, 30 October 2009.
Boro Dui Doler Achoron Triteeyo Soktike Khomotaban Korche, Interview with Imtiaz Ahmed, *Prothom-alo*, 13 November 2011.
Chadabajir Karone Poribohon Bay o Ponner Dam Barche, Khadda Montree, *Prothom-alo*, 17 August 2009.
Chaler Dam o Khadda Somossar Itibritta, *Prothom-alo*, 1 May 2010.
Club o School Er Nam Vangiye TR Er Taka Attosat, *Prothom-alo*, 23-24 August 2011.
Khadda Bivager Todonto Protibedon: Kalo Bazare Bikri Hocchhe Polisheer Ration chal, *Prothom-alo*, 19 January 2011.
Khadda Nirapottar Jonno Bikolpo Upay Khujte Hobe interview with Mahbub Hossain, *Prothom-alo*, 5 December 2010.
Khadda Ponner Jotestha Majud Ache, Somossa Sorboraher interview with Hossain Zillur Rahman, *Prothom-alo*, 10 October 2010.
Krishi Bigganee Haracchhe Desh, the daily *Kaler Kontho*, 14 November 2011.
Ramazan Mash Shurur Agei Dam Barachhe Baboshayira, *Prothom-alo*, 29 June 2012.
Ramazan Mashe Bazaar Niyontrone TCB'r Prostuti Samannoi, (*Prothom-alo*, 14 August 2009.
TR er Chal Attosat Awami League Netader, *Prothom-alo*, 3 May 2011.
TR er Name Tree-Mukhi Protarona, *Prothom-alo*, 11 November 2011.
Vejal Sare Biponna Krisok, *Prothom-alo*, 5 December 2009.

Index

For Product Safety Concerns and Information please contact our EU
representative GPSR@taylorandfrancis.com
Taylor & Francis Verlag GmbH, Kaufingerstraße 24, 80331 München, Germany

www.ingramcontent.com/pod-product-compliance
Ingram Content Group UK Ltd.
Pitfield, Milton Keynes, MK11 3LW, UK
UKHW021708270926
475702UK00054BA/688
* 9 7 8 1 0 3 2 3 7 6 9 4 3 *